Forty Three Days Of Fire
A JOURNEY INTO THE HIDDEN UNIVERSE

QUINN PATH

THRESHHOLD EDITIONS

Contents

Acknowledgments	vi
Introduction: The Monastery of Consciousness	1
Day 1 - Meeting Sayadaw	6
Day 2 — The War Within	23
Day 3 — The Medicine of Loving Kindness	38
Day 4 — The First Vision	54
Day 5 — Dancing with Death	66
Day 6 — The Ocean of Mind	80
Day 7 - The Lightning Gate	94
Day 8 - Eyes of Light	99
Day 9 - The Architecture of Inner Light	106
Day 10 - Diamond Light and the Magnetic Field of Being	115
Day 11- The Warrior's Garden: Flowers of the Heart	124
Day 12 - The Science of Light: When Wonder Meets Wisdom	135
Day 13 - The Breath's Secret Language: A Masterclass in Consciousness	144
Day 14 - The X-Ray Vision: When Consciousness Pierces the Veil	153
Day 15 - The Impossible Task: When Faith Meets Physics	164
Day 16 - The Holographic Universe: When Consciousness Becomes Cinema	175
Day 17 - Journey to the Stars: When Consciousness Becomes Cinema	189
Day 18 - Command and Control: Discovering Consciousness's Hidden Settings	201
Day 19 – Astral Tourism	211
Day 20 – The Robot's Awakening	220
Day 21 – Messages from the Void	228

Day 22 – Journey to the Celestial Realm	236
Day 23 – The Oracle's Mirrors	246
Day 24 – The Cosmic Energy Exercise	258
Day 25 – The X-Ray Awakening	273
Day 26 – The Transcendent Vision	287
Day 27 – The Crystal Body Purification	308
Day 28 – The Tranquil Paradox	314
Day 29 – The Great Deceleration	321
Day 30 – The Return of the Light	327
Day 31 – The Liquid Body	331
Day 32 - Seismic Shifts	337
Day 33- Echoes from Ancient Lives	344
Day 34 - The Invasion of Light	353
Day 35 - Glimpses of Tomorrow	358
Day 36 - The Soul's Architecture	366
Day 37 - The Cosmic Dance of Particles	372
Day 38 - Bhanga Nana	380
Day 39 - Entering the Void	387
Day 40 - Bhaya Nana	393
Day 41 - Talking	400
Day 42 - Last Interview with Sayadaw	409
Day 43 - Closing Ceremony	414
Conclusion: The Monastery of Mind	421
A Quiet Invitation	427
Pali Terms Glossary	428

Published by Quinn Path 2025

All rights reserved. No part of this book may be reproduced or transmitted in any form or by any means, electronic or mechanical, including photocopying, recording or by any information storage and retrieval system, without written permission from the author.

Acknowledgments

Every profound journey begins with a single voice calling through the darkness, and mine belonged to David Cha—a man whose words carried the weight of ancient wisdom wrapped in modern understanding. When he first spoke of the meditation centers hidden in Myanmar's verdant hills, his eyes held that particular gleam of someone who has glimpsed something beyond the veil of ordinary existence. David didn't merely provide information; he offered an invitation to transformation, his guidance becoming the first thread in a tapestry of grace that would ultimately reshape my understanding of what it means to be human.

In the sacred silence of retreat, I encountered Sayadaw Venerable Eikdi Bala, whose presence radiated the kind of stillness that makes hurricanes seem like gentle breezes. This remarkable master possessed that rare alchemy of profound wisdom and boundless compassion—a teacher whose every gesture spoke of decades spent diving into the deepest waters of consciousness. Under his patient guidance, insights bloomed like lotus flowers breaking through muddy waters, each revelation detailed within these pages emerging from his generous transmission of ancient truths. Sayadaw's teaching transcended mere instruction; it was archaeology of the soul, each session carefully excavating layers of conditioning to reveal the luminous awareness beneath.

Perhaps no acknowledgment carries more weight than the one I owe to Mr. Soemin—now the monk, Venerable Jharnote Kansa—and his extraordinary family, whose lives embodied the very teachings I sought to understand. These remarkable souls didn't simply run a meditation center; they created a sanctuary where transformation could unfold naturally, like flowers following the sun's arc across sky. Their existence became my most profound teaching, each act of service a masterclass in humility, each gesture of care a lesson in boundless generosity. Mr. Soemin served not only as mentor and interpreter during those pivotal weeks, but as a living bridge between worlds—translating not just language, but the very essence of awakened living. Through his family's example, I learned that true spirituality isn't found in grand gestures but in the countless small acts of selflessness that weave the fabric of an enlightened life.

Finally, my heart overflows with gratitude for my family, whose love forms the unshakeable foundation beneath every risk I've taken, every boundary I've crossed in pursuit of truth. Their support doesn't merely sustain; it transforms, creating a safety net strong enough to allow the kind of free-fall necessary for genuine spiritual awakening. In their boundless acceptance, I found the courage to journey to the edges of consciousness and return bearing whatever treasures I discovered there.

Each of these souls appeared in my life not as coincidence, but as essential notes in a symphony of grace—a reminder that no one walks the path of awakening alone, and that our deepest transformations are always, ultimately, gifts received through the generosity of others.

Introduction: The Monastery of Consciousness

In the unlikely setting of a meditation retreat in Australia, I encountered something that would fundamentally alter the trajectory of my life. David, a fellow practitioner with the unassuming manner of someone who worked in holistic medicine, casually mentioned that he saw lights during his meditation sessions—luminous phenomena that appeared with such regularity that he spoke of them as matter-of-factly as describing the weather.

Having studied Buddhism extensively, I immediately recognized what he was describing: the *nimitta*, those mysterious signs of deep concentration that traditional texts describe as markers of profound meditative achievement. What struck me wasn't just the phenomenon itself, but the revolutionary implications of who was experiencing it. In all my years of study, I had encountered such experiences only in ancient manuscripts or heard them attributed to monastics after decades of cloistered practice. Yet here was an ordinary person—someone with deadlines and bills and traffic jams—describing states I had assumed were reserved for the spiritual elite.

David's casual reference to meditation centers in Myanmar opened a door I hadn't known existed. The possibility that such profound experiences might be accessible to laypeople ignited something in me that I couldn't ignore—a hunger for direct experience that no amount of reading could satisfy. I made what many would consider an impractical decision: I set aside months of work and traveled halfway around the world to pursue experiences I wasn't even sure were real.

THE TERRITORY AHEAD

This book emerges from the diary I maintained during my second retreat at Mr Seomin's Monastery in Myanmar, where I spent forty-three days under the guidance of teachers who had dedicated their lives to mapping the deepest territories of human consciousness. Let me be clear about what this is and what it isn't: this is not a meditation manual. Serious practice requires the guidance of qualified teachers who can navigate the complexities and potential dangers that intensive meditation can present. Nor is this a theoretical treatise on Buddhist doctrine—such instruction extends far beyond any single book's scope. If you're genuinely interested in learning these practices, I encourage you to seek proper instruction from authorized teachers.

For years, I wrestled with whether to publish these intimate records. The rational voice in my head insisted that most readers would find the contents incredible, perhaps dismissing them as fantasy or delusion. The experiences described in these pages—witnessing subatomic particles with the mind's eye, consciousness dissolving into cosmic emptiness, past life memories emerging with documentary clarity—strain credibility even for those who lived through them.

Yet I couldn't shake the memory of a promise I made to myself during those transformative weeks. If these experiences were real, if consciousness truly possessed such extraordinary capabilities, then others deserved to know. The human potential revealed through intensive practice challenges our most basic assumptions about the nature of the mind and reality. We are far more than most of us ever imagine, and it seems tragic to live an entire lifetime unaware of our deeper capacities.

BREAKING ANCIENT BOUNDARIES

When my teacher made the revolutionary decision to break centuries of tradition by teaching laypeople—sharing knowledge previously confined to monastic communities—he did so because he understood that such wisdom belongs to humanity, not to institutions. In that same spirit, I've decided to share these records for several compelling reasons.

First, I hope they might inspire others to undertake similar journeys. The practices described here have the potential to transform lives in ways that transcend ordinary self-improvement—they offer direct access to the fundamental nature of consciousness itself. Suppose even one person reads these pages and embarks on their own exploration of these extraordinary territories. In that case, the vulnerability of sharing such intimate experiences will have been worthwhile.

Second, I believe this account offers a valuable perspective for anyone beginning serious meditation practice. Rather than presenting sanitized, theoretical descriptions, these pages reveal the messy, confusing, often uncomfortable reality of intensive inner work. Meditation isn't always peaceful; it's frequently challenging, occasionally frightening, and always unpredictable. As my mentor Mr. Soemin wisely observed, "Meditation is like a bird flying: sometimes high, sometimes low." Understanding this can help practitioners navigate their inevitable difficulties with greater perspective and persistence.

THE INNER FRONTIER

Finally, even if you never intend to meditate seriously, I hope these pages might stimulate curiosity about the nature of consciousness and human potential. In an age when we can map genomes and explore distant galaxies, we remain remarkably ignorant about the territory closest to home—our own awareness. We know more about the surface of Mars than we do about the deeper capacities of the mind that observes Mars through telescopes and contemplates its mysteries.

The experiences documented here suggest that consciousness is not merely a byproduct of neural activity, but something far more fundamental and mysterious. When properly trained, awareness can perceive realities normally invisible to ordinary perception—from the subatomic processes underlying all sensation to the vast spaces of emptiness in which all experience arises and passes away.

These are not mystical assertions but empirical observations, as verifiable through direct experience as any scientific experiment. The laboratory is consciousness itself; the instrument is refined attention; the discoveries challenge every assumption about the boundaries of human perception and the nature of reality itself.

A NOTE ON METHOD

One practical note about the narrative you're about to encounter: I wrote these entries in sections throughout each day, adding paragraphs as experiences unfolded in real time. This explains why some passages may seem disconnected or flow unevenly—they reflect the immediate, often chaotic nature of discoveries happening at the edges of human experience. I have preserved this quality while enhancing the literary elements, believing that the rawness of real-time discovery serves the truth better than polished retrospection.

You'll also notice that the early days focus heavily on the practical challenges of retreat life—the heat, the noise, the physical discomfort—while later entries venture into territories that might strain credulity. This progression mirrors the actual development of intensive practice. What begins as a struggle with basic concentration gradually evolves into access to extraordinary states of consciousness that few humans ever experience.

AN INVITATION TO WONDER

Whatever you make of the experiences described in these pages, I ask only that you approach them with an open mind. The universe may be far stranger and more wonderful than any of us dare to imagine, and consciousness may possess capacities that our current scientific paradigms have yet to acknowledge or explain.

If these records do nothing more than inspire a sense of wonder about the mystery of your own awareness—the miracle that you are conscious at all, that there is something rather than nothing reading these words right now—they will have served their purpose. For in that wonder lies the beginning of all genuine spiritual inquiry: the recognition that what we are is far more extraordinary than what we've been taught to believe.

The monastery gates are opening. The journey begins with a single step across the threshold of what you think you know about the nature of mind itself.

Day 1 – Meeting Sayadaw

The taxi's engine died with a mechanical wheeze, dust spiraling through open windows like tiny cyclones of anticipation. Heat struck my face with the weight of destiny—not merely weather but initiation, the first sacrament of a journey I couldn't yet fathom. As I stepped onto the sun-baked earth of the small courtyard, the air itself seemed to shimmer with possibility, thick with frangipani's seductive perfume and something deeper—incense perhaps, or the green breath of growing things learning to pray.

I felt like an astronaut stepping onto alien soil, my Western conditioning suddenly as useful as snow boots in the desert.

"Welcome! Welcome!"

The voice rolled across the courtyard like distant thunder made warm—deep and melodic, alive with an enthusiasm so genuine it seemed to emanate from some inexhaustible well of joy. Each syllable was shaped with the crisp precision of British English, then softened by Singapore's musical lilt, transforming ordinary words into invitations to understanding I hadn't known I was seeking.

From the shadows of a teak building emerged a man whose very presence seemed to rearrange the afternoon light. Salt-and-pepper hair cropped close, movements deliberate yet unhurried despite the urgency in his greeting—as if time itself bent around his measured grace. Even his accent carried welcome in its cultured vowels, dancing with an intonation that made conversation feel like coming home to a language I'd always known but never heard spoken aloud.

Sweat beaded on my forehead as I extended my hand to Mr. Soemin, uncertain whether a handshake belonged in this sacred geography, whether my Western gestures could translate across the invisible boundaries I was already sensing.

"Thank you. It's good to see you again."

The words emerged hoarse, unfamiliar—a voice returning from exile. I hadn't spoken much during my month at Pa-Auk Monastery, four hours south of Yangon, where silence had become a second skin and words felt like foreign objects in my mouth. It had been almost a month since I'd first stood in this very courtyard, when Mr. Soemin had gently explained that his retreat wouldn't begin for weeks and suggested I spend the waiting time at Myanmar's largest monastery, learning the fundamentals of this ancient practice.

David had been right to send me here, I realized now. His casual mention of this place back in Australia—spoken with the offhand confidence of someone describing a favorite restaurant—had launched me across oceans toward experiences I couldn't have imagined. But Pa-Auk had been the necessary preparation, the spiritual boot camp that taught me the difference between thinking about meditation and learning to wrestle my consciousness into something resembling focus.

How do you readjust your voice for human connection when you've been conversing only with your own breath for weeks, learning the secret language of air moving through nostrils like prayers whispered to no one in particular? How do you remember how to be social when you've been practicing the exquisite art of being alone with yourself?

Two teenage boys materialized from behind a flowering tree with the fluid grace of shadows given form, their bare feet silent against the packed earth. Without words—for what need had they for speech?—they swooped on my belongings like practiced dancers, one hefting my battered suitcase with surprising reverence, the other cradling my yoga mat as if it contained something precious. Their efficiency spoke of countless arrivals, countless pilgrims crossing this threshold between the world that counts minutes and the realm where time dissolved into something altogether more elastic.

The taxi driver's engine coughed back to life, already eager to escape this place where forty-three days stretched ahead like a small eternity. Dust devils followed his retreat through wooden gates that seemed to mark more than mere geographical boundaries, and I felt the last thread connecting me to ordinary life snap taut, then break with an almost audible release.

"Come, come. Sayadaw is waiting."

Mr. Soemin's sandals whispered secrets against the ground as he led me toward a low building where carved eaves cast shadows intricate as mandala designs. His voice carried the warmth of someone genuinely glad to see you—not mere politeness but authentic delight—yet underneath ran a current I couldn't identify. Anticipation? Protective concern? The suggestion that I was about to meet someone who might see straight through to whatever I'd been pretending was my authentic self?

The boys ghosted behind us, my worldly possessions suddenly insignificant in their careful hands, reduced to what they had always been: temporary arrangements of matter that couldn't contain whatever it was I'd come here seeking.

THE CELL OF TRANSFORMATION

My room waited like a monk's cell—bare walls the color of old bone, a single wooden bed worn smooth by countless pilgrims who had lain awake in the darkness, wrestling with demons whose names they couldn't yet pronounce. Each previous occupant had left invisible traces: dreams and struggles absorbed into the grain like spiritual sediment, hopes and terrors, and moments of breakthrough layered in the wood's memory.

Above the headboard, a faded Buddha gazed down with half-closed eyes, his expression suggesting he'd witnessed this same ritual of arrival and bewilderment thousands of times before. His painted serenity seemed to whisper: *You are not the first to feel lost. You will not be the last to find yourself.*

String stretched taut across the room like a spider's web, waiting for the mosquito net that would become my nightly cocoon. Through iron-barred windows, bamboo swayed in a neighbor's garden, each leaf catching and releasing light in hypnotic patterns that made me wonder: How many seekers had stared through these same bars, watching the same bamboo dance, feeling this same cocktail of excitement and terror rising in their throats like carbonated prayer?

THE HEART OF SANCTUARY

The main hall breathed around us as we entered—vast and cool, its polished teak floors gleaming like dark water that had learned to hold light without breaking. The wood creaked a familiar welcome under our feet, countless footsteps worn into its grain like prayers made solid, each board a manuscript written in the language of seeking souls.

Above, shadows played in the peaked ceiling where tropical birds sometimes nested, their calls filtering down like benedictions from another realm, another understanding of what it meant to be alive and airborne and free from the gravity of earthbound concerns.

At the hall's heart, the shrine rose like a golden island in an ocean of possibility. Fresh jasmine and marigolds spilled from crystal vases, their sweetness mixing with sandalwood incense that hung in invisible ribbons through the air, weaving scent into prayer, prayer into presence, presence into the kind of awakening that happened when you stopped trying to understand and simply allowed yourself to breathe in beauty.

The Buddha statue seemed to float in golden robes, flanked by four severe photographs of long-dead masters whose eyes followed our approach with the accumulated weight of lifetimes spent in conversation with truth. What dialogues had they conducted in the silence between heartbeats? What answers had they discovered in questions that couldn't be spoken aloud?

A mahogany throne waited empty before the shrine, its carved dragons and lotus flowers seeming to writhe in flickering candlelight. This chair had held how many enlightened beings? What transmissions of understanding had flowed from its worn velvet cushions into hearts ready to receive what couldn't be taught, only transmitted through the alchemy of presence meeting presence in the space where words became unnecessary?

MEETING THE MASTER

Mr. Soemin's knuckles barely whispered against a wooden door before it eased open on hinges that seemed to understand the difference between intrusion and invitation.

"Remember," he murmured, his voice barely disturbing the sacred silence that lived here like a permanent resident, "Sayadaw sees everything. Don't try to impress—just be honest." His warning carried the gentleness of someone who'd watched many Westerners stumble through this first encounter, armor clanking, hearts hammering with the desperate need to appear spiritually sophisticated.

Inside, the air was different—cooler, charged with something I couldn't name but that made the hair on my arms stand at attention like tiny antennae detecting frequencies my conscious mind hadn't learned to decipher. An old monk sat motionless in his chair, saffron robes draped like liquid sunlight across a frame that seemed to exist in perfect harmony with stillness itself.

When he smiled, his face transformed from weathered stone to warm honey, and I understood why people said some faces glowed. This wasn't metaphor but meteorology—the weather patterns of compassion made visible, the climate of wisdom condensed into human features that radiated something I'd never seen before but immediately recognized.

But it was his eyes that stopped my breath mid-journey—dark wells that seemed to hold both infinite compassion and unwavering clarity, as if he could see directly into the tangled confusion of my seeking heart and find there not judgment but understanding, not disappointment but patient recognition of a soul in the process of remembering itself.

His skin held the golden patina of decades spent in meditation, each wrinkle a testament to countless hours of inner stillness, the accumulated geography of a life spent in conversation with the deepest truths. This was what a human being looked like when they'd spent a lifetime learning the difference between who they thought they were and who they were when all pretense fell away.

Mr. Soemin folded to the floor like water finding its level, his forehead touching worn wooden boards with the reverence of someone who understood that humility wasn't degradation but recognition—acknowledgment of the vast spaces that opened when ego stopped insisting on its importance.

"Bow three times," he murmured, his voice barely disturbing the silence that held us all like amniotic fluid in the womb of transformation. "Show respect, but also show your willingness to learn. Show that you understand you are not here to be confirmed in what you already know, but to discover what you never suspected."

My knees found the floor with surprising grace, the wood cool and solid beneath palms that trembled not with fear but with something more like recognition. Down, up. Down, up. Down, up. Each bow felt like shedding another layer of the outside world, another piece of the armor I'd worn for so long I'd forgotten it wasn't my skin, forgotten there was anything underneath worth protecting.

"Now the vows. Repeat after Sayadaw." Mr. Soemin's translation carried new weight, the gravity of commitment. "These aren't just words—they're promises to your deepest self, contracts written in the language of intention and sealed with the breath of sincerity."

The monk's voice emerged from deep places, each Burmese syllable rolling like distant temple bells that had been cast in foundries where sound and silence were understood to be different names for the same phenomenon. I stumbled after his words, my Western tongue clumsy around sounds that had been polished smooth by centuries of repetition, each syllable a stepping stone across the river between who I had been and who I might become.

The words seemed to hang in the air long after we spoke them, as if the room itself was memorizing our promises, holding us accountable to intentions we hadn't fully understood when we spoke them but which our deeper selves recognized as the passwords to territories we'd been seeking our entire lives without knowing their names.

"*Araham.*"

The meditation word settled into my mind like a seed finding soil that had been prepared for exactly this planting—the quality of all enlightened beings, freed from the stains of greed, hatred, and delusion. I was to contemplate these purified qualities while maintaining awareness of breath flowing in and out, wedding the rhythm of respiration to the aspiration toward freedom itself.

"Three days. Keep it always." Sayadaw's eyes held mine as Mr. Soemin translated, the weight of expectation passing between us like a silent covenant, a handshake conducted in the currency of consciousness itself.

Then came an instruction that surprised me: I was to keep a detailed meditation log, recording each session's discoveries and insights. Sayadaw would give me specific exercises to practice. I was to document my experiences with each one, presenting them to him like daily homework at precisely 3 p.m. each day, with Mr. Soemin serving as my interpreter—a spiritual curriculum with assignments I couldn't yet fathom. This was radically different from every other retreat center I'd encountered, where teachers typically advised against any note-taking at all—the assumption being that writing would only strengthen the analytical mind that meditation was meant to quiet. But here, documentation was considered essential, as if the journey ahead would unfold territories so vast and unfamiliar that without careful mapping, I might lose my way entirely.

At the retreat's end, I would need to compile these notes into a comprehensive summary along with my profile. This spiritual autobiography would somehow capture whatever transformation these forty-three days might produce. The very suggestion implied that by the conclusion, I would be documenting the metamorphosis of someone I could not yet imagine becoming.

More bows, deeper this time, my body learning the rhythm of reverence as if remembering movements it had always known but had forgotten in the amnesia of ordinary life.

THE GEOGRAPHY OF AWAKENING

Outside the hall, heat struck like a physical wall. Still, Mr. Soemin seemed untouched by it as he outlined my new existence with the matter-of-fact tone of someone describing the architecture of days that would rebuild me from the foundation upward.

"Four a.m.—not a suggestion." His words carved the coming days into precise segments, each one a small eternity, each one a doorway. "Your mind is clearest then, before the world wakes up and fills it with the noise of its own confusion. Mostly alone. Group sitting, three to four, seven to eight evening—optional for you, but I recommend it. The collective energy multiplies individual effort. Interview with Sayadaw, three p.m. daily. Don't waste his time—he'll know if you've been practicing or just pretending. The difference shows in your eyes. Morning discourse, seven a.m., but it's in Burmese. Let the sounds wash over you. Sometimes understanding comes through pores instead of ears."

My stomach chose that moment to growl, loud as a temple drum in the quiet courtyard, announcing my animal needs in a place dedicated to transcending them, reminding me that enlightenment still required carbohydrates and that even the most elevated souls needed lunch.

Mr. Soemin chuckled, the sound warm and understanding, encompassing the beautiful ridiculousness of being human beings seeking the divine while still needing to urinate and clip our toenails. "Breakfast, five-thirty. Lunch, ten-thirty. Sugar drink at five—you'll hear the bell five minutes before. Don't worry, you won't starve. The body needs fuel for the inner work. Starvation is not the same as purification."

I turned toward what looked like a garden path winding between flowering bushes, but his voice stopped me like an invisible barrier I'd been about to walk through unknowingly.

"Not there! Women's side." His hand sketched an imaginary line through the air, dividing this small world into territories I was only beginning to understand, boundaries that existed not to restrict but to preserve the delicate energies that intensive practice generated, like invisible electricity that needed proper containment to accumulate into transformative force.

"Respect the boundaries. They exist for good reasons that become clear when you understand what happens when consciousness begins to purify itself."

SANCTUARY AND CHALLENGE

Back in my cell—for that's what it was, really, the kind of beautiful imprisonment that freed you from everything except the task of discovering who lived beneath your accumulated identities—I spread my yoga mat over the wooden board like laying claim to a small piece of comfort in a journey that would systematically strip away every other consolation.

The mat was a recent acquisition, purchased in desperate haste on the journey from Pa-Auk to here, my body still carrying the cellular memory of weeks spent on bare wooden planks that had branded my bones with their unforgiving geometry. That trauma had taught me the difference between necessary suffering and pointless martyrdom—one led to awakening, the other merely to chronic back pain and the kind of spiritual pride that confused discomfort with depth.

The travel pillow and thin sleeping bag from home seemed suddenly precious, links to a world that already felt impossibly distant, artifacts from a civilization I could barely remember belonging to. The mosquito net went up with practiced efficiency, a skill learned during previous weeks of monastery life. How quickly we adapt to new definitions of luxury, discovering that freedom from bloodsucking insects qualified as royal accommodation when measured against the truly essential business of awakening.

The compound revealed itself in layers as I explored, like a mandala unfolding its secret geometry. Two acres wrapped in brick and barbed wire, but somehow the barriers felt protective rather than imprisoning—a boundary between the sacred and profane, holding space for transformation like a chrysalis protecting metamorphosis that couldn't be rushed or interrupted by well-meaning interference.

Trees created natural corridors between buildings, their branches heavy with flowers that dropped petals like blessings on pathways below. Vegetables grew in neat rows, tended by invisible hands that understood the connection between outer cultivation and inner growth. Bamboo groves whispered secrets in every breeze, conducting symphonies in languages that bypassed the rational mind and spoke directly to whatever in us still remembered how to listen to the earth's deeper conversations.

The bamboo drew me like a magnet—especially the giants in the far corner that towered three stories high, their hollow stems singing wind songs as they swayed. Their shadows danced across the vegetable patch in patterns that seemed almost choreographed. When the breeze picked up, they created a symphony of wooden flutes that made my chest tight with inexplicable longing.

Was this what homesickness felt like when you'd never been to the place you were missing? Was this the soul's recognition of beauty it had been seeking without knowing beauty's proper name?

Nineteen other seekers shared this sanctuary—I glimpsed them through windows and in peripheral vision, each absorbed in their inner journey like actors in some cosmic play where everyone was simultaneously performer and audience, teacher and student, lost soul and finding guide.

Four monks in saffron robes moved like autumn leaves drifting through the compound, their presence adding gravity to the air itself. Everyone seemed to belong here in a way I didn't yet, their belongings arranged with the precision of people who had already surrendered to this place's rhythms, who had learned to move with the particular grace that comes from accepting that you are exactly where you need to be.

Would I ever move with that same unhurried purpose, or would I always feel like an imposter in borrowed robes, a tourist in the country of awakening?

THE BAPTISM OF DISCOMFORT

The men's bathing area assaulted me with its brutal functionality—an open space dominated by a massive cement tank that squatted like a gray Buddha beneath the sky, teaching lessons about dignity that didn't depend on marble fixtures or temperature control.

Toilets lined up in military precision beyond, stripping away any pretense that this journey would coddle Western sensibilities or provide the kind of comfort that let you forget you were in a body that required maintenance, that produced waste, that connected you to every other biological entity through the humble democracy of digestion.

The water shocked my system into awakeness. Despite the day's heat, it carried the chill of deep earth, of places the sun never touched, aquifers that had been conducting their meditation in subterranean temples for centuries. Each plastic bowlful poured over my head sent goosebumps racing across my skin like scattered prayers, my nervous system registering this baptism as more than hygiene—initiation into simplicities I'd forgotten were sacred.

My breath came in sharp gasps, and I found myself gritting my teeth before each deluge, as if preparing for battle with my comfort-seeking mind, as if learning that transformation always required some form of cold water thrown on the warm assumptions we'd been using as blankets.

But the water itself was revelation—sweet and mineral-rich, carrying stories of underground rivers and ancient aquifers that had never heard of chlorination or municipal treatment plants. It left my skin with a strange tackiness that no amount of toweling could erase, as if the earth itself was claiming me, marking me as its own, reminding me that for all my civilizational sophistication, I remained made of the same elements that composed stars and soil and everything in between.

Perhaps this was what baptism meant—not just symbolic cleansing but literal transformation at the cellular level, the water recognizing water, the mineral content of my body realigning itself with minerals that had never been processed through industrial pipelines.

THE TEACHING OF NOISE

Yet despite the Spartan conditions—or perhaps because of them—this place settled into my bones like coming home to a house I'd been away from so long I'd forgotten its particular way of holding light, its distinctive sounds of settling into evening peace.

The silence here had weight and substance, unlike Pa-Auk, where my roommate's every breath had been an intrusion into space that was supposed to be expanding consciousness, not navigating personality conflicts. Here, silence wasn't just the absence of sound but a presence in itself, thick as honey and twice as sweet, creating space for thoughts to surface and dissolve without the usual commentary that turned every arising into a story about me.

The only assault on this peace came from beyond the walls, where neighbors seemed locked in an eternal battle of amplification. Tinny pop music clashed with traditional Myanmar opera, creating a psychedelic symphony that would have been comical if it weren't so relentless. This soundtrack seemed designed by someone who'd never heard of the concept of "too much."

Even paradise, it seemed, came with its background noise, its reminder that the world would not arrange itself for our convenience, would not automatically provide the perfect conditions we imagined we needed for inner work.

Mr. Soemin caught me wincing as another wave of musical chaos crashed over the compound walls like acoustic surf. "Don't let the noise bother you!" he shouted over a particularly enthusiastic love ballad, his grin suggesting he'd given this advice countless times to countless foreigners who arrived expecting monastery life to resemble meditation app soundtracks.

"Noise is just another teacher. Concentrate on your meditation object! Let the sound be sound, and you be you! The problem is not what you hear—the problem is your resistance to what you hear."

But my concentration held, surprising me with its steadiness, like discovering a muscle I hadn't known existed. Nearly a month at Pa-Auk had carved new pathways in my mind, and *Araham* settled into the grooves like water finding its course, like a river remembering how to flow downhill.

Even walking the flower-lined paths, the sacred syllables pulsed with my heartbeat, weaving themselves into the rhythm of steps, breath, being itself. *Araham. Araham. Araham.* Not just repetition but incantation, not just practice but prayer disguised as technique.

Other thoughts tried to muscle in—fragments of home, worries about the days ahead, observations about my fellow pilgrims—but I pushed them aside like clearing weeds from a garden, making the meditation word louder, stronger, more present than anything else competing for space in the theater of consciousness.

This was the real work, I realized—not the sitting but the choosing, moment by moment, where to place attention in a universe specifically designed to scatter it in forty-seven different directions simultaneously.

THE FIRST NIGHT

That evening, Mr. Soemin materialized beside me as I sat in the gathering dusk, fireflies beginning their ancient dance among the bamboo. His approach was so quiet I wondered if he'd learned to walk between footsteps, to move through space without disturbing the very atoms that composed it.

"How is your meditation?" The question carried genuine curiosity, not mere politeness—the interest of someone who understood that what happened in the privacy of individual practice would determine everything that followed.

"Good." The word felt inadequate, but how could I explain the strange sense of coming awake that had been building in me all day? How could I describe feeling simultaneously more myself and less myself than ever before, as if I was finally meeting someone I'd been trying to avoid my entire adult life?

His eyes sharpened with interest, like a scientist observing a promising experiment or a doctor checking for symptoms that would reveal which medicine to prescribe next. "Did you see anything?"

The question hung in the humid air like incense smoke. "No," I replied, but his expression suggested he was hunting for something specific, something I didn't yet know to look for, some sign or signal that would indicate whether consciousness was beginning to unveil whatever it kept hidden behind the ordinary daily programming of thoughts, sensations, and mundane observations.

What did other pilgrims see on their first day? What was I missing, or not missing? Was there some cosmic television channel I hadn't learned to tune into yet?

By nine o'clock, exhaustion had seeped into my bones like monsoon rain into parched earth. My first day in this sacred container was complete. Still, already I sensed it had changed me in ways I wouldn't understand for weeks to come, alterations occurring below the threshold of conscious recognition but registering in some deeper cellular awareness that knew transformation when it tasted it.

The person who would emerge from these forty-three days was already stirring to life somewhere in the depths of my being, like something that had been in chrysalis finally beginning to push against walls that had once felt like protection but now felt like limitation.

Through my barred window, the bamboo continued its endless conversation with the wind, and somewhere in that whispered dialogue, I began to hear the first notes of my transformation. Tomorrow would bring new challenges, new dissolutions of the familiar self that had carried me this far but might not be equipped for the territories ahead.

But tonight, wrapped in my mosquito net cocoon like a spiritual larvae preparing for metamorphosis, I felt held by something larger than my small seeking heart—held by the accumulated prayers of all who had slept in this room before me, all who had made this same leap into the unknown territory of their own deepest nature, all who had discovered that the only way out was through, and the only way through was surrender.

Day 2 — The War Within

Sleep arrived like scattered coins falling through my fingers, impossible to hold, impossible to gather into anything resembling rest. The silk liner whispered accusations against my skin with each restless turn, but it wasn't the tropical heat that kept jerking me awake—it was the intruder who had claimed sovereignty over my cell's darkness.

A gecko had slipped through the gap beneath my door like a tiny burglar with perfect timing, and now it owned the night with the confidence of a landlord collecting rent. Click-click-click. The sound ricocheted off bare walls with metronomic precision, each sharp note drilling into my skull just as consciousness would begin its delicate descent toward unconsciousness. Click-click-click. I'd surface from near-sleep, heart hammering with fight-or-flight panic that seemed absurdly disproportionate to a creature no larger than my thumb, only to sink back down until the next volley of clicks hauled me up again like a fish on an invisible line.

Is this what monks called "noble suffering"? Lying there at 2 a.m., fantasizing about gecko murder with the detailed planning of a war strategist, felt distinctly ignoble.

When my alarm whispered its electronic prayer at 3:30 a.m., I felt like I'd been fighting a war all night—and losing to an opponent that weighed less than a paperclip.

THE CATHEDRAL OF DAWN

The pre-dawn air wrapped around me like cool silk as I stepped into the courtyard, my bare feet greeting the packed earth with surprising tenderness, as if the ground itself was offering comfort my bed had failed to provide. Above, the Milky Way spilled across the sky in a river of ancient light, each star sharp as a pinprick in black velvet, a celestial reminder that somewhere beyond this small compound of human struggle, the universe continued its eternal dance of beauty and indifference.

For the first time in hours, silence—real silence—settled over the compound like a blessing from the cosmos itself. Crickets wove their lullabies through the darkness while frogs added their bass notes from hidden pools, creating nature's temple music. This symphony had been playing long before humans arrived with their complications and would continue long after we departed with our resolved or unresolved seeking.

I stood there, breathing in this profound quiet that made my chest expand with something approaching reverence. This was what I'd come for—not just the absence of noise, but the presence of something vast and listening, something that didn't need to be understood to be felt, didn't need to be grasped to be received.

Araham, I whispered to the stars, and the word seemed to dissolve into the cosmic stillness above, carried away on wings I couldn't see but somehow felt brushing against my consciousness like the gentle touch of something ineffable acknowledging my small human attempt at connection.

THE SWIMMING POOL BUDDHA

At the water tank, while my toothbrush worked mechanically in my mouth like a device performing maintenance on a body I was temporarily inhabiting, the peace was shattered by a sound that belonged in a nature documentary, not a sacred compound.

Plop!

I spun toward the sound just in time to witness a massive green frog executing perfect swimming strokes across our drinking water, its webbed feet cutting the surface like a tiny Olympic athlete who'd wandered into the wrong pool but decided to make the best of it. The creature hauled itself onto the cement rim with theatrical dignity, fixed me with one golden eye that seemed to hold ancient amusement at human squeamishness, then launched itself into the darkness with the confidence of a being that owned this place far more completely than I ever would.

I stared at the ripples spreading across our water supply, toothpaste foam dripping from my chin like evidence of my Western conditioning suddenly exposed as ridiculous. Every sip, every splash on my face—suddenly I was hyperaware of sharing this space with creatures who recognized no boundaries between sacred and profane, who treated the monastery's holy water tank as their swimming pool without any sense that this might violate protocols I'd never learned to question.

Was this another teaching I wasn't ready to receive? Was the universe suggesting that purity was a more flexible concept than my cultural programming had led me to believe?

THE LIGHT BEHIND CLOSED EYES

Back in my cell, cocooned within the mosquito net's white walls like a spiritual larva preparing for transformation I couldn't yet imagine, I settled into meditation posture with the careful precision of someone performing a ritual that might matter, that might unlock doors I'd been standing in front of my entire life without recognizing them as doorways.

The mat beneath me held the memory of yesterday's practice, and my spine found its familiar alignment almost automatically, as if my body was already learning this new language of stillness, already beginning to remember something it had known before civilization taught it to slouch.

Araham. The word dropped into the silence like a stone into still water, sending ripples through consciousness that I could feel but not see, could sense but not measure.

And then—*light*.

Not the harsh glare of electric bulbs or the familiar illumination of any earthly source, but something softer, more intimate—a faint luminescence that seemed to emanate from the space behind my closed eyes, growing brighter with each repetition of the sacred syllable like some internal sunrise that had been waiting for precisely this invitation to begin.

My breath caught in my throat with the shock of recognition. This was what Mr. Soemin had been asking about yesterday with that knowing expression, that suggestion of secrets I hadn't yet learned to detect. This was what I'd read about in dusty meditation manuals but never believed could happen to someone like me —someone too ordinary, too psychologically cluttered, too fundamentally Western to access whatever mystical capabilities belonged to other people in other centuries who'd somehow been born with spiritual equipment I obviously lacked.

This was—

Ding, ding, ding.

The breakfast bell shattered my concentration like glass hitting concrete, the light vanishing as if someone had blown out a candle in a wind I couldn't feel but which seemed to carry away everything precious the moment external demands reasserted their tyranny over inner exploration.

I found myself blinking in the harsh fluorescent reality of 5:15 a.m., bereft as a child whose favorite toy had just been snatched away by cosmic forces that seemed to delight in interrupting precisely when something important was beginning to emerge from the depths of possibility.

THE SACRED CHOREOGRAPHY OF BREAKFAST

Outside the dining hall, we arranged ourselves with the precision of a military formation that had been rehearsed in previous lives—men on one side, women on the other, age granting its ancient privilege of precedence in hierarchies that felt more protective than oppressive here, more like natural order than artificial imposition.

Sayadaw emerged from the main hall like sunrise itself, his saffron robes catching what little light the dawn offered, transforming him into something between human and solar deity, someone who carried illumination wherever he moved. Behind him, a teenage monk moved with the careful grace of someone learning to inhabit sacred space, each step a small prayer offered to the earth, each gesture a reminder that even walking could be devotion when performed with sufficient attention.

A boy appeared at the entrance, hands pressed together in prayer position, his slight bow an invitation encoded in centuries of tradition. This gesture spoke languages older than words and more precise than any verbal communication could achieve. We flowed forward like a river of silent seekers, hands clasped behind backs, feet whispering against polished floors that reflected our procession like a dream of itself, like consciousness witnessing its movement through dimensions where matter and spirit learned to collaborate.

My assigned table held four other men, their faces composed in that particular way of people who had surrendered their need to fill silence with noise—or perhaps who had simply forgotten how to make small talk about the weather when the weather had become irrelevant to their inner climate, when conversation about external conditions felt like missing the point of existence itself.

We bowed in unison—three times to the Buddha whose painted eyes watched from the wall with the patience of eternity, three times to Sayadaw whose living presence blessed our simple meal with the weight of actual holiness rather than the mere symbolic gestures I'd grown accustomed to in religious contexts that had forgotten their original purpose.

THE COMMUNION OF SILENT NOURISHMENT

The dining hall breathed with quiet purpose, a pocket of calm in a world that had forgotten how to be still, a sanctuary where eating could return to its original function as communion rather than mere fuel consumption conducted while multitasking through life's endless distractions.

Sayadaw sat alone at the front like a meditation master in a classical painting. At the same time, we arranged ourselves in our designated territories—two tables of men at the front, three tables of women toward the back, geography encoding the monastery's ancient hierarchies that somehow felt like protection for delicate energies rather than restriction of human freedom.

Boys materialized beside us with the quiet efficiency of temple dancers who had learned to serve without disturbing the cathedral silence, their movements so fluid they seemed to exist in harmony with invisible currents that governed sacred space. They ladled out stir-fried noodles that steamed with the perfume of garlic and star anise, vegetables glistening with oil like precious gems, tofu cubes nestled among bean sprouts like small pillows of contentment arranged by artists who understood that presentation was prayer made visible.

The coffee arrived dark and bitter enough to wake the dead—or perhaps the spiritually dormant—while Chinese tea followed, pale green and speaking of mountain gardens where monks had perfected the art of presence over centuries, each leaf a small lesson in how patience could transform ordinary plants into vehicles for awakening.

Pickled vegetables provided a sharp counterpoint to the meal's gentle harmonies, each bite a small explosion of flavor that demanded complete attention, that made multitasking impossible and presence unavoidable. How long since I'd tasted my food instead of simply consuming it while my mind scattered itself across tomorrow's plans and yesterday's regrets?

The chanting before we ate was brief but powerful—voices joining in Pali syllables that had blessed countless meals across centuries, connecting us to an unbroken chain of practitioners who had sat in similar silence, offering similar gratitude, participating in the same recognition that nourishment was a gift, not a right, grace, not entitlement.

Then deeper silence descended, broken only by the soft percussion of chopsticks against bowls and the occasional shuffle of feet on wooden floors—sounds that belonged to the meditation rather than interrupting it. These rhythms supported the communion rather than disturbing its delicate chemistry.

Even eating became meditation here, each bite demanding presence, attention, gratitude for the hands that had prepared this simple feast, for the earth that had grown these vegetables, for the rain that had fallen, for the sun that had shone, for the vast web of interconnection that delivered sustenance to bodies temporarily inhabited by consciousness seeking to remember its true nature.

I watched Mr. Soemin orchestrate the boys with subtle gestures, a conductor managing his silent symphony of service with the grace of someone who understood that even mundane tasks could be doorways to the sacred when performed with the kind of attention that transformed everything it touched.

When we bowed our final thanks and filed out with the same reverential precision we'd entered, I felt the meal settling into my bones like contentment itself—not just physical satisfaction, but something deeper, as if I'd participated in communion with something larger than hunger, larger than individual need, larger than the small self that usually demanded to be fed first and asked questions later.

THE ASSAULT OF SOUND

Back in my room, the mosquito net hung in defeated surrender, one corner collapsed like a white flag announcing the ongoing battle between Western comfort-seeking and Eastern simplicity, between my desire for perfect conditions and reality's insistence on providing exactly the challenges I needed rather than the ones I wanted.

I wrestled it back into position, muttering minor curses under my breath that felt distinctly unholy in this sacred space, then escaped to walk the compound's leafy pathways where jasmine released its perfume to the warming air like prayers made fragrant, like beauty offered without conditions or expectations of return.

The bamboo giants whispered their morning prayers in languages older than human speech, and for a moment I felt held by something that didn't require my understanding—only my willingness to listen, only my capacity to receive whatever gifts were being offered by intelligence that communicated through rustling leaves and moving shadows rather than words and concepts.

But peace was temporary, precious as morning dew that evaporates the moment sunlight touches it with full intensity. At 10:25, the lunch bell summoned us again to our ritual of silent communion, and I found myself craving these moments of structured calm like a drug I was only beginning to understand I needed, like medicine for an addiction to chaos I'd never recognized as pathological.

The afternoon group sitting in the main hall should have been sanctuary—twenty-plus souls gathered in collective silence, our combined intention creating something larger than the sum of its parts, a field of shared seeking that felt almost tangible, like electricity generated by consciousness converging on common purpose.

I settled onto my cushion with anticipation, ready to dive deeper into the mysterious light I'd glimpsed that morning, to explore whatever doorways were opening in the architecture of my awareness, to discover what other capabilities might be awakening in consciousness that had been systematically trained to ignore its own deeper potentials.

Then the assault began.

Music exploded from the neighbors' compound like sound made violent—pounding bass that seemed designed to rearrange my internal organs, screeching vocals that clawed at my eardrums with the enthusiasm of demons celebrating their victory over peace. These electronic beats turned my skull into a percussion instrument being played by a sadistic child who understood exactly which frequencies would cause maximum spiritual damage.

The noise didn't just fill the hall; it invaded it, occupied it, colonized it, made meditation feel like trying to pray in the middle of a construction site run by people who hated silence and had declared war on contemplation itself.

Araham, I tried desperately, but the sacred syllable was no match for whatever musical war was raging beyond our walls. The harder I concentrated, the louder the cacophony seemed to grow, as if my resistance was feeding it energy, my spiritual effort providing fuel for the very forces destroying it, my determination creating exactly the tension that amplified the disturbance rather than transcending it.

Frustration bloomed in my chest like a poisonous flower, its tendrils spreading through my nervous system with toxic efficiency. My jaw clenched tight enough to crack teeth. My shoulders crept toward my ears like creatures seeking shelter. *Concentrate,* I commanded myself with the desperation of someone drowning in their inability to let go, but concentration felt impossible when my nervous system was under siege by forces that seemed designed to prevent precisely the kind of inner stillness I'd traveled halfway around the world to find.

The frustration curdled into rage—hot, helpless fury that made my hands shake and my breath come in shallow gasps. For two hours, I sat there fantasizing about storming next door with a sledgehammer, reducing their speakers to satisfying piles of plastic and wire, creating the blessed silence through violence that I couldn't achieve through peace, imposing through force the conditions I lacked the spiritual sophistication to find within the chaos.

The fantasy was so vivid I could taste the satisfaction, so detailed I could feel the weight of the imaginary sledgehammer in my hands, so compelling I had to consciously restrain myself from actually getting up and acting on impulses that felt completely reasonable under the circumstances.

What kind of meditator was I becoming? What did it say about my spiritual progress that I was sitting in a Buddhist monastery plotting the destruction of sound equipment? What did it reveal about my actual level of development that two days of practice had transformed me into someone capable of meditating violence against electronic devices?

THE SYMPHONY OF CHAOS

When the music finally stopped, my relief lasted approximately thirty seconds before new tortures began with the precision of professional psychological warfare—market vendors hawking their wares through tinny megaphones that turned human voices into robotic screeches. Someone's birthday party, complete with a karaoke machine broadcasting off-key renditions of pop songs to the entire neighborhood as if tone deafness was a virtue to be celebrated publicly.

Distant monastery loudspeakers broadcasting competing sermons that layered over each other like dueling gods arguing about enlightenment through electronic amplification, each temple convinced that volume was directly correlated with spiritual authority.

The cacophony layered itself into a symphony of chaos that made my teeth hurt and my soul feel battered, that seemed designed by someone who'd made a detailed study of exactly which combination of sounds would be most effective at preventing any possibility of inner silence. How did people live like this? How did they sleep, think, exist in this constant assault of noise that seemed designed to prevent any possibility of the contemplation required for psychological health, let alone spiritual development?

I felt my sanity beginning to fray at the edges, forty-one more days stretching ahead like a prison sentence handed down by judges who had forgotten the meaning of mercy, who had confused endurance with enlightenment, who had mistaken suffering for transformation.

When the session finally ended, I stumbled out of the hall feeling psychologically battered, like a survivor of some audio warfare that left no visible wounds but damaged everything underneath the surface, everything that mattered, everything that made consciousness feel like home rather than hostile territory.

Around me, other meditators moved with that same deliberate calm I'd noticed yesterday—slow, measured steps, eyes focused on the ground three feet ahead, faces serene as Buddhist statues that had achieved some impossible peace that seemed to operate according to entirely different laws than my nervous system had access to.

Were they deaf? Medicated? Or did they possess some secret knowledge that made them immune to the audio warfare surrounding us? I felt like an exposed nerve among beings made of stone, the only one in this sacred community who lacked the essential equipment for transcendence, the only one whose spiritual hardware was fundamentally defective.

THE DIAGNOSIS

Mr. Soemin appeared on one of the flowered pathways, taking in my shell-shocked expression with eyes that held both understanding and gentle challenge, the look of someone who'd witnessed this exact crisis countless times before and knew exactly what medicine was required.

"If you concentrate hard," he called out, his melodic voice somehow remaining warm and encouraging even as it competed with a fresh wave of pop music, "the noise will not bother you! Make the meditation object stronger than the disturbance!"

His words hit like a diagnosis I didn't want to hear but couldn't deny. Of course. I was the problem. I was the weak link in this chain of spiritual warriors, the tourist complaining about local customs in a sacred land, the foreigner who'd arrived expecting the world to arrange itself for his convenience rather than learning to find peace within whatever conditions reality chose to provide.

Everyone else had mastered the art of mental noise-cancellation while I sat there like a child having a tantrum because the world wasn't arranged for my comfort, because the universe had failed to consult my preferences before designing the circumstances that would most effectively reveal my spiritual immaturity.

THE INVENTORY OF DEFEAT

The afternoon brought more disappointment—Sayadaw was away, so no interview, no guidance, no wise words to help me navigate this acoustic hell or the psychological mess I was making of my practice. I found myself practically begging Mr. Soemin for small mercies: a chair to sit in (my spine was beginning to rebel against the floor-sitting lifestyle like a spoiled Western appendage that had never learned proper posture), a new mosquito net that might fit my bed and restore some tiny island of competence to my daily existence.

Even these tiny requests felt like admissions of failure, evidence that I lacked the basic fortitude for this path, that I was fundamentally unsuited for the kind of spiritual adventure I'd thought I was prepared to undertake but which was revealing me as someone whose self-assessment had been embarrassingly inaccurate.

As evening painted the sky in shades of saffron and gold, I sat in my room calculating despair with the mathematical precision of someone keeping score in a game they were losing by margins that grew larger with each passing hour. Day two, and I was already unraveling like a sweater with a pulled thread, each challenge revealing new ways in which my preparation had been inadequate, my expectations naive, my spiritual ambitions inflated beyond any realistic assessment of my actual capabilities.

Forty-one days remained—forty-one opportunities for my neighbors to drive me completely insane, forty-one chances to prove that I didn't belong among these serene practitioners who seemed to float above the chaos like lotus flowers rising from mud, their roots somehow finding nourishment in conditions that left me gasping for air, drowning in circumstances that revealed them as beings from an entirely different species of consciousness.

THE MOCKERY OF BEAUTY

Through my barred window, the bamboo continued its eternal conversation with the wind, but tonight their whispered wisdom sounded like mockery, as if they were discussing my failures in languages I would never understand, laughing at the foreigner who'd traveled so far to discover that he lacked the most basic equipment for the journey he'd imagined himself capable of completing.

Even the gecko had returned, claiming its territory under my door with those relentless clicks that would soon begin their nightly torture, another small creature that belonged here more naturally than I did, another reminder that this place had its own ancient rhythms that didn't require human approval or comfort to continue their eternal dance.

I pulled my thin sleeping bag up to my chin. I tried to summon something resembling hope, some thread of faith that this journey might lead somewhere other than complete psychological breakdown, some evidence that transformation was possible for someone as fundamentally unsuited to this path as I was proving to be.

Tomorrow would bring new challenges, new tests of whatever spiritual fortitude I might still possess buried beneath the rubble of my expectations, new opportunities to discover whether persistence could overcome incompetence, whether determination could substitute for the natural spiritual equipment I lacked.

But tonight, in the gathering darkness of my second day, wrapped in the cocoon of my collapsing mosquito net like a failed butterfly that would never earn its wings, that seemed like more threat than promise, more curse than blessing.

Somewhere in the distance, a temple bell rang the hour, its bronze voice carrying across the neighborhood with the authority of centuries, reminding me that at least some sounds still held beauty, that not everything in this acoustic chaos was designed to torture Western nervous systems unequipped for the democratic symphony of tropical life.

At least the darkness still offered refuge from the day's failures. And maybe—just maybe—the light I'd glimpsed that morning meant something real was trying to be born in the ruins of my comfortable assumptions about who I thought I was, something that could survive the death of illusions I'd been carrying about my spiritual sophistication, something that could grow in soil fertilized by the decomposing remains of pride that had been masquerading as readiness for transformation.

∼

Day 3 — The Medicine of Loving Kindness

Sleep arrived like mercy incarnate—deep and unbroken from 8:30 p.m. until the pre-dawn darkness called me back to consciousness at four with the gentle insistence of a lover whispering secrets. Even the gecko seemed to have declared a temporary ceasefire, its territorial clicks replaced by the softer percussion of my heartbeat against the pillow, steady as a temple drum keeping time with some cosmic rhythm I was only beginning to hear beneath the surface noise of ordinary existence.

The music from next door had continued its relentless assault past midnight. Still, somehow the volume had dropped from torture to mere annoyance—perhaps my neighbors were finally showing signs of human exhaustion, or perhaps my ears were adapting to this new acoustic reality like a soldier's hearing adjusting to the sounds of war until explosions became as natural as breathing. Either way, I surfaced from sleep feeling almost human again—a minor miracle after yesterday's psychological battlefield that had left me questioning everything from my spiritual aptitude to my basic sanity.

THE FLOWER OF AWARENESS

My first meditation session bloomed like a flower opening to sunlight, each petal of awareness unfurling with impossible grace, as if consciousness had been waiting all night for exactly this invitation to remember its capacity for beauty. From four until 5:20, I sat cocooned in my mosquito net while the world outside held its breath in that sacred space between night and dawn, when even the loudest neighborhoods fall under the spell of temporary quiet, when the universe pauses to remember what silence sounds like.

Araham dropped into the stillness like a perfectly weighted anchor. Soon the familiar light began to shimmer behind my closed eyelids—not the harsh fluorescent glare of artificial illumination that belonged to hospitals and office buildings, but something softer, more alive, like candlelight filtered through honey and held in cupped palms by someone who understood that illumination was as much about gentleness as brightness.

My breath slowed until each inhalation felt like it lasted minutes, each exhalation releasing layers of tension I hadn't even known I was carrying—the accumulated residue of a lifetime spent bracing against a world that rarely offered the gentleness I craved but had never learned to give myself. The light grew stronger, more defined, until I felt I might be able to reach out and cup it in my palms like water from a sacred spring that had been waiting centuries for someone to discover its location.

Was this what the ancient texts meant when they spoke of inner luminosity? Was this the treasure that justified all the discomfort, all the surrendering of familiar comforts, all the voluntary exile from everything that had previously defined me as successful and civilized and worthy of respect?

THE SYMPHONY OF SIMPLE NOURISHMENT

Breakfast arrived as a symphony of familiar flavors—noodles dancing with vegetables in that perfect marriage of texture and taste that made my mouth sing with gratitude for the simple miracle of nourishment, for the hands that had prepared this feast, for the earth that had grown these vegetables, for the rain that had fallen and the sun that had shone to make this moment possible.

The Chinese tea followed, pale and fragrant as mountain mist, carrying stories of high-altitude gardens where monks had learned to tend plants with the same attention they brought to consciousness, while the coffee anchored the meal with its bitter wisdom, strong enough to wake both body and spirit from whatever dreams had been postponing awakening.

Around me, my fellow seekers maintained their ritual silence. Still, I could sense a shared appreciation radiating from their careful movements, their grateful bows—these simple gifts that sustained our inner work were communion itself, evidence that the sacred could inhabit the most ordinary moments when attention was refined enough to recognize what had always been present but usually overlooked.

THE MEDICINE OF REST

After breakfast, fatigue crept up on me like fog rolling in from the sea, heavy with the weight of yesterday's struggles, carrying the particular exhaustion that comes from fighting battles against enemies that exist primarily in the landscape of resistance rather than external reality. I'd intended to meditate, but when I lay down on my mat "just for a moment," consciousness dissolved into dreamless black that felt less like failure and more like necessary healing, like medicine prescribed by some deeper intelligence that understood the difference between spiritual effort and spiritual masochism.

When I surfaced again, an hour had vanished like smoke, leaving me disoriented and slightly guilty for this unauthorized escape from awareness—but also mysteriously refreshed, as if some cosmic physician had administered exactly the treatment I needed. At the same time, my conscious mind was temporarily offline and couldn't interfere with the healing process through anxious monitoring of progress.

While the locals gathered in the main hall for their morning seminar—a river of Burmese syllables flowing through the compound like temple music in a language that bypassed my thinking mind and spoke directly to something older, something that predated the need for understanding to be nourished—I claimed my foreigner's exemption and escaped to the bathing area.

The cold well water shocked my system awake with its mineral bite, each plastic bowlful a baptism that left me gasping and grateful for this simple alchemy of purification, for water that remembered its journey through underground caverns and ancient aquifers, water that carried stories of depths my surface mind would never access but my body recognized as home.

THE FORTRESS OF INNER SILENCE

Washing clothes became a meditation in itself: the rhythm of scrubbing that synchronized with my heartbeat, the satisfaction of dirt surrendering to persistence, the simple miracle of dirty becoming clean—surely a metaphor for whatever was happening to the accumulated grime in my consciousness, the layers of conditioning and complaint and resistance that were being slowly scrubbed away through processes I couldn't control but was learning to trust.

From the hall, waves of chanting rolled across the compound like distant thunder, marking the seminar's approaching end with voices joined in devotions that had been polished smooth by centuries of repetition. I timed my retreat to my room perfectly, slipping back into solitude just as footsteps began echoing across the courtyard—a small victory in the art of monastery navigation, proof that I was starting to understand the rhythms of this place well enough to move within them rather than constantly colliding with their unexpected requirements.

An hour of sitting meditation before lunch proved revelatory in ways that surprised me with their simplicity. Despite the neighbors launching into what sounded like a mariachi band mixed with construction equipment—a sonic assault that would have shattered my concentration two days ago and sent me fleeing toward fantasies of sledgehammer-based solutions—my focus held firm as a mountain peak unmoved by storms.

Araham pulsed with my heartbeat, creating a buffer zone of inner silence that the external chaos couldn't penetrate, a fortress of awareness that no amount of amplified chaos could breach. I felt like a deep-sea diver discovering that the ocean's surface storms couldn't touch the profound calm of the depths, that there were places in consciousness the world's noise simply couldn't reach, territories of peace that remained inviolable regardless of whatever acoustic warfare raged in the shallower waters of ordinary experience.

Still, I couldn't help wondering what divine madman had chosen this location for a meditation center. Surely there were quieter corners of Myanmar where seekers could pursue inner peace without competing with what sounded like the world's loudest block party broadcast through speakers designed to wake the dead and announce the apocalypse to anyone who might have missed its arrival.

But perhaps this was the point—learning to find silence not by controlling the world but by discovering the indestructible quiet that lived beneath all disturbance, the peace that didn't depend on external cooperation but arose from some deeper source that remained unshakeable regardless of surface conditions.

THE FESTIVAL OF ABUNDANCE

Lunch transformed the dining hall into a festival of abundance that bordered on the miraculous, a reminder that even amid intensive spiritual practice, the earth continued its generous offering of nourishment and beauty. Fifteen different dishes crowded the tables like an edible rainbow—fish that flaked at the touch of chopsticks, pork that melted on the tongue like prayers made edible, vegetables that sang with spices I couldn't name but somehow recognized at a cellular level, as if my DNA carried memories of flavors from ancestors who had tasted these exact combinations centuries ago.

Each bite was a small revelation, my Western palate slowly learning to dance with complexities that had been perfected over generations of grandmothers who understood that feeding someone was the most intimate form of love, that nourishment was always sacrament when offered with attention and received with gratitude. How many meals had I consumed without really tasting them, treating food as fuel rather than a gift, as a commodity rather than communion with the vast web of interconnection that delivered sustenance to temporary biological forms inhabited by eternal consciousness?

I carried *Araham* with me as I left the dining hall, the sacred syllable weaving itself through my steps like an invisible thread connecting me to something larger than hunger or satisfaction, larger than individual need, larger than the small self that usually demanded to be fed first and asked questions about meaning later.

Under the bamboo giants, where cooling shadows offered refuge from the midday sun that beat down with the intensity of focused attention itself, walking meditation became a form of prayer written in footsteps, each placement of foot on earth a small offering to whatever intelligence had designed this intricate dance between consciousness and the physical world.

Each footfall whispered against the earth with the tenderness of someone afraid to disturb a sleeping lover, each breath synchronized with the swaying of the emerald towers above that seemed to be conducting some vast symphony only they could hear, music written in the language of photosynthesis and root systems and the patient wisdom of beings that understood how to remain still while growing toward light.

The breeze through the bamboo created its music—hollow wooden flutes singing harmonies that made my chest tight with inexplicable longing for something I'd never known but had always been missing, some home I'd never visited but whose architecture was written in my cells, whose address was encoded in the rhythm of my breathing.

Here, at least, the manufactured cacophony from beyond the walls couldn't destroy the peace. Nature still held some territory in this war between silence and noise, and I felt like a refugee who had found temporary sanctuary in her green cathedral, someone who had remembered how to listen to voices that spoke in rustling leaves and moving shadows rather than words and concepts and the endless commentary that usually passed for consciousness.

THE GIFT I DIDN'T KNOW I NEEDED

At three o'clock, I presented myself to Sayadaw like a student reporting for examination, my heart carrying both hope and the weight of yesterday's failures, the memory of psychological collapse that had revealed my spiritual preparation as far less adequate than I'd imagined when booking flights and making arrangements for this journey from the comfort of theoretical commitment.

His golden face creased into that familiar smile of approval as Mr. Soemin translated my stumbling descriptions of lights and slowing breath. I felt the relief of someone whose homework had been judged acceptable by a teacher whose standards reached toward infinity, whose expectations were calibrated according to the actual requirements for awakening rather than the consolation prizes that usually passed for spiritual progress in environments designed to make everyone feel successful.

Then came the gift I didn't know I needed.

"*Metta*," Sayadaw said, the word rolling off his tongue like a prayer that had been aged in oak barrels of compassion, like wine distilled from the suffering and healing of countless beings who had learned to transform pain into medicine, wounds into wisdom, isolation into the kind of love that included everything.

Loving kindness. Mr. Soemin's translation carried weight beyond mere language—this was medicine for a heart I hadn't realized was wounded, a prescription for an illness I'd been holding so long I'd mistaken it for my natural state, treatment for a condition that had been masquerading as personality rather than revealing itself as pathology that could be healed through the systematic cultivation of attitudes I'd never considered learnable skills.

"Start with yourself," Mr. Soemin explained, his melodic voice gentle as a father teaching a child to ride a bicycle, patient as someone who understood that the most challenging lessons often involved unlearning habits that felt like identity, dismantling defenses that had once been necessary but had outlived their usefulness. "Then extend it outward. Like ripples in a pond, but ripples of love."

THE PRACTICE OF SELF-COMPASSION

Back in my cave-like room, I began this new practice with the enthusiasm of someone discovering fire mixed with the tenderness of someone learning to touch their wounds without flinching, to approach the tender places in consciousness without the usual armor of distraction and self-criticism that had protected me from feeling too much for too long.

Metta flowed through me like warm honey, starting with the most challenging target of all—myself. *May I be happy, may I be healthy, may I be at peace.* The words felt foreign on my inner tongue, like speaking a language I'd forgotten I knew, like trying to remember the lyrics to a song I'd last heard in childhood when sincerity hadn't yet been complicated by sophistication and cynicism.

When had I last wished myself well without conditions, without the small print that required me to earn kindness through achievement, to deserve love through performance, to qualify for peace through the exhausting maintenance of some impossible standard of spiritual or personal excellence?

Then rippling outward in concentric circles of compassion: to my fellow meditators wrestling with their inner demons in the privacy of their caves, to Mr. Soemin and his family who had opened their sanctuary to broken seekers like me, to the teenage boys who served us with such quiet grace, moving through the halls like young bodhisattvas in training, their service a form of devotion that required no recognition to remain pure.

THE ALCHEMY OF LOVING KINDNESS

At 4:50, the bell's silver voice announced drink time with the authority of a church bell calling the faithful to vespers, to the kind of communion that transcended denominational boundaries and spoke to the universal hunger for connection with something larger than individual need. I emerged from my darkness blinking like a nocturnal creature discovering that daylight could be gentle rather than harsh, collected a glass of cordial that tasted like concentrated sunshine mixed with childhood memories of summer afternoons when time moved slowly and happiness required no justification.

I continued the *Metta* practice as I wandered the flowering pathways, the cold sweetness on my tongue, the warm breeze stirring the jasmine with invisible fingers, the last rays of afternoon sun painting everything golden as melted butter—all of it felt like components of a vast blessing I was finally learning to receive rather than deflect, to accept rather than analyze, to enjoy rather than evaluate according to some impossible standard of what spiritual experience was supposed to look like.

As evening descended and the group sitting began, I carried this new weapon into battle against the acoustic assault that had previously driven me to the edge of psychological collapse. But something fundamental had shifted in the geography of my inner landscape, some tectonic plate of attitude had moved in ways that changed the entire topography of experience.

When the neighbors launched into their evening concert of chaos —karaoke vocals that sounded like cats being tortured in musical time signatures by someone who'd confused volume with artistic expression—instead of tensing against it like a fist closing around pain, I found myself extending loving kindness to these invisible tormentors who were probably just trying to squeeze some joy from their ordinary lives.

May the karaoke singers be happy. May the party-goers find joy. May all beings be free from suffering, even if their celebration is destroying my meditation.

THE FEVER BREAKING

The transformation was subtle but unmistakable, like feeling a fever break—my mind felt light, expansive, as if someone had opened windows in a stuffy room that had been sealed for years, letting in air that carried the scent of possibilities I'd forgotten existed. The noise remained exactly as jarring as before. Still, its power to disturb had somehow been defanged, neutralized by an attitude that included rather than excluded, that embraced rather than resisted.

I remembered a story Ajahn Brahm had told about his teacher, Ajahn Chah, who insisted that it wasn't the music disturbing the meditation—it was the meditators disturbing the music. Tonight, for the first time, I glimpsed what he meant with the shock of recognition that accompanies truth when it finally penetrates layers of defensive thinking.

The sound simply was. My resistance to it was optional, negotiable, a choice I'd been making unconsciously but could now make deliberately. The suffering wasn't in the noise—it was in the commentary about the noise, the story about how things should be different, the demand that reality conform to my preferences before I would consent to be at peace.

THE TAPESTRY OF CONNECTION

The evening group gathering at seven felt like coming home to a family I'd never known I had, but whose love I'd been unconsciously seeking my entire life through relationships and achievements and spiritual practices that had always felt like substitutes for something more fundamental, more unconditional, more present.

Though silence bound our tongues, hearts spoke freely in this shared space where pretense felt not just unnecessary but impossible, where the usual masks and performances required by social interaction dissolved into simple presence, simple being, simple recognition of the common humanity that connected all beings who had ever wondered what they were doing here and whether their lives mattered.

Servers and meditators, Mr. Soemin's family and visitors from the village—all joined in chanting that raised the hall's rafters with collective devotion, voices weaving together like threads in a tapestry that depicted the fundamental interconnectedness of all seeking hearts, the web of longing that connected every being who had ever looked at the night sky and felt both infinite smallness and infinite possibility.

The "sharing of merit" that followed felt like watching spiritual currency being distributed among beings who understood its true value—not hoarded like material wealth that decreased when shared, but multiplied by the very act of giving it away, creating abundance through generosity rather than scarcity through accumulation.

Children peered at me with unguarded curiosity, their giggles like silver bells punctuating the solemnity, reminding everyone present that enlightenment didn't require the abandonment of joy, that awakening might restore the capacity for delight that seriousness had been slowly suffocating. A few adults offered shy smiles—small bridges built across the chasm of language and culture, proof that kindness needed no translation, required no shared vocabulary beyond the recognition of common humanity.

THE GIFT OF IMPERFECT SANCTUARY

As we filed out of the hall, Mr. Soemin materialized beside me like a guardian angel bearing gifts, his timing so perfect it felt orchestrated by forces more compassionate than coincidence, more intelligent than chance, more caring than any cosmic bureaucracy I'd previously imagined possible.

"I didn't have time for the market," he said, pressing a used mosquito net into my hands with the matter-of-fact generosity of someone who understood that small kindnesses could shift entire worlds, that practical compassion often mattered more than theological sophistication. "But perhaps this will help for now."

The gratitude that surged through me was embarrassingly disproportionate to the gift—just a piece of worn netting with a few holes, evidence of previous battles fought by other pilgrims against the same tiny adversaries that had been treating my Western blood like an all-you-can-eat buffet advertised specifically to creatures that operated according to schedules designed to maximize human misery.

But to me, this simple offering represented freedom from the nightly battle against my inadequate cocoon, liberation from one small but persistent source of suffering that had been undermining my capacity to rest, to recover, to maintain the energy required for whatever transformations were trying to emerge from consciousness that was being systematically stripped of its familiar comforts and coping mechanisms.

Back in my room, I strung up the borrowed net with the reverence of someone erecting a shrine, each knot tied with the careful attention usually reserved for sacred rituals, understanding that even the most practical acts could become prayers when performed with sufficient gratitude and recognition of the kindness that had made them possible.

The holes could wait until tomorrow; tonight I would sleep like royalty in my expanded palace of white mesh, protected by walls that let in air but kept out the tiny vampires that had been contributing to the accumulated exhaustion that made every spiritual challenge feel more difficult than it needed to be.

THE EXHAUSTION OF AWAKENING

By 8:30, my body was singing songs of protest in harmonies I'd never heard before, and hours in half-lotus position had transformed my legs into arrangements of fire and numbness, a surreal landscape where sensation and absence of sensation existed simultaneously. At the same time, my spine curved like a question mark that would never find its answer in any anatomy textbook or ergonomic manual.

The mental taxation was even more severe—maintaining one-pointed concentration felt like holding a challenging yoga pose with my mind, every moment requiring conscious effort to keep awareness from wandering off to explore the thousand fascinating distractions that consciousness seemed to generate like a mental popcorn machine designed to prevent the sustained attention that spiritual development required.

People who thought meditation was relaxation had clearly never attempted this sustained inner work, had never discovered the difference between the temporary peace that came from distraction and the profound rest that emerged from complete attention to what was happening rather than what the mind wished was happening instead.

It was like attending a ten-hour lecture while sitting in half-lotus, except the subject was the nature of consciousness itself and the final exam was enlightenment.

By nine o'clock, my mental reserves had been completely depleted, my awareness running on fumes like a car that had traveled much farther than its fuel tank should have allowed. Consciousness began dissolving at the edges like watercolors in rain, and I surrendered to sleep with the gratitude of a soldier finally granted leave from an exhausting but necessary war, from a battle that was being fought primarily against enemies that existed in the territory of resistance rather than external reality.

THE LULLABY OF ACCEPTANCE

Through my patched mosquito net, the gecko clicked its territorial claims with the persistence of someone broadcasting their existence to an indifferent universe, announcing its small sovereignty in the darkness like a tiny meditation bell reminding everyone within hearing distance that life continued its ancient business regardless of human plans for peace.

But tonight, even that sound felt like a lullaby sung by the monastery's smallest resident teacher, another voice in the symphony of existence that included everything—the beautiful and annoying, the sacred and mundane, the helpful and obstructive—in one vast composition that made sense only when heard from sufficient distance, with enough acceptance, with the kind of loving kindness that could embrace even the interruptions to loving kindness.

Tomorrow would bring new challenges, deeper dives into the mysterious territories of inner space where maps had not yet been drawn, where consciousness would continue its patient work of dismantling everything I thought I knew about the difference between self and other, peace and chaos, spiritual success and ordinary human struggling.

But tonight, wrapped in loving kindness like a protective cloak woven from the accumulated prayers of all who had walked this path before me, I felt ready for whatever tests awaited in the darkness ahead, whatever dissolution of familiar identity the journey required, whatever death of old assumptions was necessary for whatever might be trying to be born in the ruins of who I used to be.

The last thing I remembered before sleep claimed me was the feeling of my heart expanding like a balloon filling with helium, lifting me toward dreams where loving kindness might be the only language anyone needed to speak, the only currency that held value, the only skill that mattered in the end.

Day 4 — The First Vision

Dawn erupted with its familiar carnival of chaos—children's voices slicing through the morning air like miniature air raid sirens announcing the world's daily state of emergency, roosters launching into territorial arias that would humble opera singers with their raw vocal ambition, neighbors engaging in what appeared to be heated negotiations over fish prices conducted through acoustic megaphones that transformed ordinary conversation into community theater.

The compound had become a sonic bazaar where every sound hawked its wares in an invisible marketplace of attention, each noise demanding payment in the currency of consciousness, each disturbance insisting on its right to colonize whatever peace might be foolish enough to show its face.

And yet—miracle of miracles—for the first time since my arrival, I sat through this acoustic hurricane like a stone Buddha who had finally discovered the secret of selective hearing, like someone who had learned to tune into frequencies that existed beneath the surface turbulence of ordinary sensory bombardment.

THE FORTRESS OF FOCUSED ATTENTION

My hour of pre-breakfast meditation unfolded with crystalline precision, *Araham* pulsing through my consciousness like a lighthouse beam slicing through fog, each repetition of the sacred syllable creating expanding rings of silence that rippled outward from some unshakeable center I was only beginning to recognize as home.

The external pandemonium crashed against my concentration like waves against granite cliffs and simply dissolved, as if I'd stumbled upon some invisible force field that deflected sonic intrusions while allowing pure awareness to pass through unimpeded. It was like discovering that consciousness came equipped with noise-canceling technology that had been waiting all my life for someone to flip the switch.

The revelation arrived wrapped in paradox: the noisier the world became, the deeper my inner silence grew, as if chaos were feeding the stillness rather than destroying it, as if disturbance and peace were secret collaborators in some cosmic conspiracy I'd never been educated to recognize.

Consciousness, I realized with the shock of a scientist stumbling upon a new law of physics, was like a narrow-beam flashlight—it could only illuminate one object at a time with full intensity. When that beam focused with laser precision on the sacred syllable, everything else fell into darkness, not erased but simply irrelevant to the theater of attention, like background actors whose performance no longer registered once the star had claimed center stage.

I'd experienced this before in ordinary life—becoming so absorbed in a compelling book that I couldn't hear my name being called, the world beyond my focus dissolving into background static that had no power to interrupt whatever was holding my attention hostage. But this was different. This was consciousness weaponized in service of something sacred, trained like a hunting falcon to retrieve treasures from territories most people never suspected existed.

THE MEDICINE OF SUNLIGHT

Between 8:30 and nine, I emerged from my cave like a nocturnal creature learning to tolerate daylight after weeks of underground living, collecting vitamin D from the morning sun as it painted the front courtyard in shades of gold that seemed designed by artists who understood the chemistry of hope.

The warmth soaked into my skin with medicinal potency, each ray carrying promises of energy I'd need for the day's inner archaeology, my body drinking light like a plant that had been kept too long in darkness and was finally remembering its birthright of photosynthesis.

How many mornings had I rushed through without really feeling the sun's touch, treating dawn as a mere transition rather than a daily miracle? How many free doses of natural medicine had I missed while hurrying toward destinations that mattered far less than this simple communion with the source that powered every living thing?

Back in my self-imposed darkness, I settled into meditation posture with the confidence of someone who'd found their groove after days of fumbling with controls they'd never been taught to operate. This time, concentration arrived without struggle, settling over me like a perfectly tailored garment cut by invisible hands that understood exactly what my awareness needed to feel at home in stillness.

My breath began its mysterious deceleration—each inhalation stretching toward eternity, each exhalation releasing me deeper into a stillness that felt less like absence and more like presence concentrated to its purest essence, distilled into something so refined it made ordinary consciousness seem crude by comparison.

At moments, breathing seemed to pause entirely, as if my body had discovered some more efficient way of existing that transcended the need for constant oxygen exchange, like a deep-sea creature that had evolved beyond the surface world's frantic rhythms and learned to extract life from sources invisible to ordinary understanding.

When attention wandered from *Araham*—and it did, with the persistence of a child tugging at a parent's sleeve—I'd redirect it to the whisper-soft sensations around my nostrils: the barely perceptible coolness of incoming breath carrying messages from the morning air, the gentle warmth of exhalation painting my upper lip with the intimate signature of my continued aliveness.

THE SACRAMENT OF SIMPLE FOOD

Lunch arrived as a humble feast of leftovers—yesterday's dishes reborn with the kind of alchemy that only time and hunger can provide, transformed from mere sustenance into something approaching sacrament through the mysterious process by which gratitude converts necessity into gift.

Even cold rice tasted like benediction, each grain carrying the accumulated stories of hands that had planted, harvested, and prepared it with the devotion that turned farming into prayer, labor into love, the mundane business of survival into participation in the cosmic dance of nourishment.

But the revelation was the bananas: chubby little ladyfingers with skin so thin and pink they looked like they'd been blushing at their own sweetness, flesh so aromatic and intensely flavored they made supermarket bananas seem like pale imitations created by people who had forgotten what fruit was supposed to taste like before industrial agriculture replaced flavor with shelf life.

I held one in my palm, marveling at how this simple fruit contained more authentic banana essence than anything I'd tasted in years of Western abundance, each bite a small explosion of sweetness that seemed to carry the concentrated sunshine of Myanmar's soil, proof that sometimes the most profound teachings came disguised as ordinary food offered without fanfare or philosophical commentary.

THE WRESTLING MATCH WITH RESTLESSNESS

The afternoon meditation session arrived like an unwelcome guest bearing gifts of restlessness wrapped in ribbons of impatience and tied with bows of frustration that seemed designed to test every ounce of determination I'd accumulated over the previous days of practice.

My body rebelled against stillness with the determination of a teenager testing every boundary, muscles twitching with accumulated tension that had been building like pressure in a cosmic boiler, bones protesting their assigned positions like union workers demanding better conditions and threatening to strike if their grievances weren't addressed immediately.

I shifted from half-lotus to cross-legged to kneeling, then back again—a frustrated dance with discomfort that left me feeling like a meditation failure, someone who'd missed the essential instruction that would make this whole enterprise possible, someone who'd somehow been absent the day they taught the secret of sitting still without feeling like insects were crawling under your skin.

Why did everyone else seem to sit like statues carved from patience while I fidgeted like someone with a neurological condition that made stillness physically impossible? What essential piece of spiritual equipment was I missing that allowed other practitioners to inhabit their bodies like comfortable homes while I felt trapped in mine like a prisoner in a cell designed by someone who hated comfort?

Finally, mercifully, 2:45 arrived and I dragged myself to face Sayadaw's evaluation, certain that my afternoon's wrestling match with restlessness had undone whatever progress the morning had achieved. To my amazement, his golden face lit up with that familiar expression of approval, as if my internal wrestling match had somehow been exactly what my practice needed—another paradox in a path that seemed designed to confound every assumption I brought to it.

"Restlessness can be a sign of energy building," Mr. Soemin translated with his characteristic warmth, his voice carrying the authority of someone who'd witnessed this exact phenomenon countless times before. "Sometimes the mind struggles before it breaks through to new territory."

THE MOMENT THAT DIVIDED EVERYTHING

Then came the late afternoon session, and with it, the moment that would divide my spiritual life into before and after, the watershed event that would make everything I'd previously considered significant seem like preliminary exercises for this single encounter with the impossible.

I was settling into what I expected to be another ordinary meditation—*Araham* pulsing with familiar rhythm, breath beginning its mysterious deceleration like a car shifting into lower gears for a long climb—when suddenly, impossibly, something materialized in the space behind my closed eyelids.

Not imagination. Not visualization. Not memory reconstructed from wishful thinking or spiritual expectation. But vision—direct, undeniable, more real than the meditation cushion beneath me: a tendril of luminous smoke unfurling from beneath my nose like exhaled starlight made visible, like breath that had somehow learned to glow with its own internal radiance.

The color defied every blue I'd ever witnessed—electric yet ethereal, bright yet somehow soft, as if someone had liquefied sapphires and set them glowing from within by some cosmic jeweler who worked exclusively in impossible hues that didn't exist in any earthly palette. The smoky ribbon extended perhaps ten centimeters into the space before my face, undulating with its mysterious life, more present than my own breathing, more substantial than the walls surrounding my meditation cave.

I stared—if you could call this inner seeing "staring"—transfixed by beauty that seemed to belong to some other dimension of reality where artists had rewritten the laws of physics, where light could be sculpted like clay and consciousness could paint with colors that had no names in any human language.

The luminous smoke pulsed with intelligence, with presence, as if it were aware of being observed, as if consciousness itself had taken visible form to announce its arrival, to reveal capabilities that had been dormant, waiting for precisely the right conditions to emerge from whatever depths they'd been hiding in.

When my attention wavered even slightly—seduced by amazement or distracted by the rational mind's desperate attempts to categorize the uncategorizable—it vanished like smoke itself, leaving me gasping in the sudden darkness of ordinary consciousness, bereft as someone whose television had gone dead during the climactic scene of a movie they'd been waiting their entire life to see.

THE ADRENALINE OF THE MIRACULOUS

My heart hammered against my ribs like a caged bird desperate for freedom, flooding my system with adrenaline that felt completely inappropriate for someone sitting motionless on a meditation cushion in a quiet room. This wasn't the gentle light I'd experienced before—this was something else entirely, something that felt like direct contact with the miraculous, like stumbling upon a secret door in reality's basement that led to rooms no architect had ever planned.

The moment the session ended, I exploded from my cushion like a compressed spring suddenly released, my legs barely able to carry me across the compound to Mr. Soemin's office. He was just emerging as I arrived, probably drawn by the sound of my approaching footsteps—or perhaps by the electromagnetic field of excitement I was surely radiating like someone who'd just witnessed their first genuine miracle and couldn't contain the energy of revelation within ordinary behavioral parameters.

"Mr. Soemin!" The words tumbled out before I could shape them properly, my voice cracking with the effort of translating the untranslatable into syllables that might somehow convey what language had never been designed to describe. "I saw smoke!"

His weathered face transformed into a landscape of knowing satisfaction, features rearranging themselves into the expression of someone witnessing an expected miracle—a gardener whose carefully tended seed had finally broken through the soil exactly when the ancient instructions had predicted it would, right on schedule according to laws that operated beyond the reach of ordinary cause and effect.

He waited with the patient delight of someone who'd seen this moment unfold countless times before but never grew tired of watching wonder bloom in a human face, never became jaded about the moment when the impossible became visible, when consciousness finally revealed one of its hidden capabilities to someone ready to receive the shock of recognition.

"Wispy smoke—light blue—coming right out from under my nose!" My voice trembled with the effort of describing something that existed beyond the reach of ordinary language, something that belonged to vocabularies that hadn't been invented yet. "It was... it was like nothing I've ever seen. More real than real, more present than anything in this physical world."

"Congratulations!" The word burst from him like champagne from a shaken bottle, his melodic voice carrying layers of meaning I couldn't yet decode—pride, recognition, anticipation, and something else that felt like a teacher's satisfaction at watching a student finally grasp a lesson that couldn't be taught, only experienced, only discovered through the patient cultivation of conditions that allowed the miraculous to emerge from whatever dimensions it normally inhabited.

As he turned to leave, he tossed two words over his shoulder like seeds planted in fertile ground, casual as someone mentioning the weather: "More coming."

More coming. The promise hung in the evening air like incense, carrying implications that made my imagination race toward territories I didn't yet have maps for, adventures I couldn't yet imagine, capabilities I'd never suspected consciousness might possess when properly trained and systematically developed.

THE ALCHEMY OF LOVING KINDNESS

Back in my room, I dove into *Metta* practice with the fervor of someone who'd discovered fire and wanted to share its warmth with every being in existence, every consciousness that had ever struggled with the fundamental loneliness of being trapped inside individual experience without knowing how to build bridges across the apparent separation.

The loving kindness flowed through me like warm honey mixed with liquid light, and I marveled at how profoundly this simple practice had transformed my relationship with the world's abrasions, how it had alchemized irritation into compassion, resistance into acceptance, judgment into understanding.

Songs that had tortured me just days ago now seemed like offerings from neighbors who were simply trying to squeeze joy from their ordinary lives, their off-key enthusiasm suddenly touching rather than irritating, evidence of the irrepressible human need to celebrate existence despite its challenges and complications.

The construction noise became the sound of people building homes, building dreams, hammering hope into reality one nail at a time, creating shelter for families who would sleep safely because someone was willing to endure the hard work of making the abstract concrete, the planned actual.

Even the roosters' dawn proclamations felt like prayers in a language I was finally learning to understand—ancient announcements that light had once again defeated darkness, daily celebrations of the cosmic victory that made consciousness possible, made awakening possible, made this very moment of recognition possible.

THE COMMUNITY OF ALL BEINGS

During my evening walk through the flowering pathways, *Metta* transformed every encounter into a blessing, my heart radiating goodwill like a small sun that had learned to shine without discrimination, without conditions, without the usual prerequisites that limited love to approved recipients who met certain standards of worthiness.

The ants marching across the stone path became fellow pilgrims on their mysterious journeys, each carrying burdens proportionally as heavy as mine, each following imperatives as compelling and vital to them as awakening was to me. Birds singing in the durian trees were offering their own forms of devotion to the approaching night, their music as valid as any human hymn, as authentic as any prayer recited in any temple.

Even the distant voices of neighbors discussing the day's events felt like part of a vast conversation I was privileged to overhear—the ongoing dialogue between human hearts trying to make sense of existence, trying to extract meaning from the beautiful confusion of being temporarily alive in a universe that remained fundamentally mysterious despite all our scientific and spiritual investigations.

The evening group chanting at seven became a celebration I wouldn't have missed for anything—not even the promise of perfect silence or the most conducive meditation conditions. Though we remained bound by the monastery's discipline of minimal speech, hearts spoke freely in this shared space where individual practice merged into collective devotion like streams converging into a river that was stronger than any of its tributaries.

Voices joined in Pali syllables that had blessed seekers for millennia, and I felt myself becoming part of something infinitely larger than my small struggles with noise and discomfort, part of a lineage that stretched back through centuries of practitioners who had sat in similar silence, pursuing similar awakening, discovering similar capabilities hidden in the depths of consciousness.

This was what spiritual community meant—not agreement on doctrine or adherence to identical beliefs, but recognition of the shared human hunger for transcendence, the universal longing to touch something holy, to discover something real beneath the surface of ordinary experience.

THE TREASURE IN THE SECRET POCKET

As we filed out under the star-drunk sky, I carried the day's revelations like treasures in a secret pocket—the blue light that had shown me reality contained dimensions I'd never suspected, and the *Metta* that had revealed even the most irritating aspects of existence could be transformed through the alchemy of loving kindness applied with the persistence of someone who refused to give up on the possibility of peace.

Tomorrow would bring new mysteries, deeper dives into territories of consciousness that held wonders beyond imagination, capabilities that challenged every assumption about the boundaries between possible and impossible, between ordinary human awareness and whatever lay beyond the horizon of conventional understanding.

But tonight, as I settled into my patched mosquito net with the contentment of someone whose world had just expanded beyond recognition, I went to sleep feeling like an explorer who'd caught his first glimpse of a continent that would take a lifetime to map, someone who'd been granted citizenship in a realm where the miraculous was as natural as breathing and twice as essential for whatever I was becoming.

~

Day 5 – Dancing with Death

Three-thirty in the morning arrived like an unwelcome creditor, dragging me from dreams that evaporated on contact with consciousness, leaving only wisps of confusion and the humid embrace of pre-dawn darkness that felt more like a burial shroud than a blanket. My body felt heavy as waterlogged timber, each limb weighted with the kind of exhaustion that seemed to have colonized my bones during sleep rather than being healed by whatever rest I'd managed to steal from the night.

By 4:10, I'd managed to arrange myself in meditation posture with all the grace of someone assembling IKEA furniture in the dark without instructions. Still, my mind wandered like a lost tourist in a foreign city where all the street signs were written in alphabets I'd never learned. All the locals spoke in riddles designed to confuse rather than guide.

Drowsiness pressed down on my eyelids like gravity had been specifically redesigned to make consciousness impossible. I found myself nodding forward like a broken marionette whose strings had been cut by a cosmic puppeteer who'd grown bored with the performance. Each time my chin dropped toward my chest, I'd startle awake with the embarrassing jolt of someone caught sleeping during the most important lecture of their academic career.

Was this what spiritual progress looked like? Because it felt suspiciously like the opposite of enlightenment, like some cosmic joke being played on pilgrims who'd traveled too far to turn back but hadn't traveled far enough to understand the punchline.

THE SALVATION OF MOHINGA

Breakfast arrived as salvation incarnate in the form of Mohinga—Myanmar's liquid poetry served in ceramic bowls that held the accumulated stories of countless previous meals, each vessel a small museum of nourishment that had sustained seekers through identical struggles with dawn and discipline and the democratic exhaustion that made spiritual ambition feel like hubris.

The fish noodle soup sang with complexity that made my taste buds weep with gratitude: tender rice noodles swimming in broth rich with the concentrated essence of river catfish, each spoonful carrying whispers of lemongrass and ginger that had been coaxed into perfect harmony by hands that understood the alchemy of flavor, the chemistry of comfort, the physics of how ingredients could be transformed into medicine for both body and spirit.

Crispy fritters dissolved on my tongue like savory snow that had been blessed by deities who specialized in the marriage of texture and taste, while fragments of hard-boiled egg floated like tiny suns in the golden liquid, each one a small miracle of protein transformed into art by the patient application of heat and time and attention to details that mattered precisely because they seemed insignificant.

Fried onions added their sweet char—the caramelized essence of patience applied to humble ingredients that had been content to grow in dirt until someone with vision recognized their potential for transformation. Fish cakes contributed their tender chew, while tamarind's bright acidity danced with coriander's earthy embrace in a waltz that made my mouth want to applaud the choreographer who'd arranged this symphony of complementary flavors.

The dessert that followed was equally revelatory—some nameless sweet that tasted like concentrated joy mixed with childhood memories of perfect afternoons when time moved slowly. Happiness required no justification beyond its existence, the kind of flavor that made you understand why people wrote epic poems about food and called meals sacraments.

With my belly warm and satisfied, exhaustion finally claimed its due with the authority of a debt collector who'd been patient long enough and wouldn't be denied another moment of what was rightfully theirs. I collapsed onto my mat for what was supposed to be a brief rest. I didn't surface until 7:18, consciousness returning slowly like a tide filling an empty bay, bringing with it the guilty awareness that I'd been unconscious when I'd meant to be mindful, absent when I'd planned to be present.

THE REDEMPTION OF LIGHT

The morning sitting from 8:40 to 9:25 brought redemption for the earlier failure, proof that the spiritual path didn't require perfection—only persistence, only the willingness to begin again each time you discovered you'd stopped paying attention to what mattered most.

As concentration deepened like roots finally finding water after drought, reality began to shift like landscapes viewed through moving water, becoming fluid in ways that challenged every assumption about the fixity of what we called the physical world. Suddenly, above my nose, a circular burst of light exploded like a camera flash captured by equipment that photographed dimensions invisible to ordinary seeing—brilliant, instantaneous, gone before I could fully register its presence, leaving me wondering if I'd imagined the whole thing or if imagination itself had been upgraded to accommodate experiences that didn't fit previous categories.

But its afterimage burned in my inner vision, more dazzling than staring directly into the sun, more real than the physical world that seemed suddenly dim by comparison, like someone had been living their entire life in a basement and had just discovered what sunlight looked like when it wasn't filtered through layers of assumption and inattention.

This wasn't gentle illumination but something fierce and attention-demanding, like lightning that had been domesticated just enough to be contained in the space behind my eyelids but not enough to be comfortable or safe or anything resembling what I'd expected meditation to feel like when I'd booked this journey from the comfort of theoretical commitment.

The more I focused, the more the space behind my closed eyelids began to glow, as if someone were slowly turning up a dimmer switch connected to some celestial light source that had been waiting patiently for me to notice its presence, like a faithful friend who'd been standing quietly in the corner until I was ready to acknowledge that I wasn't alone in this exploration of consciousness.

By the time the lunch bell rang, the background luminosity had grown so bright I could practically read by it, transforming the darkness of closed eyes into a landscape of living light that made ordinary vision seem crude by comparison, like discovering that you'd been watching life through dirty windows your entire existence.

THE GALLERY OF SILENT COMMUNION

Lunch transformed the dining hall into a gallery of silent communion where the art was the simple perfection of shared nourishment offered without expectation, without conditions, without the usual transactions that turned even the most basic human interactions into negotiations between competing needs and limited resources.

Stewed fish flaked like tender poetry on my tongue, each bite dissolving into flavors that spoke of rivers and patience and the kind of cooking that was indistinguishable from prayer, from meditation, from the application of love to ingredients that had given their lives to sustain consciousness exploring its depths.

Vegetables carried the essence of earth and sunshine concentrated into forms that made eating feel like a conversation with the soil itself, with the rain that had fallen, with the hands that had tended these plants from seed to harvest, with the understanding that nourishment was always sacrament when offered with attention and received with gratitude.

Watermelon provided cool punctuation to the meal's warm symphony; each bite a small explosion of summer that made me grateful for the existence of seeds and rain and the mysterious process that turned dirt and sunlight into sweetness, into refreshment, into evidence that the universe was fundamentally generous despite all appearances to the contrary.

But the real treasure was the palm sugar cubes—amber jewels that dissolved into liquid nostalgia, each one a concentrated memory of tropical sweetness I hadn't known I was craving until it melted on my tongue like edible sunshine, like crystallized happiness that had been waiting in some cosmic kitchen for precisely this moment of recognition.

THE TELEPATHY OF TABLE FELLOWSHIP

The wordless ballet of our table fellowship had evolved into something approaching telepathy, a dance of attention and care that required no instruction manual, no shared language beyond the recognition of common humanity and common hunger and the common gratitude that made strangers into family when circumstances aligned properly.

Without spoken requests, my companions passed the palm sugar, knowing I'd reach for it. At the same time, I slid their preferred dishes within easy grasp of hands that had learned to speak through gesture, through timing, through the kind of attention that noticed preferences before they were expressed and needs before they were articulated.

The youngest among us had inherited the honor of rice distribution, serving the eldest first with ceremonial precision, me last as the foreign guest who was still learning the steps of this ancient choreography, then finally himself—hierarchy expressed through the simple act of ladling grain, tradition maintained through the democracy of shared nourishment.

This silent choreography felt more intimate than most conversations I'd had back home, more honest than words that often said everything except what they meant, more real than relationships that required constant verbal maintenance to survive the inevitable misunderstandings that arose when people tried to communicate complex inner states through the crude approximations of language.

We were learning each other's preferences and rhythms through pure observation, creating a wordless vocabulary of consideration and care that felt like what human community was supposed to be before we'd forgotten how to listen with our eyes, how to speak through action, how to love through the simple act of paying attention to what others needed without being asked.

THE SECRET SANCTUARY

After lunch, I escaped to explore my temporary kingdom more thoroughly, like a child given free run of a vast playground designed by someone who understood that wonder was the most critical curriculum, that curiosity was the most essential skill, that the ability to be amazed was what separated living from merely surviving.

The compound revealed new secrets with each wandering: the bodhi tree, whose ancient branches had witnessed countless seekers' struggles and perhaps even a few genuine breakthroughs. These bamboo groves sang lullabies to the afternoon breeze in harmonies that made my chest tight with inexplicable longing for something I'd never experienced but somehow recognized as home.

And finally—treasure of treasures—a hidden sanctuary tucked behind bamboo curtains near an abandoned well that looked like the setting for fairy tales about wishes that came true, about pilgrims who discovered that what they'd been seeking had been waiting patiently for them to stop looking everywhere else and notice what was right in front of them.

Here, the world transformed into living poetry that rhymed with colors instead of words, with movement instead of meter, with beauty that did not need interpretation or analysis or any of the mental activities that usually interfered with direct appreciation of what was present.

Butterflies painted the air with moving stained glass, their wings catching light and throwing it back in patterns that seemed designed by artists who worked exclusively in beauty, who understood that function and aesthetics were not opposites but different names for the same cosmic principle that made everything work by making everything wonderful.

Dragonflies hovered like tiny helicopters piloted by jeweled aviators who had graduated from some aerial academy where grace was the only subject taught, where efficiency and elegance were understood to be the same skill applied to different problems.

THE THEATER OF MORTALITY

At three o'clock, I presented myself to Sayadaw like a student reporting discoveries from an unmapped continent, my notebook filled with observations that felt simultaneously profound and inadequate, like trying to describe colors to someone who'd been blind from birth or music to someone who'd been born deaf.

His golden face lit up as I stammered through descriptions of blue light and the tingling sensations that had begun racing through my body like pleasant electricity, as if someone had plugged me into a power source I hadn't known existed, as if consciousness came with capabilities that had been dormant until the proper conditions allowed them to come online.

"*Nimitta*" he said, the Pali word rolling off his tongue like ancient music that had been composed specifically for this moment of recognition. The light visions had a name, a place in the geography of inner experience that stretched back twenty-five centuries. "*Piti*"— the pleasure, the tingling joy that accompanies deepening concentration, like flowers that bloom only in the soil of sustained attention.

These weren't aberrations or signs of impending insanity but signposts marking progress along a well-traveled path, proof that my fumbling efforts were leading somewhere recognizable to those who had walked this way before, who had left maps for pilgrims willing to trust ancient wisdom over modern skepticism.

When he asked about my *Metta* practice, honesty compelled confession: "I'm getting bored. It's repetitive. I've run out of people to send loving kindness to."

His belly laugh erupted like a small earthquake, the sound so delighted and unexpected that it transformed the formal teacher-student dynamic into something more human and warm, more real than the spiritual theater that sometimes passed for authentic interaction between seekers and guides.

The laughter was followed immediately by a sneeze that revealed his very human struggle with what appeared to be a head cold, proof that even enlightened beings had to deal with the body's small rebellions. This democratic suffering connected all biological entities regardless of their spiritual attainments.

Compassion moved me to action before thought could interfere—I hurried back to my room. I returned with Lemsip and paracetamol, small offerings to ease his discomfort. His grateful nod felt like receiving a blessing, a reminder that sometimes the most profound teachings were exchanged through simple acts of care that required no philosophy to justify their importance.

Then came the day's real teaching, delivered with the matter-of-fact tone of someone announcing the weather: *Maranasati*—contemplation of death. The preliminary exercises were ending; now came the deeper work, the kind that would rearrange not just my meditation practice but my entire relationship with existence, with time, with the preciousness of every moment I'd been squandering on concerns that would matter not at all when the final accounting arrived.

THE CARTOGRAPHY OF ENDINGS

For hours, I dove into death's many faces like an explorer mapping a terrifying continent that everyone would eventually have to visit. Still, no one wanted to think about territory that existed in every living being's future but which civilized society had conspired to keep hidden behind euphemisms and denial and the elaborate mythology that death happened to other people, in other families, in other decades.

I forced myself to visualize my corpse, drawing on every movie death scene, every funeral, every glimpse of mortality I'd ever witnessed, turning my imagination into a theater where the only show playing was the end of everything I thought I was, the dissolution of every identity that had seemed so permanent and important just hours before.

Death by shark attack: my body torn apart in a feeding frenzy, blood clouding tropical waters while my consciousness fled this vessel that had become mere meat, no different from any other item on the ocean's menu, prey indistinguishable from the tuna and mackerel that fed the same predators with less philosophical angst about the arrangement.

Death by drowning: the panic of failing lungs, water filling spaces meant for air, the terrible, slow fade of oxygen-starved consciousness as the world above grew dimmer and more distant, like watching life through a window that was gradually being painted black from the inside.

Car crashes that would turn my familiar form into twisted metal and broken bone, transforming the vehicle that had carried me safely through thousands of miles into the instrument of my destruction, proving that the same technology that extended human capability could become the mechanism of human termination with nothing more than a moment's inattention or mechanical failure.

Gunshots that would end everything in explosive finality—perhaps the kindest cut, if any death could be called kind, over before the nervous system could fully register what was happening, consciousness extinguished like a candle flame in a hurricane.

Plane crashes filled my imagination with screaming metal and the particular terror of knowing death was approaching at terminal velocity, gravity transformed from the force that kept us grounded into the mechanism of our destruction, physics becoming the enemy of the very beings whose civilization had learned to harness physical laws for survival and convenience.

Natural death from aging offered the gentlest passage—consciousness simply fading like a candle guttering out in peaceful sleep, the body finally surrendering to the entropy it had been fighting since birth, the gradual systems failure that was programmed into biological architecture from the moment of conception.

THE DEMOCRACY OF DECAY

I forced myself to watch my imagined corpse through every stage of decay: flesh swelling purple-black like fruit left too long in the sun, skin sloughing off like discarded clothing that no longer fit the changing shape of decomposition, maggots transforming my substance into their sustenance with the same enthusiasm I'd shown for the morning's breakfast, the same hunger for life that I'd never questioned when I was the one doing the consuming.

In war zones, my mental body was flattened by tanks until my head became abstract art painted in blood and bone across pavement that would be hosed clean by morning, my identity reduced to a stain that would be removed by municipal workers who'd never known my name or cared about my spiritual aspirations.

In wilderness crashes, wild animals converted my remains into their survival, nothing wasted in nature's efficient recycling program, where every death became multiple lives, every ending a beginning for creatures that didn't mourn their meals or conduct philosophical inquiries about the meaning of their consumption.

The exercise was designed to horrify, and it succeeded with the thoroughness of a nightmare that followed you into waking, that changed the flavor of every subsequent experience by reminding you that all experiences were temporary, all pleasures borrowed time, all achievements dust waiting for the wind that would scatter them.

But beneath the fear, something else emerged: a profound sense of life's fragility that made every breath feel precious, every heartbeat a minor miracle of temporary persistence in a universe that specialized in impermanence, that had designed mortality into the basic operating system of consciousness to ensure that nothing became so comfortable that it forgot to grow, to change, to evolve toward whatever came next.

THE REARRANGEMENT OF PRIORITIES

The real gift of *Maranasati* was its power to rearrange priorities like furniture in a room, suddenly seen clearly for the first time. If I had today to live, what would matter? Tomorrow? Next week? The answers shifted depending on the timeframe, revealing how much of my usual concerns were mere distractions from what truly deserved attention, what qualified as important when measured against the ultimate deadline that waited for every living being.

Unlike *Araham*, which required closed eyes and stillness, both *Maranasati* and *Metta* could accompany me on walks, turning the flowering pathways into classrooms where every step was a lesson in impermanence and love, where the beauty of blossoms became more poignant when contemplated alongside the inevitability of their withering, their return to soil that would nourish next season's growth.

I found myself visualizing faces of loved ones while contemplating their inevitable deaths, or sending loving kindness to strangers whose mortality connected them to me in the most fundamental way—we were all temporary arrangements of elements that would eventually return to the earth that had loaned them to us for this brief experiment in consciousness, this temporary dance of awareness inhabiting biological forms.

THE EQUANIMITY OF ACCEPTANCE

That night, lying cocooned in my mosquito net's white sanctuary, gazing through the mesh at silhouettes of neighbors' trees painted against star-drunk sky, I felt something I'd never experienced before: complete equanimity in the face of life's temporary nature, peace that came not from denying death but from accepting it so entirely that it no longer had the power to terrorize every moment with its inevitable approach.

The day's death contemplations had paradoxically filled me with profound contentment, as if accepting mortality had somehow made me more alive, more present to the miracle of each moment that I was still here to witness, still capable of breathing and thinking and feeling gratitude for the temporary loan of this biological vehicle.

Tomorrow would bring *Anapanasati*—mindfulness of breathing. I drifted toward sleep, anticipating this next stage of the journey like a child awaiting Christmas morning, except the gifts would be wrapped in awareness rather than paper, would be discoveries about consciousness rather than acquisitions of objects that would eventually join everything else in the great democracy of decay.

Death, I was learning, was not the enemy of life but its most honest teacher, the one who never lied about what was permanent and what was just borrowed time, who stripped away every pretense and forced attention toward what mattered when all the distractions of ordinary existence were revealed as elaborate methods of avoiding the only question that ultimately mattered: what did it mean to be temporarily alive in a universe where nothing lasted forever but everything participated in the endless transformation of energy from one form to another?

Tonight, I felt grateful for the lesson, grateful for the breath that would carry me into dreams, thankful for the temporary vessel that would wake tomorrow ready to explore new territories of consciousness. In accepting death, I had somehow found a way to fall in love with being alive, to appreciate impermanence as the very quality that made every moment precious, every experience sacred, every breath a small victory against the entropy that would eventually reclaim all victories for the vast recycling project that connected every being to every other being through the shared destiny of return.

Day 6 – The Ocean of Mind

Two forty-five in the morning—consciousness surfaced from sleep's depths like a pearl diver breaking through layers of dreams that dissolved on contact with awareness, each stratum of unconsciousness peeling away like silk scarves falling from a magician's hands. Though brief, the rest had been profound, leaving me strangely refreshed as I emerged from my mosquito net cocoon at 3:45, feeling like someone who invisible artisans had rebuilt while I slept, every component cleaned and recalibrated for optimal performance.

At four, I dutifully returned to *Maranasati*, but death contemplation had lost its power to move me, like a medicine that had worked its cure and was now just bitter liquid without purpose. The practice felt as stale as yesterday's incense, arousing neither fear nor insight—just the mechanical repetition of visualizations that no longer carried emotional weight, like prayers recited so often they'd become muscle memory rather than communication with the divine.

Some medicines, I was learning, worked best in small doses before the mind developed immunity to their bitter wisdom, before familiarity bred not contempt but simple indifference to what had once been revelatory.

THE RETURN TO LOVING KINDNESS

Metta proved more rewarding, like returning to a favorite garden after wandering through barren landscapes, like discovering that home had been waiting patiently for my return from expeditions that had taught me to appreciate what I'd left behind. As loving kindness flowed through my consciousness like warm honey mixed with liquid starlight, *piti* returned with renewed intensity —an expanding constellation of tingling sensations that transformed my body into a living instrument of joy, each nerve ending singing in harmonies I'd never heard before but somehow recognized as the music my cells had been waiting their entire existence to perform.

The *nimitta* manifested as a yellowy-orange sphere that pulsed with its own inner light, breathing like a small sun that had taken residence in the space behind my closed eyes, a celestial companion that had decided my skull was suitable real estate for cosmic phenomena. Before gradually fading, it was replaced by swirling blue smoke that danced before my inner vision like ethereal cigarette wisps painted by artists who worked exclusively in impossible colors, who had access to pigments that existed only in the palette of consciousness exploring its creative capabilities.

THE FEAST OF SIMPLE TEXTURES

Breakfast arrived as a feast of textures that spoke to every sense simultaneously: coconut milk congee that slid down my throat like liquid silk woven from morning clouds by deities who understood that nourishment should be poetry, sticky rice studded with peanuts and sesame seeds that provided satisfying resistance between my teeth—each grain a small meditation on the pleasure of simple things prepared with love rather than mere efficiency.

Coffee awakened every nerve ending like a gentle alarm clock designed by someone who understood that consciousness needed coaxing rather than shocking into alertness, that awakening was a conversation between beverage and biology rather than a chemical assault on the nervous system.

Tea whispered of distant mountains where elderly hands had picked leaves in the pre-dawn darkness, each sip carrying stories of soil and rain and the patient alchemy that transformed bitter leaves into comfort, into medicine, into liquid contemplation that connected every drinker to the vast web of cultivation and care that made civilization possible.

Each spoonful felt like receiving communion from Myanmar's generous earth, reminders that nourishment was always a gift rather than an entitlement, always grace rather than a simple transaction between hunger and satisfaction.

THE SANCTUARY OF SHADE

This morning brought welcome permission to abandon the sweltering group hall—thirty-two degrees of humid stillness that made concentration feel like swimming through molasses while wearing winter clothes designed by someone who'd never experienced tropical heat. My room, shaded by neighbors' trees whose branches reached across walls like green hands offering protection from a sun that seemed determined to melt every meditator into puddles of good intention, offered blessed coolness that felt like sanctuary itself.

Though proximity to the primary school meant trading heat for an increased symphony of children's voices—their laughter and shouts filtering through my window like aural sunshine that painted the air with colors I couldn't see but could somehow feel warming the atmosphere—it seemed a fair exchange for the comfort that made sitting possible without feeling like I was being slow-cooked in my spiritual ambition.

THE GATEWAY TO DEEPER MYSTERIES

At three o'clock, Sayadaw delivered the teaching I'd been unconsciously preparing for, though I hadn't realized until this moment how much I'd been anticipating it: *Anapanasati*—mindfulness of breathing. His reminder to maintain meditation logs felt like a sacred charge, documentation of an inner journey that would unfold in ways I couldn't yet imagine, a cartographic project mapping territories that existed only in the geography of consciousness.

The interview ended, but the rest felt impossible—not from anxiety but from the kind of eagerness a child feels on Christmas morning when presents wait downstairs, when anticipation has transformed ordinary time into a countdown toward something that might change everything. Anticipation pulled me back to my cave, where I arranged myself like an explorer preparing to dive into uncharted waters, except the ocean I was about to explore existed entirely within the space between my ears, vast as any external sea but infinitely more mysterious.

Anapanasati—the breath as gateway to concentration's deeper mysteries, the key that unlocked doors I hadn't even known were closed, the bridge between ordinary consciousness and whatever lay beyond the horizon of typical human awareness.

Unlike Pa-Auk's direct approach, this tradition honored the wisdom of preliminary practices with the reverence of master gardeners who understood that soil must be prepared before seeds could flourish, that rushing toward goals often prevented their achievement, that patience was not delay but proper timing applied to processes that couldn't be hurried without being harmed.

The mind, like a wild horse that had never known bridle or saddle, needed gradual taming before attempting the subtle work of breath awareness that required cooperation rather than conquest, partnership rather than domination. Without proper preparation, years of practice could yield nothing—or worse, create harm through misguided effort applied with the best intentions but the worst timing.

THE TREASURE WORTH DYING TO PRESERVE

This reverence for authentic transmission explained Myanmar's profound respect for teachers, a culture where even kings bowed before monks who carried Buddha's original instructions like precious heirlooms passed down through twenty-five centuries of careful preservation, each generation understanding that they were custodians rather than owners of wisdom that belonged to all beings seeking liberation from suffering.

Here was wisdom that had survived wars and empires, protected by people who understood that some treasures were worth dying to preserve, that certain knowledge was more valuable than personal safety, that the transmission of liberation techniques justified any sacrifice required to keep the lineage intact.

Gratitude washed through me for David's recommendation to seek this practice in its homeland, recognition that some gifts could only be received in their proper context, like languages that lost essential meaning when translated, like music that required specific acoustics to reveal its full beauty.

Isolation had protected Myanmar's meditation traditions like amber preserving ancient insects—here survived methods that had vanished elsewhere, techniques taught exactly as Buddha had shared them when the world was young and enlightenment felt like a reasonable goal for anyone willing to sit still long enough to discover what stillness might reveal.

THE SPIRITUAL TELESCOPE

A senior monk's words echoed in memory like temple bells that continued ringing long after they'd been struck: "To study nature, you use a powerful microscope. Concentration is infinitely more powerful than any microscope—it reveals not just your body and others nearby, but truth itself." Concentration wasn't the goal but the tool, the spiritual telescope that made insight possible, the lens that brought reality into focus sharp enough to see what was there instead of what we thought was there based on assumptions accumulated over lifetimes of imprecise observation.

The mechanics were elegantly simple, like all profound truths that had been distilled to their essence through centuries of experimentation and refinement: consciousness required an object, and usually that object was thinking—the endless internal chatter that most people mistook for the voice of wisdom rather than recognizing as mental static that obscured deeper sources of knowledge.

Since you couldn't command thoughts to cease—the mind doesn't work through direct orders any more than the heart responds to commands to stop beating—the solution was redirection rather than suppression, aikido rather than wrestling, gentle guidance rather than forceful control.

Tie consciousness to a single point—the breath—and thoughts naturally subsided, not through force but through the simple fact that attention could only be in one place at a time with full intensity. Perfect focus made thinking impossible; lingering thoughts revealed imperfect concentration, like static on a radio indicating the need for better tuning rather than fundamental equipment failure.

THE MOST FAITHFUL FRIEND

For thousands of years, sages had chosen breath as meditation's foundation. The wisdom was profound in its elegant simplicity: breath accompanied us everywhere, more faithful than any friend, more reliable than any external support, reflecting the mind's every state with the honesty of a mirror that never lied about what it showed.

Agitation made breathing rapid and shallow; calm created subtle, barely perceptible respiration that seemed to disturb the air barely, that whispered rather than shouted, that demonstrated the possibility of existence that required minimal disturbance of the environment while maintaining perfect aliveness.

Following breath was like using a guide rope to descend into consciousness's deepest caverns, each level revealing new territories of inner space that most people never suspected existed within the familiar geography of their awareness, chambers and corridors, and vast halls that had been waiting patiently for exploration but which ordinary attention never had time to visit.

THE HIDDEN TREASURE

When thoughts—those mental defilements that masqueraded as important insights—finally quieted, you reached the mind's true nature: naturally luminous Buddha-nature existing in all beings like hidden treasure buried beneath layers of accumulated confusion, beneath the archaeological deposits of conditioning and habit and the endless commentary that usually passed for consciousness.

But reaching those depths required the dust to settle, like waiting for pond sediment to reveal the bottom's clarity, or clouds to part and expose the moon's full radiance that had been shining all along but had been obscured by atmospheric conditions that had nothing to do with the moon's essential nature.

This explained Zen's impossible koans—puzzles designed to exhaust logical thinking until practitioners surrendered completely, allowing insight to emerge from stillness beyond thought, from spaces in consciousness that existed prior to language and would continue after language ceased to be necessary for whatever came next in the evolution of awareness.

While thinking served daily life admirably, it became insight's greatest obstacle, like wind churning pond water until you couldn't see through to the depths where wisdom waited in perfect silence, where understanding existed without need for explanation or justification.

THE GATEWAY TO ABSORPTION

Strong concentration produced *nimitta*—light arising in the mind's eye as concentration's visual signature, proof that consciousness had reached territories where different laws applied, where the impossible became routine and the miraculous felt as natural as breathing.

The ancient Chinese called it "wisdom's light," but it served multiple functions: confirmation of concentrated states, a spiritual microscope revealing minute details invisible to ordinary perception, and most importantly, the gateway to *jhanas*—absorption states essential for enlightenment, territories of consciousness that existed beyond the reach of normal human experience but which proper training could make accessible.

Without *nimitta*, those purified consciousness states remained unreachable, like trying to enter a house when you couldn't find the door, like attempting to navigate without instruments through territories that required enhanced perception to avoid the dangers of unconscious wandering.

THE DEMOCRACY OF SPIRITUAL TIMING

Everyone's timeline differed dramatically, like flowers that bloomed according to their internal seasons rather than external calendars, each practitioner carrying their unique constellation of spiritual genetics that determined when capabilities would emerge from dormancy into active expression.

Some monks developed *nimitta* in days, while others required years. One monk, for instance, had taken fifteen years of daily practice before catching his first glimpse of inner light, proving that persistence mattered more than natural talent and that determination could eventually overcome any obstacle that wasn't an absolute impossibility.

It depended entirely on *parami*—spiritual accumulations from countless previous lives, karmic interest accrued through lifetimes of patient effort that had created conditions for current breakthrough, even when the mechanism of that accumulation remained invisible to conscious understanding.

Like eggs hatching, the process couldn't be predicted or forced through willpower alone. Some treasure chests lay in shallow water, easily grasped by anyone willing to wade in; others rested in depths requiring tremendous effort to reach, demanding the kind of spiritual diving equipment that could only be developed through sustained practice.

THE FLYING CARPET OF DISTRACTION

At Pa-Auk, we'd all received breathing meditation as our foundation, hundreds of meditators sitting cross-legged for seven hours daily, battling wandering minds while yearning for *nimitta's* first glimpse like children pressing faces against windows hoping to catch sight of distant relatives coming home from journeys that had lasted longer than anyone expected.

Months passed without signs, and doubt crept in with the persistence of water finding cracks—did this light exist, or were we all victims of elaborate spiritual placebo effects designed to keep us sitting still long enough for some other kind of transformation to occur without our conscious participation?

The cushion became my flying carpet, consciousness traveling everywhere except where it belonged, exploring every corner of memory and imagination while breath waited patiently for my return like a faithful dog whose owner had become distracted by shiny objects that promised more entertainment than simple presence.

Closing eyes was like opening floodgates that had been holding back an ocean of mental activity. Without visual stimuli keeping consciousness occupied with the immediate world, thoughts emerged like nocturnal predators who had been waiting for darkness, swooping in to hijack attention with the precision of practiced thieves who knew exactly which valuables to steal.

THE BROKEN JUKEBOX

These weren't thoughts you created—they arose automatically, propelled by their own momentum like wheels set spinning long ago by causes you couldn't remember or control, each mental formation carrying its agenda that had nothing to do with your current intentions or spiritual goals.

You had to guard carefully what you fed your mind, because it would replay everything endlessly, like a jukebox with a broken repeat button that couldn't stop playing the same songs, that treated every input as worthy of infinite repetition regardless of its actual value or relevance to present circumstances.

The mind stored everything—every glimpse, every fleeting image witnessed throughout life, filed away in archives more comprehensive than any library, more detailed than any database, cataloguing experiences with the obsessive thoroughness of a cosmic accountant who never threw anything away because you never knew when some random detail might prove essential for survival.

During one retreat, I spent days seeing magazine pages featuring hair products and women's accessories, complete with vivid colors and detailed layouts that reproduced themselves with photographic accuracy despite my having no conscious interest in either beauty products or fashion accessories.

Eventually, I realized these came from an in-flight magazine I'd barely glanced at months earlier. Yet my consciousness had photographed every page, filing them away for later, random retrieval when I least expected or wanted them. The mind was a hoarder of the highest order, keeping everything because it had never learned to distinguish between useful information and mental junk.

THE TYRANNY OF THOUGHTS

Mind craved constant stimulation, variety, something to grasp and manipulate like a child who couldn't sit still without toys, who treated every moment of boredom as a crisis requiring immediate resolution through entertainment or distraction or any activity that prevented the kind of stillness that might reveal uncomfortable truths about the nature of existence.

When concentration finally reached sufficient strength, I could observe this mental chaos objectively—thoughts bubbling like boiling soup, each demanding attention in an endless, automatic process that revealed the mind's true nature as something that operated primarily without conscious oversight or voluntary control.

This revealed the "not-self" nature of thinking: thoughts arose without a thinker, autonomous mental formations oppressing consciousness through constant demands that felt personal but weren't, that seemed important but were just habit patterns left over from evolutionary survival mechanisms that had outlived their usefulness.

Recognizing this tyranny allowed me to discard "important" ideas without guilt and avoid unnecessary suffering, like learning to ignore the demands of a dictator who had no real authority beyond what I chose to give him, who ruled only through the consent of the governed.

THE ECSTASY OF PERFECT CONCENTRATION

Perfect concentration was rare—perhaps once per day during Pa-Auk's five sessions, usually in the pre-dawn darkness when the mind was naturally quiet, like finding moments of perfect calm in an otherwise stormy ocean, windows of stillness that opened without warning and closed just as unpredictably.

One morning brought meditation so exquisite it felt like discovering my natural state, the way consciousness was meant to function when not clouded by the accumulated debris of ordinary mental activity, when awareness operated at peak efficiency rather than being handicapped by constant internal interference.

Following breath became effortless pleasure, body calming until breathing reduced to tiny hiccups of air that barely disturbed the profound stillness that had settled over everything like snow muffling all sound except the essential rhythms that kept life functioning.

After two hours, no pain disturbed this lightness—the body had somehow transcended its usual demands for position changes and comfort adjustments, as if flesh had remembered how to exist without complaint, how to serve consciousness without demanding constant attention to its needs and preferences.

Cool tingling sensations—waves of tiny bubbles bursting against skin—spread from the spine's base or the head's crown throughout my entire form, transforming flesh into something that felt more like energy than matter, more like music than solid substance, more like light condensed into biological form than ordinary physical architecture.

This was clean, lucid ecstasy beyond any worldly pleasure, joy that didn't depend on external circumstances or temporary satisfactions but arose from the simple fact of consciousness recognizing its pure nature beneath all the modifications and complications that usually obscured its essential clarity.

THE GENEROSITY OF BREAKFAST

When the breakfast bell rang, I couldn't abandon such bliss—it felt like being asked to leave paradise to attend a mundane business meeting, like choosing ordinary consciousness over direct contact with whatever intelligence had designed awareness to be capable of such extraordinary states.

Thirty minutes later, finally emerging with the reluctance of someone leaving a perfect dream, I discovered that concentration had sharpened perception dramatically, like someone had replaced my ordinary eyes with high-definition cameras that revealed details, colors, and spatial relationships that had been invisible to previous levels of attention.

A monk passed, speaking urgent Burmese that meant "hurry, they're closing the kitchen!" But arriving at the serving area, I found every pot scraped clean—not even congee dregs remained in the enormous barrel's bottom, proof that meditation's gifts sometimes came with practical costs, that transcendence didn't exempt you from the requirements of ordinary logistics.

As I turned away empty-handed, resigned to a morning without breakfast, my roommate appeared like an answer to prayers I hadn't thought to pray. Without words, he poured his cup of vermicelli noodles into mine before walking away, giving me his only food access for the morning with the casual grace of someone for whom generosity had become as natural as breathing, as automatic as kindness itself.

He'd given me his breakfast. His only breakfast. At that moment, I understood what it truly meant to embody spiritual practice—generosity arising naturally from a heart that had transcended the tyranny of self-concern, kindness offered without calculation or expectation of return, love expressed through the simple act of ensuring that others' needs were met even when meeting them required personal sacrifice.

THE OCEAN WITHIN

Tonight, as I settled into meditation posture once again, breath became my teacher, my anchor, my guide into territories of consciousness that promised revelations I couldn't yet imagine but was finally ready to receive. The ocean of mind stretched infinite and deep, and I was finally learning to navigate its mysterious currents, discovering that the most profound journeys happened while sitting perfectly still, that the most incredible adventures took place in the space between thoughts.

Each inhalation was an invitation to go deeper, each exhalation a release of everything that wasn't essential, everything that belonged to the surface turbulence rather than the depths where wisdom waited in perfect silence. In this simple rhythm, older than thought and more reliable than hope, I was beginning to find what I hadn't even known I was looking for—not enlightenment as achievement but consciousness as home, not transcendence as escape but awareness as the most natural state of being that had been obscured by everything except itself.

Day 7 – The Lightning Gate

Dawn broke with the tenderness of recognition, consciousness emerging from sleep's embrace like a lover greeting a familiar face. I approached my meditation cushion with the quiet confidence of someone who had finally learned the difference between forcing and allowing, between grasping after states and letting them arise like morning mist from still water.

The early sessions bloomed with their authority—incandescent fountains cascading from my skull's apex, spiraling ribbons of amber light weaving through the theater of closed eyes, my respiratory rhythm so refined it felt like conversing with angels through whispered exhalations. Each breath seemed to carry me deeper into territories where the ordinary laws of physiology held less dominion than the mysterious currents of concentrated awareness.

But the afternoon session would shatter every assumption I'd developed about the boundaries of human experience.

One o'clock found me settling into what I expected would be another pleasant exploration of familiar inner landscapes. The twin solar phenomena returned—those blazing orbs that had become my reliable companions, one burning with the fierce intensity of summer noon, the other glowing with autumn moon's gentler radiance. Both commanded such visceral respect that my body instinctively recoiled despite knowing they existed only in consciousness's deeper chambers.

Then reality began its most elegant dissolution.

White light emerged like dawn breaking across infinite horizons—not the focused beam I'd grown accustomed to, but an encompassing luminosity that transformed the very medium of perception. Breathing became so ethereal it seemed I might have evolved beyond the need for crude atmospheric exchange, existing instead on whatever celestial substances sustained beings who had learned to metabolize light itself.

The luminous background intensified beyond anything previously witnessed, brightness escalating until I felt my awareness detaching from its familiar moorings, consciousness becoming both utterly concentrated and simultaneously scattered across dimensions that had no coordinates in ordinary space.

I existed everywhere and nowhere, rooted in this moment yet floating through eternities that stretched beyond temporal measurement. Sound began its retreat from perception, external volume diminishing as if cosmic engineers were gradually reducing the input levels on reality's mixing board, creating an acoustic cocoon where only the most essential frequencies could penetrate.

Without warning, my cardiovascular system launched into percussive chaos—*thum-thum-thum-thum*—a rhythm that belonged more to emergency rooms than meditation halls. Fear and exhilaration collided in my chest cavity like opposing weather systems, creating internal storms that threatened to scatter whatever concentration had made this moment possible. *Stay calm,* I instructed myself with the authority of someone who had no control over what was unfolding, *simply witness whatever emerges.*

Even as the illumination dimmed in response to my physiological rebellion, I could sense it gathering momentum for something that would redefine every assumption about the possible.

I became aviation incarnate, consciousness piercing cloud banks of pure radiance.

The whiteness enveloped me with maternal completeness—tender, cool, infinite—wrapping awareness in quilts woven from concentrated starlight. At its epicenter, a more intense core pulsed with the rhythm of whatever heartbeat sustained the universe itself. Then *piti* arrived like electricity, discovering flesh, cascades of cosmic pleasure flooding through my nervous system in waves that made earthly joy seem like a pale approximation.

My physical form transformed into an earthquake epicenter, half-lotus posture rocking with tectonic force as if the meditation hall's foundations were liquefying beneath me. Eyelids became hummingbird wings while my inner vision filled with a supernatural electrical storm—lightning bolts crackling through dimensions like special effects from films about interdimensional travel, reality fragmenting into component elements of energy and illumination.

High-pitched ringing crescendoed until it overwhelmed even the neighborhood's relentless musical assault, creating a sonic cathedral built from frequencies that belonged to no terrestrial instruments. Within this otherworldly orchestration, gratitude arose unbidden—profound appreciation for Sayadaw and Mr. Soemin's inexhaustible patience. The instant this recognition touched consciousness, the white radiance blazed with renewed intensity, stabilizing into something that felt like discovering home for the first time.

I floated in this luminous ocean while temporal measurement became irrelevant.

Then, at the brilliance's heart, a vertical fissure materialized—a cosmic doorway barely ajar, streaming with radiance that suggested entire universes waiting beyond the threshold. I gazed with the fixation of someone certain they were about to witness creation's most guarded secrets, that this portal would expand to reveal whatever truths had been hidden since time began. But it simply pulsed there, tantalizing me with possibilities before gradually fading like dreams dissolving at awakening's edge.

Mundane time reasserted its jurisdiction. *The interview*—suddenly I remembered my obligation. Pressing palms together in reverence to the Buddha, eyes remaining sealed, the tingling electrical storm erupted once more—the third time this session had transported me beyond ordinary reality's boundaries.

When my eyelids finally parted, wonder cascaded through me like champagne through crystal. One hour and twenty minutes had evaporated like morning dew, my form feeling weightless despite the extended immobility, liberated from the usual protests that typically accompanied such duration on unforgiving surfaces.

At the interview, my fumbling attempts at description felt like trying to paint sunsets with charcoal. Sayadaw's golden features radiated knowing satisfaction. "The white light—that was authentic *nimitta*. You are approaching *jhana* now."

Exhilaration detonated in my ribcage like celestial fireworks, but Mr. Soemin's intervention sliced through my euphoria with laser precision: "Don't become attached to it, or progress will cease!" His matter-of-fact delivery suggested this counsel was standard protocol, but I recognized the wisdom embedded in his warning even as my excitement completely disregarded it.

Throughout the remaining hours, that luminous realm haunted my awareness like the fragrance of perfect flowers whose source remained mysteriously hidden. I attempted to summon the uniform white radiance in subsequent sessions. Still, only faint echoes manifested—pale whispers of the afternoon's cosmic revelation.

That evening, the acoustic warfare reached unprecedented intensity. Bass frequencies achieved such power that my window glass became a percussion instrument, vibrations transforming into a tangible presence that pressed against the compound's barriers until well beyond midnight. Yet somehow, insulated by memory of that afternoon's transcendence, even their most aggressive compositions felt like distant weather systems from alternate dimensions.

I settled into my mesh sanctuary, cataloguing every nuance of the lightning gate that had opened for me, wondering what lay beyond that brilliant threshold and when consciousness might prove worthy of crossing it. Tomorrow would offer fresh opportunities to explore that realm of pure radiance. Still, tonight I floated on the afterglow of glimpsing what saints across centuries had died hoping to witness.

The *nimitta* had finally revealed its true nature, and existence would never feel quite the same.

Day 8 – Eyes of Light

Sleep had become a casualty of acoustic warfare—merely two hours salvaged from the wreckage of rest before the neighbors' sonic terrorism finally overwhelmed my body's heroic attempts at adaptation. At 2:37 a.m., I raised the white flag of surrender, consciousness emerging into darkness while my nervous system thrummed with the paradoxical combination of bone-deep fatigue and electric hyperstimulation.

I dragged myself to the meditation cushion like a wounded soldier reporting for duty, arranging limbs that felt disconnected from any central command. The morning session opened doorways into territories that challenged every assumption about the stability of human perception.

THE IMPOSSIBLE LIGHT

Luminescence materialized—not the pure radiance I'd grown familiar with, but something more complex, shot through with pewter shadows like thunderheads pregnant with celestial lightning. The visual display suggested storm systems brewing in dimensions where meteorology obeyed different laws than earthly weather patterns.

My auditory world began its mysterious retreat, sounds becoming muffled as if invisible hands were packing cotton batting around my eardrums, creating an acoustic isolation chamber that separated me from the monastery's ambient symphony. More disturbing was the sensation that my skull was undergoing alchemical transformation—bone and flesh liquefying into molten metal that reshaped itself according to geometric principles I couldn't decode.

My mouth vanished from sensory existence entirely, becoming as numb and disconnected as prosthetic anatomy that had never learned to communicate with its host nervous system. The dissociation was so complete that I found myself touching my lips to confirm they remained physically attached to whatever my face was becoming.

As the session approached its conclusion, those familiar wisps of colored vapor emerged at my nostrils—azure and golden smoke that had become reliable indicators of deepening states. But when I finally opened my eyes and lifted my head, reality revealed its most stunning magic trick yet.

Brilliant blue radiance flooded my entire visual field—not the pale afterglow of retinal persistence, not the wishful projections of an overstimulated imagination, but vivid luminescence streaming from my nose like some ethereal dragon breathing starlight instead of fire. The illumination possessed substance and presence that made ordinary vision seem crude by comparison.

But the light itself was merely the stage for an impossible performance: with eyes sealed behind cloth barriers, I could perceive the ghostly silhouettes of my hands and arms moving through space like underwater dancers performing in an ocean of liquid sapphire.

I experimented with tentative arm movements, watching these spectral appendages navigate the blue medium with the fascination of someone discovering they possessed limbs made of concentrated moonbeams. *This must be elaborate self-deception,* my rational mind protested. *Proprioceptive awareness is simply creating visual projections of known body positions.* But then my gaze drifted toward the bed's terminus, where the headboard's unmistakable outline materialized—a long horizontal shadow suspended in the azure background, positioned exactly where physical reality insisted it should exist.

My scientific worldview began developing stress fractures as I struggled to construct explanations that wouldn't require abandoning everything I thought I understood about the relationship between consciousness and perception.

EYES BEHIND EYES

The subsequent session escalated these revelations into a full-scale assault on the boundaries of possible experience. Opening my eyes beneath the blindfold produced only expected darkness—the normal visual void that should accompany blocked photons. But closing them again immediately restored the extraordinary sight, as if some dormant organ of perception had awakened that operated independently of optical nerve pathways.

I possessed greater visual acuity with eyes sealed and covered than with them open beneath identical conditions, suggesting that consciousness had access to sensory channels that existed beyond the five-sense model that Western education had taught me to consider complete and exhaustive.

The irony wasn't lost on me—here I was, an optometrist by profession, experiencing visual phenomena that would have sent me reaching for my prescription pad if a patient had walked into my clinic describing identical symptoms. I would have been deeply concerned about what psychoactive substances they might have ingested, or worse, what neurological catastrophe might be unfolding behind their retinas. Yet here I sat, stone-cold sober, witnessing my visual system operate according to principles that violated everything I'd learned about ocular anatomy and the mechanics of sight.

EXPERIMENTS IN IMPOSSIBLE SIGHT

During another sitting, I conducted systematic experiments with the methodical curiosity of someone documenting phenomena that might revolutionize neuroscience if properly understood. Repeatedly opening and closing one fist, I observed my fingers performing their aquatic ballet in the blue luminescence, each digit visible despite existing behind multiple layers of cloth and flesh barriers that should have rendered such observation impossible.

That evening in the main hall, surrounded by fellow practitioners whose presence created amplified spiritual resonance, I discovered I could perceive my legs through clothing when adjusting meditation posture. Yet the person sitting directly beside me remained entirely invisible for this supernatural vision, while my wristwatch —positioned mere inches from where this enhanced sight should have maximum clarity—revealed nothing beyond empty void.

This new faculty operated according to principles I was only beginning to decipher, with limitations and capabilities that seemed to follow laws unknown to conventional ophthalmology.

The *nimitta* itself was undergoing evolutionary transformation, its usual azure hues deepening into brilliant turquoise that possessed the luminous intensity of tropical seas illuminated by alien suns. Most remarkably, it had achieved sufficient stability to manifest even before formal meditation commenced, extending outward from my nostrils like a radiant tongue sampling atmospheric energies that remained invisible to ordinary awareness.

I could sustain observation of this phenomenon for twenty uninterrupted minutes before it gradually dissolved, serving as an interdimensional bridge connecting mundane perception with territories that existed beyond the reach of conventional sensory experience.

THE TEACHER'S WISDOM

At the afternoon interview, Sayadaw's melodious laughter greeted my fumbling attempts to articulate experiences that challenged every vocabulary designed for ordinary reality. "This development is entirely predictable," he observed with the casual demeanor of someone discussing routine weather patterns rather than phenomena that belonged in peer-reviewed journals of consciousness research.

"Avoid becoming fascinated by observation and analysis. Maintain patience. Persist with diligent effort." His matter-of-fact response somehow transformed the impossible into standard curriculum, suggesting that what felt like personal miracles were predictable stages in consciousness development that countless practitioners had navigated before me.

EVENING REVELATIONS

The 5:45 p.m. session unveiled fresh dimensions of visual pyrotechnics that began with cascading illumination resembling celestial fireworks—simultaneously distracting, beautiful, and overwhelming in their complexity. My facial muscles contracted into unfamiliar configurations as if my skull were being remodeled by invisible sculptors working from blueprints I couldn't access.

For the first time, the *nimitta* emerged as brilliant emerald vapor before metamorphosing into electric blue radiance that extended with substantial presence until I felt confident I could direct it toward the wall like some cosmic dragon exhaling luminous mist across dimensions that connected inner vision with external reality.

The day's most enigmatic gift manifested as a recurring holographic display: a vertical wall that appeared to be a fragment of some vast crimson carpet-like structure suspended in space, its center dominated by a perfect void that seemed to absorb light rather than reflect it. The entire formation undulated as if caught in cosmic breezes, floating through dimensions that bore no relationship to my meditation room's familiar Euclidean geometry.

This image returned with insistent regularity throughout the session, demanding attention I struggled to spare from breath awareness while simultaneously refusing to be dismissed as random mental static or meaningless hallucination.

Evening brought the familiar fatigue that marked the depletion of whatever internal resources sustained such intensive spiritual phenomena. Later sessions felt dense and unfocused, as if I'd exhausted some hidden reservoir of concentration that required restoration before reaccessing these extraordinary states.

BLESSED SILENCE

But then, like answered prayers from gods who specialized in perfect timing, the acoustic torture finally ceased. The neighbors' relentless musical assault surrendered to blessed silence, creating the first authentic quiet I'd experienced since arriving at this monastery, where external peace had seemed like an impossible luxury.

That night, sleep enveloped me with the tenderness of a long-absent lover returning home, carrying me through restorative depths for the first time in seven days. I surfaced only twice from habitual alertness before consciousness naturally emerged at 3:30 a.m., my body feeling genuinely refreshed and prepared for whatever fresh impossibilities might emerge from the darkness preceding dawn.

Through my mesh sanctuary, the world outside maintained its beautiful, merciful silence. Even the territorial gecko appeared to have negotiated a temporary armistice with whatever cosmic forces governed nocturnal disturbances. As I prepared for the day's inaugural sitting, curiosity bloomed about what additional senses might awaken as concentration achieved deeper refinement, what other dormant capabilities lay sleeping within human neural architecture, awaiting optimal conditions to blossom into experiences that transformed ordinary existence into ongoing miracles.

Day 9 – The Architecture of Inner Light

The pre-dawn darkness surrendered to consciousness at 3:43 a.m., carrying with it a quality of alertness that felt borrowed from another species entirely—crystalline and unwavering, as if my mind had suddenly remembered that perfect focus was its birthright rather than its aspiration. When I settled onto the meditation cushion, concentration didn't arrive as the hard-won prize of mental effort but as a gift offered by the morning itself, effortless as breathing, complete as sunrise.

Behind closed eyelids, the *nimitta* that bloomed possessed an almost architectural precision. This wasn't the fuzzy glow I had grown accustomed to, but something with the structural integrity of celestial engineering—a luminous background that graduated like light falling across cosmic topography, more brilliant in its upper reaches, with the top left corner blazing like a distant star system viewed through the Hubble telescope's unwavering eye.

For nearly two hours, until the breakfast bell shattered the monastery's crystalline silence at 5:25, I inhabited this inner planetarium. The light shifted and breathed with each cycle of attention, responding to the rhythm of consciousness like aurora responding to solar wind. The colorful wisps of smoke that had previously danced through my visual field had vanished, replaced by something more focused and substantial—a light-colored disc no larger than my palm, hovering in the darkness with the serene presence of a miniature moon. When I searched for the familiar smoke patterns, I found only tiny stars twinkling at the periphery, scattered like diamond dust across the velvet of inner space.

THE FLOODGATES OPEN

The second session at 7:05 a.m. opened floodgates I hadn't known existed within the geography of mind. Lights erupted across my inner vision with such explosive profusion that witnessing them became exhausting labor. I struggled to maintain proper meditation technique, to resist being drawn into these compelling visual narratives unfolding behind my eyelids. But it was like trying to ignore the aurora borealis while standing beneath its dancing curtains—a feat of willful blindness that felt almost offensive to the majesty presenting itself.

First came what could only be described as sunrise itself—a brilliant disc floating above orange clouds that stretched across my inner horizon with photographic precision. The resemblance to dawn breaking over earthly landscapes was so perfect it made me question the boundary between inner vision and outer memory. Had my mind simply projected some remembered dawn, or was I witnessing the archetypal sunrise from which all earthly mornings drew their light?

Then emerged something far more otherworldly: a blue sphere that swirled and pulsed like the bamboo footballs I had watched children kick through Yangon's dusty streets, but transmuted into something cosmic and electric. This celestial orb possessed a blazing core that emitted long azure rays, crackling with the energy of captured lightning as it spun and drifted away from me. It resembled an electrostatic crystal awakened to impossible life, so vivid and three-dimensional that my fingers twitched with the phantom sensation of reaching toward its surface.

As I watched, mesmerized by its alien beauty, the sphere began to contract, growing smaller and smaller until it simply popped out of existence like a soap bubble touched by wind, dissolving into a broad band of blue light that stretched across the lower portion of my visual field like some impossible horizon where sky meets space.

This blue band became a living thing, sometimes stretching itself thin as stratified clouds, other times billowing into cumulus formations that seemed to breathe with their own meteorology. But even this spectacle paled before what emerged next—a funnel-shaped blue cloud viewed from its wider mouth, the narrow end receding into infinite distance like a corridor leading to the edge of the known universe. The background transformed into what appeared to be deep space itself: black infinity populated by billions of tiny blue stars, so sharp and vivid that I felt my consciousness had been launched beyond Earth's atmosphere into the cold clarity of the cosmic void.

The sensation of flying through space was so convincing that my rational mind had to work actively to remember I was sitting on a meditation cushion in a Yangon monastery, surrounded by the mundane sounds of breakfast preparation filtering through monastery walls. This was the most spectacular vision I had ever witnessed—more real than reality, more beautiful than any earthly sunset or starfield captured by astronomical photography. How could one ignore such magnificence? It was like being commanded not to look while witnessing the birth of galaxies, the dance of cosmic forces that most humans never glimpse even in their most vivid dreams.

THE TUNNEL OF LIGHT

The noon session began with another eruption of luminosity, but this time the lights arranged themselves into something unprecedented—a bright tunnel extending roughly thirty centimeters from my nose, as if someone had constructed a corridor of pure illumination leading directly into the hidden chambers of consciousness. I found myself staring down this passage of light, wondering what lay at its terminus, what destination it might reveal if I possessed the courage to follow it completely.

The tunnel pulsed with its own inner rhythm, walls made of concentrated photons that seemed more substantial than the physical matter surrounding my body. It invited exploration with the magnetic pull of a mystery that had waited eons for discovery. Part of me wanted to dive headfirst into that luminous corridor, to surrender completely to whatever lay beyond its far end.

But meditation, like all profound experiences, follows its own mysterious rhythms, obeying laws that exist beyond human will or desire.

THE CRASH

The afternoon session after lunch crashed like a tsunami wave against granite cliffs, leaving behind only scattered foam and debris where once had been a cosmic ocean. By 4:30 p.m., the inner cosmos had vanished entirely—no lights, no smoke, no *nimitta* of any kind—just darkness, ordinary and disappointing as a theater after the final curtain falls. The contrast was so stark it felt like visual death, as if some essential organ of perception had simply ceased functioning without warning or explanation.

Panic crept up my spine with cold fingers, each vertebra registering the ascending dread. Was this regression? Had I somehow broken the delicate mechanism that produced these visions? The morning had been my Everest; the afternoon felt like free fall into an abyss. The emotional whiplash was almost unbearable—like experiencing the most beautiful sunrise of your life followed immediately by permanent blindness.

WISDOM IN THE DARKNESS

Fortunately, the young assistant teacher was available, standing in for Sayadaw, who had returned to his village for ten days to tend to matters that belonged to the world beyond monastery walls. The assistant's English flowed with the fluency of someone who had learned not just vocabulary but the subtle architecture of meaning, and he had invited questions whenever problems arose, approaching each student's confusion with the patience of someone who understood that bewilderment was simply another stage in the journey.

When I found him during the break, walking with the measured pace of someone who had nowhere urgent to be, I approached with the desperation of someone whose world had suddenly gone dark.

"Why did everything disappear?" I asked, unable to keep the distress from coloring my voice like blood in water. "This morning I saw the universe itself, but now there's nothing."

His smile carried the patient wisdom of someone who had heard this lament countless times before, who had watched dozens of meditators ride the same roller coaster of celestial visions followed by crushing emptiness. "It's completely normal," he said, his voice carrying the reassuring authority of someone who had navigated these waters himself. "The *nimitta* comes and goes, varying with conditions, moods, the countless factors we cannot control or predict. When you see beautiful visions, don't become excited. When they disappear, don't become downhearted. Both responses create obstacles to deeper practice."

His words landed like medicine on an open wound—not immediately healing, but beginning the slow work of restoration.

THE BIRD'S FLIGHT

Mr. Soemin must have noticed my dejected demeanor—or perhaps had spoken with the assistant teacher about the foreign meditator who looked like he'd lost his best friend—because at day's end, he summoned me to his office with the gentle concern of someone tending a wilting plant.

"How's it going today?" he inquired, settling behind his desk with the patient attention of someone prepared to listen to whatever confession might emerge.

"Well, in the morning, I saw the universe," I replied, still bewildered by the day's contradictions, "but later all I saw was black!"

Mr. Soemin's face twitched with barely suppressed laughter—perhaps at the dramatic way Westerners tend to narrate their inner experiences—but seeing my somber mood, he quickly covered his mouth and composed his features into appropriate seriousness.

"Meditation is like a bird flying," he said, making a graceful undulating motion with his hand that captured the essence of flight better than any ornithology textbook. The gesture rose and fell through the air between us, tracing invisible thermals and wind currents. "Sometimes high, sometimes low. Don't worry—you have not lost the *nimitta*."

He opened his desk drawer and withdrew a small flashlight, clicking it on to cast a bright circle on the wall like a teacher preparing a simple but profound lesson. "The *nimitta* is like a torch," he explained, moving the beam across the surface in slow, deliberate arcs. "It is used to see things."

Then, in a gesture both simple and revelatory, he turned the light toward his face, illuminating features that immediately became harsh and distorted in the direct glare—shadows carving unfamiliar valleys across familiar terrain, eyes becoming hollow caverns, the gentle teacher suddenly transformed into something alien and severe.

"But you don't look at the torch!" he said, his voice carrying the emphasis of someone delivering a truth that could change everything.

He switched off the light and returned it to the drawer with the finality of someone concluding a lesson that had been taught in classrooms of consciousness for millennia. "Look," he said, his voice carrying new instruction like a prescription for the soul, "for the rest of the day, just do *Metta*."

So I spent the remaining hours cultivating loving-kindness, letting go of my attachment to spectacular visions in favor of the gentler work of opening the heart—a practice that felt like tending a garden instead of scaling a mountain.

THE HOLOGRAPHIC NIGHT

That night, as I lay in bed with eyes closed, expecting only the ordinary darkness that precedes sleep, the most extraordinary phenomenon yet began to unfold in the space around me. Holographic images started projecting themselves throughout my room—not behind my eyelids like the day's visions, but apparently into the three-dimensional space around my physical body, transforming my simple monastery cell into what I could only compare to Star Trek's holodeck.

The entire room filled with vivid, colorful, impossibly detailed images that seemed to possess independent existence, as if someone had installed a cosmic projector that drew its material from dimensions beyond the visible spectrum. These weren't mere mental pictures flickering across the screen of imagination, but full environmental experiences that engaged every aspect of perception.

Bas-reliefs carved from pure light floated through the air, their surfaces catching illumination from sources I couldn't identify—phantom suns casting real shadows, creating depth and texture that challenged everything I thought I knew about the relationship between mind and matter. Black skies populated with twinkling blue stars stretched across my ceiling, then gave way to rolling landscapes that materialized and dissolved like time-lapse geography viewed from the window of a spacecraft traveling at impossible speeds.

Sailing ships moved majestically through the space above my bed, their sails filled with winds from other dimensions, rigging detailed down to individual ropes, crew members moving across decks with the purposeful motion of beings going about important business in worlds that existed only in the theater of inner space.

The three-dimensional quality was so convincing that I repeatedly had to remind myself these images weren't physically present—that if I reached out, my fingers would encounter only empty air instead of the masts and sails that seemed solid enough to touch. Some images bore resemblance to earthly things I had encountered in waking life—landscapes that echoed places I had visited, faces that seemed familiar from dreams or distant memories.

But others appeared utterly alien—geometric patterns that seemed to follow mathematical laws I didn't recognize, creatures that moved according to biological principles from other worlds, architectural structures that defied gravity and conventional engineering with the casual confidence of beings who had never heard of Isaac Newton.

Most puzzling were the images I was certain I had never encountered in waking life, dream, or fantasy. Where had my mind acquired these templates? What vast library of impossible forms was my consciousness accessing in the deep hours of night? Was I somehow tuning into frequencies that broadcast from the collective unconscious, or had meditation unlocked storage chambers in the brain that contained the blueprints for worlds that existed only in potential?

I lay there marveling at this nocturnal cinema, watching alien worlds parade through my sleeping quarters like a private screening of creation's deleted scenes, until practical wisdom finally reminded me that even the most extraordinary visions were no substitute for the sleep my body would need for tomorrow's practice.

But as I drifted toward dreams, one question lingered in the space between waking and sleeping: if the mind could generate realities this vivid and detailed without any external stimulus, what did that say about the nature of the reality I took for granted when my eyes were open? Perhaps the real lesson wasn't about spectacular visions at all, but about the malleable nature of experience itself—the way consciousness shapes and reshapes the raw material of existence moment by moment, creating worlds upon worlds from the inexhaustible mystery of awareness itself.

The last image I remember before sleep finally claimed me was a simple one: a bird soaring through infinite sky, riding thermals that existed nowhere and everywhere, following flight patterns that had been traced by countless wings across the vast democracy of air that connects all breathing things. Sometimes high, sometimes low, but always, somehow, exactly where it needed to be.

Day 10 – Diamond Light and the Magnetic Field of Being

Sleep arrived in fragments throughout the night—consciousness surfacing and diving like a restless swimmer caught between the pull of dreams and the insistent tug of wakefulness. Each emergence brought with it the electric afterglow of the previous day's cosmic theater, my nervous system still humming with the residual frequency of visions that had stretched the boundaries of what I thought possible. When I finally surrendered to full wakefulness around four a.m., I felt like a radio receiver that had been tuned too close to a powerful transmitter, every cell still vibrating with phantom signals.

THE SHY RETURN

Morning meditation limped along without much grace, though it surpassed yesterday afternoon's barren void with the modest victory of someone learning to walk again after an injury. The faint *nimitta* appeared as wispy smoke—pale and tentative, like a shy animal testing whether it was safe to emerge from hiding after some great disturbance had passed through its territory.

I watched this fragile luminosity with the careful attention of someone coaxing a wild creature closer, afraid that too much eagerness might send it scurrying back into whatever hidden realms had sheltered it during yesterday's crash. The light flickered uncertainly, neither fully present nor completely absent, occupying that liminal space where possibility hovers on the edge of manifestation.

But later sessions revealed *Metta*'s healing power with the clarity of a medical diagnosis finally explaining mysterious symptoms. After bathing my consciousness in loving-kindness—deliberately cultivating compassion for all beings, including the frustrated meditator who had watched his cosmic visions vanish like smoke—the *nimitta* brightened considerably, as if loving-kindness had polished some inner lens that allowed light to shine more clearly through the accumulated dust of disappointment and attachment.

The correlation felt too consistent to be coincidence, too immediate to be imagination. Loving-kindness seemed to prepare the ground for deeper visions the way rain prepares soil for new growth, softening the hardpan of a heart that had become too focused on spiritual achievement rather than spiritual surrender.

THE STRATEGIC REST

A post-lunch nap proved strategic rather than lazy—a tactical retreat that restored something essential to the meditation mechanism. Rest recharged whatever batteries powered the inner light show, and the afternoon session bloomed with renewed vitality, like flowers opening after the heat of midday had passed.

Lights cascaded like gentle fireworks across the landscape of closed eyes, each burst of illumination more sustained than the desperate flickers of morning. The *nimitta* manifested as a brilliant cylindrical form wreathed in wispy blue aureoles, spinning slowly in the darkness with the serene rotation of a celestial body that had found its perfect orbit.

The turquoise radiance pulsed with intensity beyond anything found in nature's visible spectrum—a color that existed only in consciousness's secret palette, mixed from pigments that had no names in any earthly language. It was the blue of impossible oceans, of skies that belonged to worlds where different laws of physics allowed light to behave in ways our sun had never taught it.

BENEDICTION AND DIAMONDS

Mr. Soemin's summons to his office brought unexpected gifts wrapped in the quiet authority of someone who had witnessed countless spiritual emergencies and knew exactly which medicines each required. He demonstrated his slow breathing technique with the patience of someone who'd guided countless seekers through these mysterious territories, his own breath becoming a teaching tool more eloquent than any textbook.

"Don't worry," he said, reading the doubt that must have been written across my face like headlines announcing my spiritual incompetence. "Your *parami* has brought you this far."

The word landed like a benediction I hadn't known I needed. *Parami*—the accumulated spiritual merit from lifetimes of practice, the invisible momentum that carries beings toward liberation. His words suggested I'd achieved something even monks struggled to attain, that the *nimitta* itself was proof of spiritual accumulations gathered across incarnations like interest compounding in some cosmic bank account.

His encouragement felt like sunlight breaking through storm clouds, warming places in my heart I hadn't realized had grown cold during yesterday's emotional winter. The relief was almost physical—tension I hadn't recognized dissolving from muscles that had been braced against the possibility of complete spiritual failure.

But the day's most spectacular gift arrived as an entirely new form of *nimitta* that made all previous visions seem like rough sketches compared to finished masterpieces. Instead of the usual discs and tunnels of light, a handful of diamonds scattered themselves across my inner vision, each fragment blazing with crystalline fire that cut through darkness with the precision of laser surgery.

These weren't metaphorical diamonds or approximate resemblances—they possessed the exact optical properties of precious stones viewed under perfect illumination, each facet catching and refracting light according to the same mathematical principles that governed earthly gems. Sharp-edged and brilliant beyond description, they sparkled against the black backdrop of consciousness as if some cosmic jeweler had spilled the contents of heaven's treasure box across the darkness of my closed eyes.

Each diamond pulsed with its own inner radiance while simultaneously reflecting light from sources I couldn't identify, creating a light show that seemed to follow crystallographic laws I'd never studied but somehow recognized as fundamentally correct. The beauty was so intense it bordered on painful, like staring directly into the essence of what humans had always tried to capture in their most precious ornaments.

THE MAGNETIC FIELD OF BEING

Evening brought an experimental mood born from confidence that today's practice had earned me the right to explore territories mentioned in ancient texts but rarely explained in detail. After the diamond *nimitta* stabilized into reliable brilliance, I decided to test something I'd read about but never attempted—micro-orbit circulation meditation, the Taoist practice of moving energy through specific pathways in the body.

Shifting attention from the visual spectacle to the subtle geography of energy channels, I felt currents beginning to move in patterns that seemed older than memory, as if my consciousness were remembering dance steps learned in some previous existence. The sensations were delicate but unmistakable—warmth and tingling following invisible highways through my torso, energy moving according to laws I couldn't articulate but somehow trusted.

Then, following an impulse that felt like remembering rather than discovering, I directed the *nimitta's* brilliant focus back toward my face, allowing the diamond light to merge with these subtle energy currents.

What happened next defied easy description, pushing language beyond its comfortable boundaries into territories where words became crude approximations of realities too subtle for speech.

A magnetic force emerged—not physical magnetism measurable by instruments, but something deeper and more fundamental, an energy that seemed to exist in the space between matter and spirit. It felt like standing between two invisible magnets powerful enough to bend space itself, consciousness becoming the medium through which these mysterious forces operated.

The sensation was both utterly familiar and completely alien, as if I'd accessed some forgotten faculty of human perception that evolution had buried beneath layers of survival-focused awareness. My face felt simultaneously pulled and pushed by energies that obeyed no laws I'd learned in physics class, yet the experience carried an undeniable authenticity that made ordinary reality seem thin and insubstantial by comparison.

The magnetic field—for lack of a better term—seemed to emanate from the intersection of visual *nimitta* and energy circulation, as if these two practices together had created conditions for phenomena that neither could produce alone. I felt like an accidental scientist who had mixed chemicals and discovered an entirely new element, beautiful and strange and unmistakably real.

THE DIMINISHING CIRCLE

Our meditation family had quietly diminished over recent days, departures so subtle they barely registered until empty spaces began accumulating like gaps in a smile. The older man with the walking stick—always first to finish his meals despite being the oldest among us—hadn't appeared for lunch, his customary place at the table now occupied only by absence.

In his seventies, he'd been our group's dignified patriarch, moving through the monastery routines with the measured grace of someone who understood that spiritual practice was a marathon rather than a sprint. His disappearance left a hole in our small community's geometry, a reminder that these intimate bonds could dissolve as quietly as they'd formed.

Meanwhile, the youngest layman remained our gentle straggler, perpetually wiping sweat from his forehead as he tried to match our eating pace, his considerate struggle to keep up touching in its earnestness. His persistence in the face of obvious discomfort spoke to something admirable in human nature—the willingness to endure minor suffering rather than inconvenience others.

I realized belatedly that we'd lost another monk as well, departures so quiet they'd barely registered in the focused absorption of daily practice. Now only four laymen remained alongside three monks, our meditation hall feeling spacious in ways that suggested loss rather than luxury.

These departures cast subtle shadows over the evening, reminders that spiritual practice unfolds in community even when pursued in silence. Each empty cushion told its own story of inner journeys interrupted or completed, of beings following mysterious callings back to the world beyond these flowering monastery walls.

Some left because they'd found what they came for; others because they'd discovered the path was longer or more difficult than anticipated. A few might have been called away by family emergencies or work obligations that wouldn't wait for enlightenment's schedule. Each departure was a small death in the life of our temporary sangha, a dissolution that made the remaining bonds feel both more precious and more fragile.

THE AFTERGLOW

Tonight, as I settled into my mosquito net sanctuary—that gossamer fortress that had become as familiar as home—the diamond *nimitta* lingered in my peripheral vision like stars refusing to fade with dawn. Even with eyes open and attention focused on the mundane task of arranging bedding, the crystalline brilliance persisted at the edges of awareness, a reminder that some experiences leave permanent residue in consciousness.

The magnetic force experiment had opened new questions about consciousness's hidden capabilities, revealing pathways of energy that traditional meditation texts hinted at but rarely explained in detail. These were territories where ancient wisdom met direct experience, where practices developed over millennia suddenly became as real and immediate as breathing.

I found myself wondering how many human beings throughout history had stumbled upon these same phenomena, these intersections of mind and energy that existed beyond the boundaries of conventional understanding. How many had felt the magnetic pull between consciousness and cosmos, had watched diamonds of light scatter across inner darkness, had discovered that the body contained highways for forces that science couldn't yet measure?

Tomorrow would bring new opportunities to explore these territories where mind met energy, where ancient practices revealed capabilities that modern understanding could barely accommodate. The diamond light had shown me that consciousness possessed faculties I'd never suspected, tools for perception that made ordinary awareness seem like black-and-white photography compared to full-spectrum vision.

But tonight, I was content to rest in the afterglow of diamond light and mysterious forces, grateful for *parami* that continued carrying me deeper into realms I'd never imagined existed. The retreat was transforming from a meditation practice into an exploration of consciousness itself, each day revealing new rooms in the vast mansion of human awareness.

As sleep approached—more gently than the previous night's fragmented arrival—I reflected on how quickly the impossible had become familiar, how readily consciousness adapted to experiences that would have seemed like science fiction just days earlier. Perhaps the most profound discovery wasn't the visions themselves, but the recognition that human awareness contained infinite potential for expansion, endless capacity for perceiving realities that existed just beyond the narrow bandwidth of ordinary perception.

The diamond light continued to pulse softly behind my eyelids as I drifted toward dreams, a gentle beacon marking territories of consciousness I was only beginning to explore. In the morning, I would sit again on the cushion, open again to whatever mysteries awaited in the vast laboratory of mind. But for now, it was enough to rest in gratitude for this glimpse behind the curtain of conventional reality, this preview of capabilities that belonged to every human being willing to sit still long enough to discover what consciousness could become when freed from its ordinary constraints.

FORTY THREE DAYS OF FIRE

Day 11 – The Warrior's Garden: Flowers of the Heart

Three-thirty in the morning found me hauling consciousness from sleep's sticky depths like a deep-sea diver surfacing too quickly, nitrogen bubbles of drowsiness still fizzing through my awareness. The pre-dawn sitting from 3:40 to 5:25 dissolved into a meditation that felt more like wrestling with quicksand than dancing with breath—my mind wrapped in cotton wool, concentration slipping through my fingers like water through a broken cup.

I even had to surrender to horizontal defeat mid-session, lying down as exhaustion rose from my bones like heat from sun-baked stones. My left nostril throbbed with soreness from breathing too intensely, the delicate tissues inflamed from attention focused like a laser beam on that tender gateway. Now I understood why teachers warned against concentrating inside the nostrils—they weren't designed to withstand such relentless scrutiny. I resorted to plugging the nostril with tissue, grateful for the privacy of solo practice that allowed such unglamorous adaptations.

Light-headedness followed me through the morning like a persistent shadow, sessions limping along without inspiration while the diamond-shaped *nimitta* flickered occasionally like a distant lighthouse signaling through thick fog. My meditation felt like trying to tune a radio with broken knobs, catching only fragments of the clarity I'd tasted in recent days.

THE STRATEGIC SURRENDER

Lunch brought the wisdom of strategic retreat—a thirty-minute nap that felt like medicine for an overtaxed nervous system, followed by walking meditation that combined *Metta* and death contemplation. These practices worked like tuning forks on consciousness, each step calibrating my awareness to frequencies that made deeper states possible.

When I finally settled into *Anapanasati*, everything shifted with the sudden grace of tumblers falling into place in a cosmic lock.

A bright blue bubble materialized at my nose's tip, expanding gradually until it filled my entire visual field with hazy azure radiance that seemed to pulse with its own gentle breathing. For twenty minutes—an eternity in meditation time—this luminous sphere remained perfectly stable at my vision's center, a breakthrough that felt like discovering a new continent floating in the ocean of consciousness.

When it finally shifted, a blue background *nimitta* sustained itself for the session's remainder, providing a canvas of light against which breath could paint its subtle masterpiece. Most remarkably, I could simultaneously watch the *nimitta* and maintain breath awareness—skills that had previously felt as mutually exclusive as looking in two directions at once.

Moving fluidly between meditation objects became like speaking multiple languages simultaneously, each practice carrying its own luminous signature. Death contemplation dimmed the colors like storm clouds passing over the sun, while loving-kindness brightened them like dawn breaking over a clear horizon.

THE EXPERIMENT IN EXTREMES

The four o'clock session brought the day's major revelation, born from the assistant teacher's emphasis on one-pointedness that had been echoing in my mind like a persistent bell. Suddenly, I decided to test concentration's absolute limits—to discover what lay beyond the boundaries of ordinary focused attention.

Starting with *Metta*, I developed a blue background *nimitta*, then shifted to *Anapanasati* while maintaining attention so laser-focused it felt like consciousness itself had been compressed into a surgical instrument. The strategy worked with dramatic precision —colors remained brilliant even as my breathing became gossamer-soft, barely perceptible wisps that seemed more like memory than actual respiration.

When breath sensation disappeared entirely, something extraordinary occurred: the *nimitta* blazed even brighter, as if perfect stillness had unlocked some deeper source of inner light that had been waiting beneath the surface chatter of ordinary breathing. It was like discovering that the gentle candleflame I'd been tending contained the compressed energy of a star.

A Pa-Auk monk's words surfaced from memory like a life preserver thrown to someone drowning in confusion: not feeling breath's touch was perfectly acceptable—simply knowing you were breathing mattered more than physical sensation. This paradox felt like receiving permission to dive deeper into stillness than I'd ever dared, to trust that consciousness could navigate waters where ordinary perception failed.

THE TANGIBLE LIGHT

The 6:40 p.m. session pushed these experiments even further into territories where meditation became sculptural, almost architectural in its solidity. Forcing one-pointedness on the sacred syllable

Araham produced a brilliant blue smoky rod extending twenty centimeters from my face—meditation's most tangible manifestation yet, so substantial it seemed I could lean against it for support.

Even when concentration wavered, colors remained vivid, as if I'd accessed some sustainable source of inner luminosity that didn't depend on perfect mental stillness. The light had become self-generating, powered by some renewable energy source hidden in consciousness's depths.

The intensity left my mind alert and humming until bedtime, consciousness charged with electric clarity that made ordinary thoughts feel crude and heavy by comparison.

THE MIND'S REBELLION

I'd spent the entire day maintaining wholesome thoughts with the discipline of a Tibetan monk in retreat, and the effort paid dividends in states of consciousness so refined they felt borrowed from another species. My mind had become impossibly sensitive and subtle, like a precision instrument capable of detecting the most delicate spiritual frequencies.

But achieving this state required constant warfare against consciousness's rebellious nature—a battle that made medieval sieges seem like gentle negotiations.

The mind yearned to be anywhere except focused on the breath's subtle gateway. Thoughts of family back home would arise like gentle sirens, calling me to remember Sunday dinners and familiar laughter, the warmth of my mother's kitchen and the sound of my father's laugh echoing through childhood memories. These weren't crude distractions but tender invasions that felt like love itself, making the act of dismissing them feel like severing pieces of my heart with each redirection back to breath.

Missing loved ones became another enemy to vanquish—the ache of separation disguising itself as reasonable concern that could consume entire meditation sessions if left unchecked. The homesickness would present itself as virtue: A loving son should worry about his parents. What kind of person abandons family for selfish spiritual pursuits?

Even simple physical pleasures became elaborate psychological traps. Walking past the courtyard's sun-drenched patches, my consciousness would whisper seductive suggestions with the voice of apparent wisdom: Just sit here for a few extra minutes. Feel the warmth on your skin. What harm could there be in basking in these golden rays a little longer? The desire felt so innocent, so wholesome, yet I'd learned to recognize it as another clever distraction from the breath's subtle teachings.

Every comfort the mind had ever known became ammunition in its campaign against one-pointed concentration. Thoughts of soft beds, favorite foods, air conditioning, hot showers—a parade of sensual memories designed to make the hard wooden floor and tropical heat feel unbearable. The mind behaved like a spoiled child denied its toys, throwing increasingly creative tantrums to reclaim its accustomed freedoms.

THE ARSENAL OF CONCENTRATION

Controlling consciousness for entire days required enormous effort—pulling attention back to breath thousands of times like a trainer working with an impossibly willful animal that had memorized every escape route from discipline's cage. Early in the retreat, I'd spent hours lost in mental quicksands, jumping unconsciously from one of the Buddha's five hindrances to another—from missing home to craving comfort to worrying about the future to feeling drowsy to doubting the entire enterprise. It was an exhausting carousel of distraction that left me dizzy and depleted.

Now, with established concentration and mindfulness, I could recognize these formations as they emerged and avoid their gravitational pull. But vigilance was essential—these mental formations disguised themselves as legitimate concerns, slipping past awareness through cunning camouflage that would have impressed military strategists.

A thought about family would masquerade as caring love: I should check if everyone's okay. A loving son would be concerned about his parents' health. The desire for physical comfort would present itself as reasonable self-care: My back is aching—surely the Buddha wouldn't want me to suffer unnecessarily. A wise practitioner knows when to rest. The urge to abandon difficult practice would arrive dressed as wisdom about balance and moderation: This intensity isn't sustainable. True spiritual growth comes from gentle, consistent effort, not this exhausting pushing.

Each deception felt so reasonable, so spiritually mature, that I had to develop increasingly sophisticated defenses against my own mind's treachery.

When breath awareness began slipping away, I'd deployed an escalating arsenal of concentration tools. First, I'd switch to verbalizing *Araham* internally—the sacred syllable becoming a lifeline when the subtle breath proved too elusive to hold. The word would pulse with my heartbeat, each repetition pulling scattered attention back into focus like a magnet gathering iron filings.

If even *Araham* couldn't penetrate the mental fog, I'd resort to more direct commands: "Concentrate, concentrate," spoken firmly in my mind's voice, each word a gentle slap to wake up wandering awareness. Sometimes this internal coaching was enough to restore order to chaotic consciousness.

But when thoughts proved particularly stubborn—when family memories or comfort cravings launched full-scale invasions—I'd turn up the volume. "CONCENTRATE, CONCENTRATE," shouted silently but with increasing intensity, the words becoming louder and more continuous in my mental landscape, drowning out all other chatter like a battle cry overwhelming the enemy's morale.

When even this failed—when sitting still became a losing battle against distraction's well-organized army—I'd surrender the position and change tactics entirely. Standing up, I'd begin walking meditation while internally shouting concentration commands even louder and more continuously: "CONCENTRATE! *ARAHAM*! CONCENTRATE! *ARAHAM*!" The movement helped discharge restless energy that made stillness impossible, while the rhythmic verbalizations created an impenetrable wall of focused intention.

Walking around the compound with this internal war cry echoing in my mind, I'd gradually feel control returning—scattered attention gathering itself like soldiers regrouping after battle. The combination of physical movement and aggressive mental discipline usually restored enough concentration to return to sitting practice, my mind finally ready to submit to the breath's subtle guidance.

By day's end, I felt like a warrior who'd fought a thousand small battles, each victory over wandering attention earned through conscious effort. The exhaustion was profound but satisfying—the fatigue of someone who'd given everything to stay present, to keep consciousness tethered to the simple reality of each breath.

THE IMPOSSIBLE GARDEN

The evening's group sitting at seven brought the day's most extraordinary gift, a revelation that transformed everything I thought I knew about the relationship between mind and reality.

While extending *Metta* to the assistant teacher—sending waves of loving-kindness toward his gentle, patient presence—something impossible bloomed in my inner vision: a perfect bunch of lotus flowers suspended in space, so real I could have reached out and touched their delicate petals.

But "real" was an inadequate word for what I witnessed, like calling the ocean "wet" or the sun "bright"—accurate but utterly insufficient to capture the magnitude of the experience.

These flowers possessed a solidity that made the meditation hall seem like a faded photograph in comparison, a mere sketch of reality compared to their blazing, three-dimensional presence. Each lotus petal was rendered with crystalline precision that surpassed anything earthly photography could capture—every vein visible, every curve catching light that seemed to emanate from within the blossoms themselves rather than falling upon them from external sources.

They hung suspended directly in front of my face, perhaps eighteen inches from my nose, occupying space with such undeniable presence that the wooden floor beneath me and the walls around me felt suddenly insubstantial, like stage props in a dream I was just beginning to wake from. The contrast was so stark it made me question which reality was more fundamental—the solid world I'd always trusted, or these impossible flowers that seemed more real than anything I'd ever encountered.

The lotuses radiated their own luminescence, each flower glowing with pearl-white light edged in the softest pink, more vivid than any bloom that had ever opened to earthly sun and rain. They seemed carved from condensed starlight, their substance denser than matter, more present than presence itself.

Then, in a transformation that left me breathless with its casual magic, the lotuses morphed into vivid red roses. The metamorphosis unfolded like divine time-lapse photography—petals reshaping themselves with fluid grace while maintaining their supernatural solidity, each movement choreographed by laws that existed beyond physics.

These roses blazed with crimson fire, each bloom flawlessly formed and radiating color so intense it seemed to burn itself into my retinas like afterimages of impossible suns. Their presence was overwhelming, commanding, as if the entire universe had suddenly reorganized itself around these floating miracles, making everything else peripheral to their blazing beauty.

The roses hung there with such substantial reality that they cast shadows in my inner vision—not metaphorical shadows, but actual areas of deeper darkness that proved these flowers occupied genuine space in some dimension that intersected with ordinary reality. I could see individual droplets of dew trembling on their petals, could perceive the velvet texture of each crimson surface, could almost smell their perfume saturating the space between us with fragrance that had no earthly equivalent.

They were more present than my own hands, more solid than the cushion supporting my body, more real than anything I'd ever encountered in ordinary life. For precious seconds that felt like eternities compressed into moments, these divine offerings from consciousness's hidden gardens dominated my entire reality, making everything else seem like mere sketches compared to their blazing, three-dimensional presence.

Then, slowly, reluctantly, they began to fade—not disappearing so much as receding into whatever impossible realm had birthed them, leaving me gasping in ordinary darkness that now felt hollow and impoverished by comparison, like returning to black-and-white television after experiencing reality in colors that had no names.

THE TRANSFORMED INSTRUMENT

Satisfaction flooded through me as the day concluded, washing away the accumulated frustration of recent struggling sessions. After several days of feeling like I'd lost my footing on the spiritual path, today restored my confidence in the journey's trajectory with the authority of undeniable experience.

Meditation's ups and downs were natural—I understood this intellectually—but recent struggles had triggered primal fears of permanent regression, of having somehow broken the delicate mechanism that produced transcendent states. Tonight, those doubts dissolved in the afterglow of breakthrough sessions and impossible flowers that had bloomed from loving-kindness like orchids growing in the soil of the heart.

Even sleep brought continued revelations. When neighbors' music jarred me awake at 11:50 p.m., smoky *nimitta* lingered in my peripheral vision despite not actively meditating—orange flashes glinting at my eyes' corners like cosmic fireflies, reminders that concentration's effects now extended beyond formal practice into the liminal spaces between waking and sleep.

Consciousness itself was transforming, becoming a more sensitive instrument capable of perceiving beauty and light that existed beyond ordinary perception's narrow bandwidth. The flowers had been gifts from my own awakening heart, proof that even the most impossible visions could blossom from disciplined practice and one-pointed attention.

As I drifted back toward sleep, the day's lessons integrated themselves into something approaching wisdom. The mind's rebellion against concentration wasn't an obstacle to overcome but a dragon to befriend, its fierce energy transformed through patient discipline into the very power that fueled transcendent states. The warrior and the gardener were the same person—one who fought for the stillness that allowed impossible flowers to bloom in the fertile darkness of a heart opened beyond its ordinary boundaries.

Tomorrow would bring new battles and new blossoms, new opportunities to discover what consciousness could become when freed from its habitual constraints. But tonight, it was enough to rest in the afterglow of roses that had been more real than reality, lotuses that had taught me that the heart's capacity for beauty was literally infinite, limited only by the depth of attention I was willing to bring to the mysterious garden that had been growing in the darkness of my own awareness all along.

Day 12 – The Science of Light: When Wonder Meets Wisdom

Three-thirty arrived like an unwelcome alarm clock, dragging me from dreams into the humid predawn darkness with all the gentleness of a fishing hook pulling consciousness from the depths of sleep. But sleep's tentacles still wrapped around my awareness like some benevolent octopus reluctant to release its catch, making meditation feel like trying to hold water in cupped hands—every attempt at concentration simply leaked away through the gaps between my fingers.

The first session dissolved into a fog of drowsiness so thick I couldn't summon even basic one-pointedness, my mind scattered like leaves in a windstorm, thoughts tumbling over each other with no discernible pattern or purpose. It was the kind of meditation that made me question whether enlightenment was possible for someone whose consciousness felt as organized as a pile of laundry.

STRATEGIC RECOVERY

After breakfast, I orchestrated a tactical retreat that felt more like battlefield medicine than spiritual practice: fifteen minutes of surrendering to sleep's demands without guilt, followed by coffee's bitter medicine and a reviving walk around the monastery's flowering pathways. Sometimes the body needed tending before the spirit could soar—a lesson that seemed obvious in hindsight but required hard experience to truly understand.

The second session emerged from mediocrity's depths like a flower pushing through concrete—better than expected given the morning's complete failure, though exhaustion still clung to my awareness like morning mist refusing to burn off under a clouded sun.

Following lunch, I deployed my full arsenal of energy restoration with the systematic precision of someone who'd learned to treat meditation like any other demanding craft: a brisk walk to circulate stagnant qi through pathways that felt clogged with lethargy, a brief strategic nap to reset my nervous system's overwhelmed circuits, and three-in-one coffee that tasted like liquid alertness poured directly into my bloodstream.

The day had been unproductive so far—a string of failed experiments that made me feel like a scientist whose equipment kept malfunctioning at crucial moments. I needed at least three hours of quality sitting to salvage something worthwhile from these scattered hours, to prove that yesterday's breakthroughs hadn't been flukes or accidents.

THE COSMIC EYE OPENS

Then the afternoon session exploded into revelation with the sudden force of a dam bursting.

A blue circle *nimitta* materialized like a cosmic eye opening in the darkness of inner space, expanding from two to five centimeters in diameter with the organic precision of a blooming flower filmed in time-lapse photography. It wobbled initially—uncertain, finding its balance in the strange physics of consciousness—before stabilizing at my vision's center with the confident presence of a planet settling into perfect orbit.

For twenty magnificent minutes, this luminous disc held its position like a meditational lighthouse, casting steady beams of azure radiance across the landscape of closed eyes. Then came the transformation that left me breathless with its casual impossibility: the circle dissolved into blue sky, infinite and clear, becoming the perfect backdrop for *Anapanasati* breathing practice—as if my inner vision had suddenly opened a window into some pristine dimension where air itself was made of crystallized serenity.

I'd discovered something crucial through this accidental experiment: *Araham* made *nimitta* emergence far easier, even when I had to force concentration initially, like jump-starting a reluctant engine that needed just the right combination of patience and persistence. The pattern became predictable as any natural law—a tiny dot would appear first, gathering electrical sparks around its edges like a miniature star being born in the nursery of consciousness. As concentration deepened, this cosmic seed would expand into a light orange orb before morphing into the familiar large blue *nimitta*, each transformation following laws I couldn't articulate but was learning to trust.

THE LABORATORY OF CONSCIOUSNESS

Scientific curiosity seized me with the intensity of a fever. If I could reliably produce these visions, perhaps I could study their mechanics more systematically—turn my meditation cushion into a laboratory where ancient wisdom met modern investigative methodology. Armed with a stopwatch and the methodical mindset of someone conducting crucial research, I began timing *nimitta* manifestation using *Araham* as the catalyst.

Fourteen minutes—that's how long it took consciousness to shift from ordinary awareness to luminous display, as consistent as any chemical reaction following predictable kinetics. The discovery thrilled me with its implications: if these experiences followed measurable patterns, perhaps they operated according to discoverable principles rather than random mystical occurrences.

The first controlled experiment yielded a wobbly, hollow, transparent blue tube extending twenty centimeters from my nose—like some ethereal telescope protruding into space, designed for viewing dimensions invisible to ordinary sight. The second attempt produced wispy blue smoke that danced before my eyes like incense from invisible censers, following air currents that existed only in the meteorology of inner space.

Each trial added data points to my growing understanding of consciousness's hidden mechanics, the replicable conditions that allowed the mind to transcend its ordinary boundaries and access realms that felt more real than reality itself.

THE TEACHER'S WISDOM

When I reported these experiments to the assistant teacher with the enthusiasm of someone who'd discovered a new species, his response was swift and definitive, cutting through my scientific excitement with the blade of traditional wisdom: "The most important thing is one-pointedness on breath. Ignore the *nimitta*."

His words carried the weight of centuries, the accumulated experience of countless practitioners who'd traveled this path before me and learned to distinguish between helpful stepping stones and beautiful distractions. The *nimitta*, however spectacular, was like admiring the finger pointing at the moon instead of seeing the moon itself.

Not long after, Mr. Soemin summoned me to his office, his expression mixing exasperation with paternal concern—the look of a teacher who'd watched too many eager students fall into the same captivating trap. "Every day you ask about *nimitta*, and every day we tell you not to focus on it!" He rolled his eyes with the long-suffering patience of someone who'd guided countless enthusiastic but misguided seekers down this same rabbit hole of spectacular distraction.

"I'm sorry," I mumbled, feeling like a child caught playing with forbidden toys, my scientific curiosity suddenly seeming naive and misguided under his patient but firm gaze.

Mr. Soemin demonstrated his breathing technique with movements so slow and subtle they seemed to barely disturb the air around him, each inhalation and exhalation flowing like honey poured from an infinite jar. The rhythm was so measured and deliberate that it made my own breathing feel rushed and crude by comparison, like a jackhammer operating next to a whisper.

His demonstration was a wordless teaching more eloquent than any lecture: true meditation wasn't about producing spectacular visions but about cultivating the kind of refined attention that could find infinity in the simple act of breathing.

THE REFINED APPROACH

From that moment, I committed to emphasizing *Anapanasati* with the reverence it deserved, allowing breath to become gossamer-light and infinitely patient. Instead of forcing concentration like a battering ram against the gates of consciousness, I learned to approach each breath with the delicate touch of someone handling butterfly wings.

The evening session brought immediate rewards for this refined approach, proving that sometimes the gentlest methods produce the most dramatic results. Slow, gentle breathing produced a brilliant blue *nimitta* that blazed like a blowtorch flame shooting from my nose's tip—intense, focused, impossibly bright, yet arising effortlessly from the marriage of proper technique and patient attention.

The vision was so stable that it persisted even when I lay down to rest, manifesting spontaneously without any meditation effort, as if some inner fire had been ignited that now burned with its own sustainable fuel. As I relaxed on my wooden bed, the *nimitta* continued firing toward the ceiling like my nose had become a lighthouse beacon, shooting luminous rays into the darkness above.

The phenomenon felt both amusing and profound—like discovering that proper meditation technique had transformed my entire respiratory system into some kind of spiritual laser, broadcasting light into dimensions I was only beginning to understand.

THE RHYTHM OF SACRED TIME

The retreat's rhythm had become as predictable as breathing itself, yet time moved with dreamlike fluidity through these structured days, following laws that had nothing to do with ordinary chronology. We rose in darkness to sit with the breath, gathered for breakfast as dawn painted the sky in watercolor pastels, then flowed through walking and sitting meditation sessions punctuated by meals and brief restorative exercises.

Although five hours separated breakfast and lunch by the monastery's clocks, time seemed to compress like accordion music, each moment saturated with presence that made ordinary duration irrelevant. Minutes could feel like hours when concentration was poor, while entire sessions could pass like single breaths when awareness found its perfect focus.

The afternoon sweet drink break at five arrived with surprising swiftness, cordial and orange juice tasting like liquid sunshine after hours of inner work that left the palate refined and sensitive to subtleties that would normally pass unnoticed.

This became my favorite ritual of the day—carrying my glass of cordial to the hidden sanctuary near the abandoned well, where bamboo giants swayed in their eternal dance with the evening breeze. Here, in this secluded corner of the compound that felt like a secret garden designed by consciousness itself, I'd complete one final walking meditation round.

My bare feet whispered against the earth while towering green columns creaked their wooden songs overhead, a natural symphony that seemed composed specifically for contemplative minds. Purple butterflies fluttered through the dappled light like living jewels, their wings catching the golden hour's radiance as they danced from stem to stem with the purposeless purpose of beings who existed purely to add beauty to the world.

Dragonflies hovered with helicopter precision, their iridescent bodies flashing emerald and sapphire as they patrolled their bamboo kingdom with the authority of creatures who knew they belonged exactly where they were. Each glimpse of these delicate beings felt like receiving small blessings, reminders that beauty existed everywhere for those with eyes refined by meditation practice.

The cordial's sweetness mingled with jasmine perfume carried on the evening breeze, while bamboo shadows painted shifting patterns across the vegetable patches where monks cultivated both food and mindfulness. This was my daily communion with the natural world that supported our inner journey—a moment of grateful appreciation before returning to the evening's deeper work of consciousness archaeology.

THE SUSPENDED ELEMENTS

Evening group sitting at seven felt like a natural conclusion to each day's spiritual arc, the final movement in a symphony that began in darkness and resolved in the shared silence of practitioners gathered around the invisible fire of collective concentration.

Even weather seemed suspended in this timeless bubble—not a single drop of rain had fallen since my arrival, as if the elements themselves respected our need for uninterrupted inner exploration. Each day unfolded exactly like the last in terms of external structure, yet each sitting brought new territories of consciousness to explore, new experiments in the laboratory of awakening mind.

The paradox fascinated me: how routine could be the perfect container for revolution, how the most predictable schedule could create space for the most unpredictable discoveries. Perhaps this was meditation's deepest teaching—that transformation happened not through dramatic external changes but through the patient refinement of attention applied to the most ordinary experiences.

Tonight, as *nimitta* flames continued shooting toward my ceiling like prayer made visible, I marveled at how scientific curiosity and ancient wisdom were learning to dance together in the theater of my awakening awareness. The teachers had been right to redirect my fascination with spectacular visions toward the breath's subtle teachings, but my experimental nature had also served a purpose —teaching me that consciousness operated according to discoverable principles, even if those principles transcended ordinary understanding.

The blue light streaming from my nose as I lay in the darkness felt like a bridge between two ways of knowing: the mystic's direct experience and the scientist's systematic investigation. Both approaches honored the mystery while trying to understand it, and both recognized that consciousness contained territories vast enough to support infinite exploration.

As sleep approached with the gentleness that only came after days of proper meditation, I realized that tomorrow would bring new opportunities to balance wonder with wisdom, to maintain the beginner's mind that made discoveries possible while cultivating the discipline that made progress sustainable. The laboratory of consciousness would continue its experiments, but now with the refined tools that came from listening to teachers who had walked this path long before I'd ever imagined it existed.

Day 13 – The Breath's Secret Language: A Masterclass in Consciousness

Four extraordinary sessions unfolded between 4:15 a.m. and 1:40 p.m., each one a masterclass in the subtle art of *Anapanasati* that transformed my understanding of what it meant to breathe consciously. My body had become a laboratory of breath, every inhalation a controlled experiment in consciousness, each exhalation a data point in the vast research project of awakening.

I deliberately resisted the temptation to cultivate *nimitta* through *Araham* or *Metta*—those familiar pathways to luminous visions that felt like taking shortcuts through a sacred maze whose every turn was designed to teach specific lessons. Instead, I chose to dive deeper into breath meditation's hidden curriculum, to become a scholar of breathing's most intimate secrets.

My nostrils transformed into hypersensitive instruments capable of detecting the most microscopic variations in air temperature, humidity, and velocity. If concentration was truly the key to unlocking consciousness's deeper chambers, then I needed to become a detective of the invisible, an investigator of the space between breaths where the real mysteries lived.

THE BLUE SKY OF INNER SPACE

All three sessions bloomed into "blue sky" *nimitta*—vast expanses of azure luminosity that stretched beyond vision's boundaries like finding myself standing inside a cloudless summer heaven where the horizon had dissolved into infinite possibility. The blue wasn't flat or uniform but vibrantly alive, pulsing with depth and dimension that made my retinas ache with beauty too intense for ordinary perception.

Sometimes, blue bubble vortices would spiral through this celestial landscape like cosmic weather systems, each one carrying its own gravitational pull that threatened to drag my attention away from the breath's delicate anchor. These spiraling formations moved with the hypnotic grace of galaxies viewed through time-lapse photography, beautiful enough to make forgetting the breath feel like the most natural thing in the world.

THE PEDAGOGICAL TREASURES

Through careful experimentation that felt like learning a new language whose grammar was written in the rhythm of respiration, the breath began revealing its pedagogical treasures, each discovery earned through hours of microscopic attention applied with surgical precision:

THE SACRED TRANSITIONS

Continuous mindfulness became absolutely essential, especially during breath's turning points—those hair-trigger moments where inhalation became pause, pause became exhalation, and exhalation dissolved into the next inward journey like waves meeting shore in endless repetition. These transitions felt like standing on the edge of cliffs where consciousness could either maintain its footing or tumble into the abyss of mental wandering.

Missing even one transition was like dropping a single stitch in an intricate tapestry—the entire fabric of attention could unravel from that single lost moment, sending awareness spinning into the familiar chaos of uncontrolled thinking. Each transition required the vigilance of a guard watching for enemy infiltration, ready to catch the exact moment when breath changed direction and consciousness faced its greatest vulnerability.

KNOWING BEYOND FEELING

A profound discovery emerged that shattered my assumptions about meditation's fundamental mechanics like a scientific revolution overturning centuries of accepted truth. Feeling breath's physical touch—that cool kiss of incoming air against nostril walls, the warm caress of exhalation painting my upper lip—mattered less than simply knowing I was breathing.

This knowing existed somewhere beyond the five senses, operating through a sixth faculty that dwelt in consciousness's deeper chambers like some ancient organ of perception that modern humans had forgotten how to use. Even distinguishing between inhalations and exhalations proved secondary to maintaining awareness of breath's continuous presence, like a radio operator tuned to a frequency that transcended specific transmissions while remaining connected to the source of all signals.

This knowing became an unbreakable anchor for consciousness, more reliable than any physical sensation that could fade or shift with changing conditions. It was awareness aware of itself being aware—a recursive loop of attention that created stability from its own recognition of its own presence.

RHYTHM AS MEDICINE

Smooth transitions proved far superior to abrupt ones, like choosing silk over sandpaper against raw nerves that had become sensitive enough to register the texture of air itself. By deliberately setting slower breathing rhythms—sometimes leaving two or three agonizing seconds between inhalation and exhalation where my lungs screamed for the next breath like a drowning person reaching for the surface—the respiratory system would eventually adopt this gentler pace naturally.

The process felt like training a wild horse to match its rider's preferred gait, requiring patience and persistence until the animal's natural rebellion transformed into willing cooperation. Those pause-moments suspended between breaths became spaces of pure potential, consciousness hanging in the void like a diver floating in the ocean's depths where pressure and silence created perfect conditions for profound stillness.

MOVEMENT AS METAPHOR

Visualization transformed everything, turning abstract awareness into vivid cinema playing behind my closed eyelids with the clarity of high-definition television. Imagining breath as a graceful dance made my diaphragm move like a ballet dancer's controlled rise and fall, each movement choreographed with divine precision.

The smooth sawing motion turned each breath into carpentry of the spirit, consciousness as master craftsman shaping awareness with precise strokes that revealed the grain hidden in the wood of experience. The swinging pendulum metaphor created a hypnotic rhythm that seemed to slow time itself, each breath-swing marking meditation's deeper descent into stillness like a grandfather clock measuring eternity in moments of perfect presence.

THE RIVER OF AIR

Most powerfully, I began experiencing breath as a flowing river requiring the intense focus of a naturalist studying water ecology with scientific precision and poetic sensibility. Every inhalation became a current to observe, every exhalation a downstream flow carrying away mental sediment that had accumulated in consciousness's backwaters.

The eddies and vortices—those mysterious pauses where breath seemed to pool before continuing its ancient journey—became landmarks in the geography of presence, recognizable features in the landscape of awareness that helped me navigate the subtle territories of deep concentration. I could feel the air's temperature shifts like seasonal changes in this inner river, cool mountain streams of inhalation warming into tropical exhalations that painted my lips with the breath of distant summers.

ANATOMICAL ALCHEMY

A practical breakthrough emerged when I discovered that pressing my tongue firmly against my mouth's roof—that soft palate landscape behind my teeth—directed breath onto my upper lip like adjusting a garden hose's angle to create the perfect spray pattern. This simple repositioning solved the throbbing nostril soreness that had plagued earlier sessions like a persistent headache, transforming pain into pleasure through the alchemy of proper technique.

The adjustment felt like finding the right key for a stubborn lock that had been refusing to open for days, suddenly revealing doorways to longer, more comfortable practice sessions where physical discomfort no longer competed with concentration for attention's limited resources.

THE LUMINOUS GEOGRAPHY

The *nimitta's* brightness could be sustained across different breathing rhythms, even the slowest ones that left my lungs burning for more oxygen, like a swimmer pushing the limits of underwater endurance. However, softer breaths demanded concentration so intense it made my skull feel like it might crack from the pressure—a delicate dance between effort and effortlessness that required the precision of a tightrope walker suspended between trying too hard and not trying hard enough.

At each session's end, that familiar gift returned with startling clarity: the outlines of my legs visible through closed eyelids, as if meditation was slowly awakening dormant organs of perception buried in consciousness's deeper strata like archaeological treasures waiting to be discovered.

I could see the curve of my shins, the angles of my knees, even the position of my feet tucked beneath me—all rendered in ghostly blue luminescence that seemed more real than the physical limbs themselves, more substantial than the matter I'd always trusted as solid and dependable. This vision felt like proof that consciousness possessed capabilities that ordinary waking awareness couldn't even imagine, perceptual tools that made normal sight seem crude and limited by comparison.

THE CASCADING LIGHT

The 4:30 p.m. *Araham* session brought unprecedented phenomena that left me gasping with amazement, like someone witnessing the birth of new stars in real time. After fifteen minutes of sacred syllable repetition—each *Araham* pulsing through my consciousness like a mantra-powered heartbeat that synchronized with rhythms deeper than cardiac muscle—a bright blue bubble began pouring from my left eye's upper corner.

The luminous flow cascaded down toward my vision's center like a waterfall made of liquid starlight, defying every law of physics I'd ever learned while following some deeper logic that consciousness recognized as fundamentally correct. The movement was viscous, almost honey-like in its deliberate progress, leaving trails of light that lingered in my inner vision like phosphorescent wake behind some celestial swimmer.

Later, the flow shifted with the unpredictability of divine caprice—streaming from my left temple like a spring suddenly opened in consciousness's mountainside, then from my head's crown, all rivers of light converging toward the epicenter of awareness like tributaries feeding some impossible lake of luminosity. These starting positions were completely novel, uncharted territories in my *nimitta* geography that made my scalp tingle with electric anticipation of what might emerge next.

At one point, blue light blazed from my nose's tip with the intensity of a welding torch cutting through the darkness of ordinary perception, and I discovered I could extend it through pure intention—willing it to stretch further into space like some ethereal appendage under conscious control. The light responded to my mental commands like a perfectly trained pet, lengthening and brightening according to the intensity of my focus with immediate obedience that suggested a direct connection between will and luminous manifestation.

THE TEACHER'S ECHO

The temptation to experiment further was overwhelming, like a child discovering they could control lightning with their thoughts and wanting to see what else was possible in this playground of impossible physics. But my teachers' warnings echoed clearly through the intoxication of these spectacular displays: observe without attachment, witness without manipulation, remain the scientist rather than becoming the subject of the experiment.

These lights were signposts pointing toward deeper territories, not destinations for spiritual tourism—tools for investigation rather than toys for ego's entertainment. Each manifestation was meant to teach something about consciousness's capabilities, not simply to dazzle awareness with cosmic special effects that could become their own form of subtle imprisonment.

The discipline required to observe these wonders without being seduced by them felt like the ultimate test of meditation maturity—the ability to witness miracles while maintaining the inner posture of someone for whom miracles were simply natural phenomena occurring in consciousness's expanded laboratory.

THE UNIVERSITY OF BREATH

Tonight, as I reflected on the day's discoveries while my body still hummed with residual energy from intensive practice like a tuning fork struck by invisible mallets, I marveled at breath meditation's infinite subtlety and inexhaustible curriculum.

What had seemed like simple awareness of breathing revealed itself as an entire university spanning physiology, psychology, and mystical experience—each department offering courses that could occupy lifetimes of study. The breath was simultaneously the most ordinary and most extraordinary phenomenon in human experience, the one constant that connected every moment of life while serving as a gateway to dimensions of consciousness that most people never suspected existed.

Each session was peeling back new layers of this ancient practice like an archaeologist uncovering civilization's hidden depths, revealing why sages throughout history had spent entire lifetimes exploring the simple miracle of conscious breathing that sustained every heartbeat, every thought, every moment of existence. The breath was both the most familiar and most mysterious aspect of being alive—intimate enough to take for granted, profound enough to serve as a vehicle for complete transformation.

In tomorrow's sessions, I will continue this exploration of breathing's secret language, learning to read the subtle grammar of inhalation and exhalation with the fluency that came only from devoted practice. Each breath would become both teacher and teaching, simultaneously the path and the destination, the question and the answer written in the universal alphabet of air moving through conscious awareness.

The blue lights streaming from my face as I settled into sleep felt like love letters from consciousness to itself, proof that attention applied with sufficient precision and patience could unlock capabilities that existed beyond the boundaries of ordinary human experience. The laboratory of breath would continue its experiments tomorrow, revealing new secrets in the endless curriculum of awakening that used the simplest possible material—the air we breathed—to teach the most profound possible lessons about what it meant to be conscious in a universe where consciousness itself was both the greatest mystery and the most intimate reality.

Day 14 – The X-Ray Vision: When Consciousness Pierces the Veil

The night shattered around me like glass breaking in slow motion, each fragment of attempted rest pierced by sonic shrapnel from my neighbors' sadistic symphony of unconscious cruelty. Just as deep sleep finally claimed my exhausted consciousness around 2 a.m.—that precious moment when my battered nervous system began its healing descent into darkness—the neighbors behind my room launched their acoustic warfare with the precision of psychological torturers who'd earned advanced degrees in human breaking points.

Bass frequencies punched through the brick walls like invisible fists made of pure sound, each thump reverberating through my skeleton until my bones became tuning forks vibrating at frequencies designed by hell's most creative orchestra director. The wooden bed frame beneath me transformed into a percussion instrument, every beat transmitted directly into my spine, my skull, the delicate liquid chambers of my inner ears, where equilibrium dissolved into nauseous chaos that made the room spin like a carnival ride designed by sadists.

When they cranked up the volume again at 4:30 a.m.—apparently deciding that dawn's natural silence was an insult to their musical philosophy and needed immediate correction—I lay there feeling like a prisoner strapped to an electric chair powered by decibels and operated by demons with perfect timing. My teeth ached from unconsciously clenching my jaw into a vise, my temples throbbed with the rhythm of someone else's celebration, and my eyeballs felt like they were being massaged by jackhammers operating at the speed of light.

THE PHOENIX OF PERCEPTION

But in those fragmented moments between sleep and waking, when consciousness floated in that liminal ocean between dreams and dawn like a deep-sea diver suspended between ocean floor and surface, something extraordinary emerged from the wreckage of my rest like a phoenix born from sonic ashes.

My eyes remained sealed shut by exhaustion's lead weights, yet clear as an X-ray technician's screen viewed through supernatural focusing equipment, a complete human skeleton materialized in my inner vision. Not some random anatomical illustration lifted from a medical textbook gathering dust in some forgotten library, but my own living, breathing framework of bone rendered in luminous detail that made my retinas sing with impossible clarity.

Every joint articulated with mechanical precision that would have impressed Swiss watchmakers, each rib curved like parentheses around the cavity where my heart hammered its desperate protest against the sleepless night. The skeletal architecture glowed with its own internal light source, each bone outlined in phosphorescent radiance that seemed more real than the flesh that supposedly contained it.

When I shifted my body to one side—rolling away from a particularly offensive bass line that seemed designed to liquify my internal organs through pure vibrational assault—the skeletal form turned in perfect synchronization, each vertebra and rib following my physical motion with the fluid grace of underwater ballet choreographed by consciousness itself.

The spine twisted like a segmented snake made of calcium and phosphate, while my ribcage expanded and contracted with breath like some prehistoric bellows feeding fire to the forge of awareness. Every movement tracked with absolute precision, as if my inner vision had discovered the blueprint from which my physical form had been constructed.

Ah ha! This is my skeleton!

The revelation struck like lightning, illuminating a darkened landscape that had always existed but never been seen, never been suspected, never been imagined possible. My mind reeled with the implications—this wasn't a hallucination born from sleep deprivation or dream-logic filtered through exhaustion's fevered imagination, but meditation's gift of inner sight, concentration so refined it could penetrate flesh and muscle to reveal the mineral architecture beneath.

THE BLUEPRINT BENEATH

Here was the calcium scaffolding that held my consciousness upright like some ancient cathedral made of living bone, the protective cage that shielded my frantically beating heart from the world's constant bombardment, the articulated framework that allowed movement through space with the grace that humans took for granted every waking moment. All of it is visible now, like looking through my skin with supernatural X-ray vision that made medical imaging seem crude and primitive.

For days, I'd glimpsed these bone structures in the liminal space between sleep and consciousness, dismissing them as half-dreams born from exhaustion's fertile imagination running wild in the hours when rational thought surrendered to fatigue's creative madness. But now I understood with crystalline clarity that felt like cold water thrown on my face—this was the fruit of intensive practice, concentration so laser-focused it had unlocked dormant faculties of perception buried in consciousness's deeper strata like archaeological treasures waiting for the right tools to unearth them.

Each day, the visions had lingered longer, growing from fleeting glimpses into sustained displays that tracked perfectly with my deepening practice like some internal barometer measuring spiritual pressure. Today, for the first time, the skeleton held its luminous presence for five full seconds that felt like geological epochs, each moment stretching into eternity before dissolving back into ordinary darkness that suddenly seemed impoverished by comparison.

I could see the elegant curve of my ribs expanding and contracting with breath like an organic accordion played by invisible hands, the articulated precision of my spine's vertebral column stacked like ancient coins in a cosmic bank vault that had been accumulating value across lifetimes. The hollow sockets where my eyes sat like surveillance cameras in a skull's command center, monitoring reality through windows that were themselves being observed by some deeper seeing that had no need for physical apertures.

It was beautiful and terrifying simultaneously, like discovering that beneath the warm flesh and flowing blood, I was already a museum exhibit waiting to happen—a collection of bones temporarily animated by some mysterious spark that might extinguish at any moment, leaving only this mineral framework as evidence that consciousness had once inhabited this particular arrangement of matter.

THE LOBOTOMIZED MORNING

The sleepless night had lobotomized my concentration with surgical precision that would have impressed neurosurgeons specializing in the complete destruction of mental focus. Morning sittings collapsed into a series of abbreviated disasters, my mind scattered like leaves caught in a hurricane's fury, each thought blown away before it could take root in awareness's barren soil.

Exhaustion wrapped around my consciousness like wet wool soaked in molasses, making even basic breath awareness feel like trying to thread a needle while wearing boxing gloves in a room full of strobe lights operated by enemies of concentration. My skull felt stuffed with cotton batting that had been soaked in some consciousness-dulling chemical, my neurons firing in random bursts like a broken electrical system throwing sparks into the darkness.

Every attempt at sustained focus crumbled within minutes like sand castles built too close to an incoming tide of mental chaos, leaving me frustrated and depleted, staring at the meditation cushion like a defeated general surveying a lost battlefield where all his finest strategies had been reduced to smoking ruins.

THE UNINVITED GUEST

When I surrendered to horizontal recovery after breakfast and lunch, my body collapsing onto the yoga mat like a marionette whose strings had been severed by exhaustion's sharp scissors, trying to steal fragments of rest from the day's acoustic carnage, the *nimitta* announced its presence uninvited like an old friend arriving without knocking but bringing spectacular gifts.

Blue rockets launched themselves toward the ceiling of my inner vision, each projectile leaving trails of luminous exhaust that lingered like meteor showers playing in reverse, gravity-defying fireworks celebrating in the theater of my closed eyelids with the enthusiasm of children on New Year's Eve. The colors were so vivid they seemed to burn themselves into my retinas—electric blue so pure it made sapphires look muddy by comparison, trailing streams of light that moved with liquid grace through the space behind my skull.

Then came the familiar funnel formation—that cosmic tornado I'd witnessed days earlier, spinning lazily in the space behind my closed eyelids like a galaxy being born in slow motion, following laws of physics that existed only in consciousness's hidden dimensions. The vortex pulsed with its own internal rhythm, drawing imaginary debris into its luminous maw while casting shadows that had no right to exist in the realm of pure light.

These visions emerged spontaneously, without any meditation effort on my part, perhaps because horizontal relaxation had unlocked some deeper reservoir of concentrated energy that had been building pressure like steam in a cosmic boiler throughout days of intensive practice. My body had become so sensitized by continuous sitting that even rest produced extraordinary phenomena, like a radio receiver so finely tuned it could pick up distant stations long after being turned off, catching transmissions from frequencies that didn't officially exist on any terrestrial broadcast schedule.

THE MASOCHISTIC EXPERIMENT

The afternoon session from 3:50 to 4:30 became an experiment in respiratory extremes that bordered on the deliberately masochistic, a test of how far concentration could be pushed beyond the boundaries of comfortable practice. I deliberately slowed my breathing until it barely qualified as breathing—microscopic sips of air that left my lungs screaming like drowning victims begging for oxygen, each inhalation stretched across geological periods while my cardiovascular system went into panic mode.

My diaphragm cramped with the effort of maintaining such unnatural rhythm, like a muscle being asked to move underwater against the resistance of liquid that had replaced air. The space between breaths expanded into chasms of time where my body's every cell cried out in protest, demanding the life-giving rush of oxygen that I was deliberately withholding like some internal tyrant starving his own kingdom.

Saliva pooled in my mouth as my nervous system sent increasingly urgent distress signals, my heart rate dropping to funeral procession pace as my body shifted into some primitive survival mode designed for meditation monks and pearl divers who had learned to exist in the spaces between normal human limitations.

The technique was masochistic but revealing, demonstrating how concentration could function independently of breathing's normal rhythms, like discovering that consciousness could operate on backup power when the main generator was deliberately shut down for maintenance.

Initially, only a "white cloud" *nimitta* appeared—diffuse and unremarkable like looking through fog generated by dry ice, lacking the vivid definition I'd grown accustomed to expecting from deeper states. But when I laser-focused attention on a single point within that cloudy expanse, pouring every ounce of available concentration into a space smaller than a pinprick, blue light erupted like a sapphire star being born in the heart of a nebula.

The explosion was brilliant and perfectly defined against the white background like a cosmic jewel set in cotton, the transition violent and beautiful—from misty nothingness to blazing clarity in the span of a heartbeat, as if someone had suddenly focused a cosmic telescope and brought distant galaxies into sharp relief for the first time in universal history.

THE LIMITED SUPERPOWER

By session's end, the familiar gift returned with startling clarity that made my breath catch in my throat like a surprised gasp: my legs and arms visible through closed eyelids, rendered in that ghostly blue luminescence that seemed more substantial than flesh and blood, more real than the physical matter I'd always trusted as solid and dependable.

I could see the curve of my shins like architectural drawings rendered in light, the angular architecture of my knees designed by some divine engineer, the delicate bones of my feet tucked beneath me like origami sculptures carved from phosphorescent starlight.

Emboldened by these X-ray capabilities that made me feel like some kind of meditation-powered superhero equipped with impossible vision, I attempted to look through the meditation room's wall, straining this inner sight toward territories beyond my physical boundaries. I focused with laser intensity on the brick barrier that separated my space from the neighbor's musical kingdom, willing my supernatural vision to penetrate mortar and clay to reveal whatever acoustic weapons lay beyond.

Nothing. Absolute darkness met my probing consciousness like a black wall designed specifically to stop psychic intrusions, impermeable as lead shielding in a nuclear facility. The wall remained stubbornly opaque, my supernatural vision apparently limited to my own body's geography like a flashlight with a very particular range and frequency.

Perhaps this ability required years of development to extend beyond personal boundaries, or perhaps walls belonged to a different category of perception entirely—matter that existed in dimensions my current level of realization couldn't access, territories that demanded different keys than the ones I'd managed to forge through weeks of intensive practice.

THE CONCENTRATION NIGHTMARE

Today had been a concentration nightmare—the worst performance since the retreat began, a spiritual disaster of epic proportions that left me feeling like a meditation fraud who'd somehow fooled teachers and himself into believing progress was possible. My mind felt like a broken instrument, a violin with snapped strings incapable of sustaining the one-pointed focus that made these extraordinary experiences possible.

Yet I continued practicing like a soldier following orders in a losing war, because my teacher's words echoed like a sacred commandment burning in the depths of my consciousness: maintaining focus on the meditation object was my "job" here, regardless of conditions or results, regardless of neighbors who seemed determined to drive me insane with their sonic terrorism disguised as innocent music appreciation.

The discipline required to sit through complete concentration failure felt like its own form of meditation—the practice of practicing when practice felt impossible, the commitment to commitment when commitment felt meaningless, the faith in process when process produced only frustration and scattered awareness.

THE SECRET TREASURE

Exhaustion saturated every cell of my being as evening approached like a slow-moving storm front gathering strength from the accumulated fatigue of countless sleepless hours. My nervous system felt frayed and overstimulated, like electrical wiring that had been carrying too much current for too long without proper maintenance or rest.

Sleep deprivation had turned my brain into a fuzzy television screen where thoughts appeared as static-filled images that dissolved before they could be adequately identified or understood, leaving only the vague impression that something important had been attempting to broadcast but couldn't break through the interference.

But even in this depleted state, I carried the morning's skeleton vision like a secret treasure locked in my heart's vault—irrefutable proof that consciousness possessed capabilities far beyond anything ordinary imagination could conjure, even in its most creative moments. The bones had been real, more real than the meditation cushion beneath me, more present than the walls surrounding this small room where impossible things happened with increasing frequency.

The experience had shattered another assumption about the relationship between inner and outer reality, between mind and matter, between what seemed possible and what actually was possible when awareness was refined to sufficient precision. The skeleton hadn't been a symbol or metaphor but a direct perception of actual structure, consciousness learning to see through flesh the way X-rays penetrated tissue—but using attention instead of electromagnetic radiation as the penetrating medium.

Tomorrow would bring fresh opportunities to explore these territories where inner sight penetrated matter's veil like radiation, revealing hidden structures that had always been there but never been perceived. Tonight, I collapsed into my mosquito net sanctuary like a wounded bird seeking shelter from storms beyond its control, hoping for merciful silence from my musical neighbors who seemed to view sleep as humanity's greatest weakness requiring immediate correction.

I drifted toward whatever dreams might come, carrying visions of the day when concentration would be strong enough to see not just through flesh and bone, but perhaps through the very walls that confined us all—and maybe, just maybe, through the veils that separated this dimension from whatever lay beyond the reach of ordinary perception, waiting to be discovered by consciousness brave enough and skilled enough to look directly through the apparent solidity of everything we'd been taught to accept as the limits of the possible.

FORTY THREE DAYS OF FIRE

Day 15 – The Impossible Task: When Faith Meets Physics

Dawn arrived like a hangover made of light, dragging my consciousness from the wreckage of another fractured night into a reality that felt disconnected from my own body, as if someone had performed an amateur soul transplant while I slept. I woke feeling like I'd been systematically poisoned—not just tired but drained, as if some invisible parasite had been feeding on my life force through tiny straws inserted into my dreams.

My skull felt hollow yet heavy, a contradiction that made no anatomical sense but described perfectly the fog bank that had settled between my ears like weather from another dimension. Walking became an exercise in applied physics, each step requiring conscious calculation to avoid stumbling into walls or furniture that seemed to have migrated during the night according to laws that mocked ordinary spatial relationships.

The world tilted at strange angles, gravity pulling from directions that physics hadn't invented yet, leaving me gripping doorframes like a sailor in rough seas trying to maintain basic equilibrium while the ship of consciousness pitched and rolled beneath me.

THE GEOGRAPHY OF NUMBNESS

When I attempted *Anapanasati*, my face began transforming into a geography of numbness that spread like digital static across a malfunctioning television screen, each dead pixel representing another nerve pathway going offline. The left cheek went first—a dead zone where sensation simply vanished, as if someone had injected novocaine directly into the nerve highways that carried feeling from surface to brain.

Then the temporal areas joined the rebellion, those tender spots near my ears where pulse usually thrummed its steady rhythm, becoming vacant lots in my sensory landscape where nothing registered except a strange absence that felt louder than presence. The occipital area at the back of my skull followed suit, that crucial junction where spine met brain going offline like a computer system experiencing cascade failure, each circuit shutting down in sequence.

Finally, my right jaw surrendered to the spreading anesthesia, leaving me feeling like half my head had been amputated by an invisible surgeon who'd forgotten to mention the procedure, let alone obtain consent for this unauthorized neurological experiment.

Was this some exotic headache variant, or had my intensive meditation practice finally triggered a neurological meltdown? The sensations felt too specific to be ordinary illness, too systematic to be random malfunction. Perhaps I'd pushed concentration beyond safe limits, like overclocking a computer processor until it started glitching in fascinating but dangerous ways that threatened the entire system's integrity.

I swallowed two paracetamol tablets like offerings to whatever medical gods might be listening from their distant clinical olympus, hoping chemistry could solve what consciousness had broken. The pills went down like bitter prayers, my throat feeling disconnected from the swallowing reflex as if the numbness was spreading to systems I hadn't even known could go numb.

THE RETREAT TO LOVING-KINDNESS

Concentration became impossible under these circumstances, like attempting surgery while wearing mittens—technically possible but practically absurd. Trying to focus on breath while half my face felt like it belonged to someone else created a disorienting split-screen experience where awareness kept getting confused about which signals belonged to my actual nervous system.

So I retreated to *Metta*'s familiar embrace, hoping loving-kindness might heal whatever internal warfare was raging behind my malfunctioning facial nerves. The practice felt like applying salve to wounds I couldn't see, sending compassion toward territories of my body that had gone dark and silent.

Worry gnawed at the edges of my consciousness like acid eating through metal, each anxious thought creating new holes in my already damaged confidence. What if this numbness were permanent damage? What if intensive meditation had rewired my nervous system in ways that couldn't be undone? The retreat suddenly felt less like a spiritual adventure and more like a dangerous medical experiment conducted without proper supervision or informed consent.

WATER AS MEDICINE

But salvation arrived through the ancient ritual of cold water, shocking my system back to life like defibrillators applied to the soul. The monastery's well water hit my overheated skin like liquid electricity drawn directly from underground lightning storms, each plastic bowlful I poured over my head sending goosebumps racing across my flesh in waves of involuntary awakening.

The mineral-rich water carried stories of underground rivers and ancient aquifers, its earthy sweetness somehow penetrating deeper than mere surface cleansing, reaching nerve endings that had forgotten their function and reminding them of their purpose. As I squatted beside the cement tank, scooping bowl after bowl of this precious liquid like a desperate prospector panning for gold, the numbed territories of my face began tingling back to consciousness.

Each splash restored sensation to areas that had gone dark, water pressure massaging feeling back into numbed nerve pathways until my face gradually returned to its normal operational status. The cold was brutal but medicinal, like shock therapy administered by nature itself to systems that had overloaded on too much intensity.

THE SOLAR REVELATION

I was dreading another day of meditation disaster, my confidence shattered like glass hitting concrete at terminal velocity. After forcing down breakfast and lunch—meals that tasted like cardboard seasoned with anxiety and garnished with defeat—I collapsed into horizontal recovery, my body demanding rest like a union worker refusing overtime until working conditions improved.

Then, as I reluctantly arranged myself in meditation posture, having forced myself through sheer stubborn will to attempt another sitting despite every instinct screaming for retreat, the afternoon delivered its redemption in the form of the most spectacular *nimitta* I'd ever witnessed.

A "sun" blazed into existence behind my closed eyelids—not some pale approximation of solar radiance, but a perfect replica of the actual star that ruled our solar system with thermonuclear authority. It appeared with both *Anapanasati* and *Metta*, floating in the space of inner vision with the same majestic presence that the real sun commanded in Earth's sky, as if consciousness had somehow accessed the cosmic blueprint from which all stars were constructed.

Each manifestation lasted approximately five minutes, during which I felt like an astronaut who'd somehow gotten close enough to our star to study its architecture without being incinerated, protected by some impossible meditation suit that allowed direct observation of fusion itself.

The center blazed with intense white light so brilliant it made my retinas ache even through closed eyelids—the kind of radiance that existed at the core of fusion reactions, where hydrogen atoms danced their nuclear ballet to create the light that sustained all life from photosynthesis to human dreams. The outer corona pulsed with slightly gentler luminosity, like the sun's atmosphere made visible to inner sight, creating layers of brilliance that seemed to extend infinitely into the darkness surrounding this impossible solar display.

This was the first time I'd encountered such overwhelming luminous intensity, light so pure it seemed to contain the essence of illumination itself. Looking at it felt like staring directly into the source of all energy, the cosmic furnace that powered planets and consciousness alike. The appearance of this stellar *nimitta* lifted my spirits from the morning's medical horror show into something approaching cosmic euphoria, motivation flooding back like blood returning to frostbitten extremities.

THE IMPOSSIBLE ASSIGNMENT

At three o'clock, I presented myself to Sayadaw like a student reporting from the frontlines of consciousness research, ready to receive whatever instructions might advance my education in the graduate-level curriculum of awakening. His golden face registered satisfaction at my descriptions of the solar *nimitta* before delivering new instructions that would push my practice into territories that challenged every assumption about the nature of perception itself.

"Place a circle on the wall one to two feet away," he said through Mr. Soemin's translation, his voice carrying the casual authority of someone assigning basic homework. "Once you have *nimitta*, try to see the circle."

The instruction seemed simple enough until I began attempting its execution, like being asked to jump across a canyon that looked narrow from a distance but revealed itself as impossibly wide once you reached the edge. Hours dissolved into frustration as I strained my inner sight toward the small dot I'd drawn on my meditation room's wall, willing my consciousness to extend beyond the boundaries of closed eyelids and somehow perceive physical objects through supernatural means.

Nothing. Absolute darkness met every attempt to project awareness beyond my skull's confines like radio signals hitting a dead zone where no transmission could penetrate. The wall might as well have been located on Mars for all my ability to perceive anything beyond my own internal light shows, which suddenly seemed like parlor tricks compared to this impossible task.

THE CONFERENCE OF DEFEAT

Defeat drove me back to Mr. Soemin's office, where I presented myself like a failed student seeking remedial instruction, hoping there might be some basic principle I'd misunderstood that would explain my complete inability to perform what seemed to be considered elementary meditation.

"Mr. Soemin, am I supposed to see the dot when my eyes are still closed and blindfolded?" I asked, hoping there'd been some translation error that would explain my complete failure to achieve what sounded like science fiction.

"Yes," he smiled with the casual confidence of someone describing how to tie shoelaces or breathe air, as if seeing through solid matter were as natural as any other human function.

"Uh... is that even possible?" The question burst out before diplomatic filters could edit my disbelief, revealing the full extent of my bewilderment.

"Yes!" His laughter suggested I'd asked whether water was wet or whether fire was hot—questions that revealed fundamental misunderstandings about reality's basic operating principles, the kind of confusion that amused teachers who dealt with beginners daily.

I shook my head like a dog trying to clear water from its ears, struggling to integrate this information with everything I thought I knew about the relationship between consciousness and physical matter. "Well, I tried and tried, but I just couldn't do it."

He fixed me with a stare that seemed to penetrate directly into my doubt-riddled consciousness, reading the skepticism that was sabotaging my efforts before they could even begin. "You *have* to believe it! You *have* to have confidence. You *have* to have faith. *Otherwise*, it won't work!"

The words hit like a diagnosis that explained everything: my failure wasn't technical but philosophical, not a problem of method but of faith. I was trying to accomplish something I didn't actually believe was possible, like attempting to fly while remaining convinced that gravity was absolute. The deeper issue wasn't my concentration or technique—it was the invisible wall of skepticism I'd erected that made the physical wall seem impenetrable by comparison.

But as his words settled into my consciousness, I found myself reflecting on everything that had happened since my arrival. I'd witnessed phenomena I wouldn't have thought believable before coming here—skeletal visions through closed eyelids, cosmic suns blazing in inner space, diamond *nimittas* cascading like celestial jewelers had spilled their wares across the darkness of my awareness. Every single thing Sayadaw had taught me had proven precisely correct, his predictions unfolding with the reliability of natural law.

His casual confidence in assigning this impossible task suddenly made perfect sense. This wasn't experimental territory for him—it was routine, evident in the way he delivered instructions with the same matter-of-fact tone someone might use to explain basic arithmetic. He had clearly guided countless others down this exact path, watched them discover these same capabilities with the predictable progression of students mastering any well-understood curriculum.

There was no logical reason for me to doubt this ability existed, not when everything else he'd promised had materialized exactly as described. My skepticism wasn't protecting me from delusion—it was the delusion, a stubborn refusal to accept evidence that had been accumulating for days.

"Okay," I said, this time with genuine conviction replacing my earlier hesitation. If Sayadaw said it was possible, then it was possible. My job was to align my belief with the evidence of my own experience.

THE ANALOGY OF KEYS

"Look," he continued, searching for metaphors that might bridge the gap between ordinary perception and whatever impossible ability he was describing, like a translator working between languages that had no common vocabulary.

"Just imagine you are watching TV and you suddenly remember that you've left a key at school. Now, that spot on the wall is like the key you left at school."

His analogy felt like trying to explain quantum physics through interpretive dance—creative but not immediately helpful in any practical sense. Yet something in the comparison intrigued me: the idea that seeing through walls required the same mental mechanism involved in remembering distant objects, as if consciousness could reach through space the way memory reached through time. Perhaps the barrier wasn't the wall itself but my lingering assumption that physical distance mattered to properly focused awareness.

I nodded with the focused attention of someone receiving crucial technical instruction, determined to approach this with the same faith I'd applied to every other impossible-seeming task that had somehow become possible.

THE LABORATORY OF FAILURE

I returned to the meditation cave with renewed determination, arranging myself in the posture that had become the launching pad for so many impossible discoveries. For hours, I attempted to project my awareness onto that spot on the wall, now approaching it not as an impossible task but as the next logical step in a curriculum that had consistently delivered on its promises.

My concentration became a laser beam aimed at that precise point in space, consciousness reaching beyond the boundaries of flesh and bone with the same confidence I'd learned to apply to breath meditation. I visualized the spot with photographic precision, imagined my awareness extending through solid matter the way it had learned to penetrate my own body to reveal the skeleton beneath.

But despite my newfound faith, the effort remained exhausting. I could feel my consciousness pressing against what seemed like limits, though now I wondered whether these barriers were residual doubt, insufficient technique, or simply the natural resistance that any new skill encounters before a breakthrough occurs. The wall remained opaque to my supernatural vision, but I no longer interpreted this as evidence of impossibility—merely as an indication that I hadn't yet developed the precise focus required.

Hours of effort yielded no breakthrough, leaving me frustrated but not devastated. This felt like the early days of breath meditation, when concentration seemed impossible—difficult, yes, but not evidence that the ability didn't exist. I was learning that even with complete faith, some skills required time to develop, like muscles that needed conditioning before they could perform what eventually became effortless tasks.

THE COMPLETE ABANDONMENT

By evening's end, my familiar *nimitta* had also abandoned me—no solar radiance, no blue flames, no cosmic fireworks—just ordinary darkness that felt temporary rather than permanent. The absence felt like the natural ebb and flow I'd learned to expect from intensive practice, not evidence of fundamental failure.

All I'd achieved was a tension headache that felt like someone had been using my skull as an anvil, the familiar fatigue of consciousness working at its limits. But this exhaustion felt productive now, like the soreness that follows a good workout rather than the pain of injury.

The day no longer felt like a cruel joke but rather like a necessary stage in learning something that challenged the very foundations of ordinary perception. Morning's medical mystery had given way to afternoon's solar breakthrough, which had led to evening's patient attempt at an ability that clearly required more development.

The contrast between cosmic vision and current limitation didn't represent whiplash between success and failure, but rather the natural progression of someone learning skills that operated in different dimensions of consciousness. Some abilities emerged quickly; others demanded more cultivation.

Tomorrow would bring fresh opportunities to develop this ability, and tonight I went to sleep with curiosity rather than despair. The real lesson had been about recognizing the walls I'd built inside my own mind—assumptions about possibility and impossibility that created barriers more impenetrable than any physical matter.

The retreat had become an education in both the extraordinary capabilities and the patience required to develop them, a curriculum that revealed how belief was the foundation, but practice was the process through which belief became reality. I'd learned to trust the teachings; now I needed to trust the timeline, understanding that consciousness revealed its secrets according to its own mysterious schedule, not my impatient demands for immediate results.

Day 16 – The Holographic Universe: When Consciousness Becomes Cinema

Dawn broke with the "blue ray" *nimitta* already blazing behind my closed eyelids like some internal lighthouse that had been burning through the night, its beam cutting through the darkness of ordinary consciousness with unwavering intensity. I experimented with moving it up and down toward the ceiling, this luminous beam responding to mental commands like a perfectly trained pet made of concentrated starlight, obedient to will in ways that physical matter never seemed to be.

When I attempted to direct it toward that spot on the wall—yesterday's assignment that had tested my faith more than my technique—it still refused to penetrate solid matter. But this morning, the limitation felt different, less like evidence of impossibility and more like a skill that required patient development. I approached the practice with the same steady confidence I'd learned to apply to breath meditation, trusting that a breakthrough would come when consciousness was ready.

THE DROWNING SESSION

The 3:55 a.m. session stumbled through fog banks of drowsiness, my consciousness wrapped in cotton wool that made even basic breath awareness feel like trying to thread a needle while underwater in a swimming pool filled with molasses. Sleep's tentacles still clung to my awareness with the persistence of an octopus that had found something precious, dragging attention into murky depths where meditation became more like controlled dreaming than focused practice.

Breakfast arrived like salvation delivered by angels disguised as monastery cooks, the ritual of eating solid food anchoring my drifting consciousness back to the reliable shores of physical reality. Rice and vegetables never tasted so much like medicine for a mind that had been floating too long in liminal spaces between waking and sleeping, between ordinary awareness and whatever strange territories consciousness explored when freed from its usual constraints.

THE SPONTANEOUS GIFT

The second session began with me surrendering to horizontal recovery, my exhausted nervous system demanding rest like a battery that had been drained beyond its recommended limits and was now sending warning signals through every nerve ending. But as I lay there trying to steal fragments of peace from the morning's chaos, something extraordinary announced itself uninvited—a powerful *nimitta* emerging spontaneously from the depths of relaxed awareness, blazing with such sudden intensity that I bolted upright like someone receiving an electric shock from a cosmic outlet.

I shifted immediately into formal *Anapanasati* posture, recognizing this gift from consciousness's deeper strata with the gratitude of someone receiving unexpected treasure. As breath awareness deepened, something clicked into place with the precision of a cosmic tumbler falling into position in some universal lock—total one-pointedness achieved with such sudden completeness that my mind transformed from scattered leaves in a hurricane into laser-focused diamond cutting through reality's fabric.

That "sweet spot" immediately birthed the most spectacular *nimitta* yet witnessed: a "moon" that blazed with intense, pure white luminosity unlike anything existing in terrestrial experience. This wasn't the harsh, warm radiance of yesterday's solar display, but something infinitely softer yet twenty times brighter than Earth's actual satellite hanging in its ordinary darkness.

The light seemed to emanate from dimensions where photons obeyed different laws, creating illumination that caressed rather than burned, gentle yet so brilliant my inner retinas ached with beauty beyond the ordinary spectrum. For twenty magnificent minutes, this lunar perfection remained stable at the center of my inner vision like a meditation hall's most honored guest, radiating serene presence that made everything else seem secondary.

Then, with the unpredictability of divine artistry operating according to laws I couldn't fathom, its shape began shifting—becoming irregular, organic, alive with its own mysterious agenda. I attempted to redirect this luminous masterpiece toward the wall spot, but it maintained its independence like light itself, refusing to be commanded by mere human will or desperate spiritual ambition.

Yet I could still see my arms and legs through closed eyelids with crystalline clarity, this X-ray vision now as reliable as ordinary sight, perhaps more so—a supernatural faculty that had somehow become as natural as breathing.

THE JOY OF DISCOVERY

Suddenly, *Anapanasati* transformed from spiritual labor into pure joy, each session bringing new territories of impossible experience like an explorer discovering continents that shouldn't exist according to any known maps of human capability. Mr. Soemin's cryptic prophecy echoed with new meaning that reverberated through my understanding: "More coming." He'd known the *nimitta* would continue evolving, consciousness revealing layers of capability according to its own mysterious timeline. Yesterday's lesson about faith had been the key that would unlock not just this ability, but whatever other capabilities lay waiting in consciousness's vast curriculum.

After lunch, I awoke from restorative napping with another powerful *nimitta* blazing uninvited behind my closed lids like some cosmic alarm clock designed to wake consciousness rather than ordinary sleep. Playfulness seized me—I began experimenting with this luminous tool, shooting it toward the ceiling like some kind of meditation-powered laser cannon that responded to pure intention.

Each attempt extended its range further, consciousness learning to project light beyond the boundaries of skull and skin, discovering that awareness itself might have no fixed borders when properly directed. Yesterday's conversation with Mr. Soemin had shifted something fundamental—I now approached these experiments with the patience of someone who understood that extraordinary abilities developed through practice, not force.

THE GREEN CIRCLE BREAKTHROUGH

Emboldened by these successes and armed with yesterday's lesson about the power of genuine belief, I sat up with renewed determination to complete the wall-seeing assignment. This time, directing focused attention toward that spot with the same faith

I'd learned to apply to every other seemingly impossible task, something miraculous occurred: a beautiful, vivid, fluorescent green circle materialized in my inner vision.

Not the solid black dot I'd drawn with marker, but a luminous emerald ring pulsing with its own internal radiance like some cosmic target finally acquired by supernatural radar operating beyond the electromagnetic spectrum. The circle blazed with electric vitality, more real than the physical mark it somehow represented.

Finally! The assignment was complete, not through desperate effort, but through the natural unfolding of an ability that had been waiting for the right combination of technique and trust. Yesterday's lesson about faith had been the missing ingredient, transforming what seemed impossible into the inevitable result of proper practice.

THE HIGH-DEFINITION WORLD

Pleased with this breakthrough that felt like the natural flowering of yesterday's hard-won wisdom, I granted myself celebratory freedom—strolling through the compound's flowering pathways and bamboo cathedral with the satisfaction of someone who'd learned to trust a process that consistently delivered results, even when those results challenged everything they'd previously believed about consciousness and reality.

But the walk revealed something even more extraordinary than successful supernatural vision: the entire world had been upgraded to high-definition reality, as if someone had replaced my eyes with advanced optical equipment capable of detecting frequencies I'd never imagined existed.

Everything blazed with enhanced clarity, colors so vivid they seemed to burn with their own internal fire rather than simply reflecting external light. Leaves weren't just green but contained entire symphonies of emerald, jade, forest, and lime dancing together in harmonies my eyes had never been sophisticated enough to detect. Floor tiles revealed intricate textures and grain patterns that had been invisible to ordinary perception, each surface telling geological stories written in mineral and clay languages that spoke directly to refined awareness.

I felt taller, more present, as if meditation had somehow increased my physical dimension or at least my awareness of occupying space with conscious intention. The transformation reminded me viscerally of stepping off an airplane in New Zealand years earlier, where pollution-free air had revealed distances I'd never known were visible, making me realize how much atmospheric contamination had been limiting vision everywhere else.

Now, mental pollution had been suppressed with a similar dramatic effect, creating the same shocking clarity. The compound hadn't changed—my perception had undergone fundamental renovation, consciousness itself becoming a more sensitive instrument capable of detecting beauty that had always existed but remained hidden behind the static of untrained awareness.

I couldn't help wondering how magnificent reality must appear through enlightened eyes, if this preliminary cleaning of perceptual windows could produce such dramatic enhancement of ordinary experience.

THE ARSENAL OF *NIMITTAS*

Returning to my meditation cave, I immediately found myself bombarded with an entire arsenal of new *nimitta* formations, each one a different experiment in consciousness's artistic capabilities, as if awareness had suddenly discovered it was equipped with a vast studio of creative tools:

The "Ring" *Nimitta*: A perfect smoke ring hovering in inner space—cigarette smoke's ghostly geometry rendered in luminous white against black void, about half a tennis ball's diameter with a hollow center that seemed to extend infinitely inward. It maintained its perfect circular integrity for twenty minutes like some cosmic donut made of condensed light, spinning slowly in dimensions that had no names.

The "Cannonball" *Nimitta*: Pure surreal warfare—cotton wool projectiles firing rapidly from both sides of my head, exploding just in front of my eyes like fireworks made of pillow stuffing and operated by invisible artillery units. Each impact burst into fragments of white softness that dissolved into the darkness surrounding this impossible military display.

The "Blowtorch" *Nimitta*: A brilliant blue flame extending twenty centimeters from my nose with industrial precision, so realistic I could almost hear the hissing sound that should accompany such intense combustion. The flame held steady like some spiritual welding torch preparing to fuse consciousness with reality's deeper metals through heat that burned without destroying.

The "Star Trek" *Nimitta*: Bright white diamond and square formations flashing on and off with the rhythm of cosmic Morse code—on/off, on/off—resembling special effects from science fiction television where reality bends according to different physical laws. Each flash lasted precisely two seconds before fading, only to be replaced by the next geometric burst in an endless sequence of mathematical poetry.

THE THRESHOLD OF *JHANA*

The *Metta* practice that concluded this session produced a swirling blue light that alternated between ray-like beams and nebular spirals, sustaining itself for over thirty minutes like some benevolent cosmic lighthouse guiding ships across the ocean of consciousness. During this extended display, I could clearly see my foot and that triumphant wall spot, consciousness now capable of simultaneous internal and external perception that made ordinary vision seem limited and crude.

The sensation suggested that *jhana* states lay just beyond the next breath, with absorption levels waiting like unopened doors that required only slight additional concentration to unlock. But the interview bell summoned me away from these threshold territories, duty calling from the world where teachers waited for progress reports on consciousness's ongoing research project.

THE IMPOSSIBLE ASSIGNMENTS

Sayadaw's golden face radiated satisfaction at my completed assignment before issuing new challenges that pushed supernatural vision into even more impossible territories that seemed designed to test the absolute limits of what awareness could accomplish:

1. Try seeing objects at least five feet away with your eyes closed.
2. Use *nimitta* to locate the three Buddha statues in the main hall—two I'd observed with ordinary sight, one that remained mysteriously hidden.

After a brief walking meditation to discharge excitement and prepare consciousness for deeper work, I settled back into the cave where awareness had been revealing its hidden curricula with increasing generosity.

Intense concentration produced faint outlines of the giant Buddha painting decorating the hall wall ten meters away— ghostly impressions that required such focused attention that my forehead began aching with the effort of projecting awareness across physical space. Then came a dim but unmistakable image of one Buddha statue, its familiar form materializing in inner vision like a photograph developing in slow motion in consciousness's darkroom.

The mental exhaustion was profound, like trying to lift weights with cognitive muscles I'd never known existed, muscles that apparently needed training before they could handle the load of supernatural perception. Tension gathered between my eyebrows where this supernatural effort seemed to originate, as if consciousness had discovered it possessed its own physical location.

Still, at least one of the three target statues had been successfully located through means that would make neuroscientists weep with confusion about everything they thought they knew regarding perception's mechanisms.

THE BROWN BUDDHA VISION

During the evening group sitting, surrounded by fellow meditators whose silent presence created amplified spiritual resonance like instruments in a cosmic orchestra, I approached Sayadaw's assignments with the steady confidence that had replaced yesterday's desperate effort. After generating a powerful *nimitta* that revealed both my foot and the monk sitting directly ahead of me, I directed laser-focused attention toward one of the Buddha statues I needed to locate.

What happened next felt like the natural progression of abilities that had been developing systematically throughout the retreat, each breakthrough building logically on the last.

A solid brown Buddha statue materialized with shocking completeness, suspended in a bubble of luminous mist directly in front of my closed eyes. Not some vague impression or wishful visualization, but photographic reality rendered in three-dimensional perfection—every fold of the robes visible, every curve of the serene face detailed with sculptural precision that surpassed anything my ordinary vision had ever captured.

The statue appeared so substantial I could have reached out and touched its wooden surface, so real it seemed more present than the meditation hall containing my physical body. The clarity was profound but no longer shocking—this was what consciousness could achieve when approached with proper understanding and patient development.

I had finally learned to work with awareness as a trainable faculty rather than a fixed limitation, discovering that what seemed supernatural was simply natural abilities that most people never learned to access through systematic practice.

THE HOLOGRAPHIC ENTERTAINMENT SYSTEM

Ten hours of intensive sitting meditation had somehow compressed into what felt like a single extended session of pure enjoyment, time flowing according to different laws when consciousness operated at these refined frequencies. This was the most satisfying day of practice since the retreat began, awareness finally operating with the confidence that came from understanding rather than hoping, from trusting a proven process rather than fighting against perceived limitations.

That night, as I settled into the mosquito net's white sanctuary, closing my eyes brought immediate activation of the most extraordinary entertainment system ever devised by consciousness or cosmic intelligence.

Vivid holographic images filled my entire visual field with the precision of advanced virtual reality technology that had somehow been installed directly into my nervous system. These weren't ordinary mental pictures but three-dimensional displays so detailed and colorful they seemed more real than physical experience, each scene rendered with edges that softened into misty borders like dreams achieving unusual solidity.

The holograms moved in continuous procession, one landscape seamlessly transforming into the next like scenes from an endless documentary about impossible worlds that existed in dimensions parallel to ordinary reality. Most were devoid of human or animal life—pure geography expressing itself through consciousness—though one sequence featured elephants moving with majestic grace through terrain that belonged to no earthly continent.

A massive waterfall cascaded directly toward me with such convincing reality that I nearly raised my arm for protection from the approaching deluge. Water seemed to carry actual weight and momentum, each droplet rendered with photographic precision as it plummeted from heights that disappeared beyond vision's upper reaches into territories where physics apparently followed different rules.

THE COSMIC DOCUMENTARY

Endless processions of temple bas-reliefs floated past like ancient stone walls come alive, their carved surfaces telling stories in languages I couldn't read but somehow understood at levels deeper than intellectual comprehension. Landslides rolled across impossible mountains while explosions bloomed on distant planets, their shock waves seeming to ripple through the meditation room's actual atmosphere.

Most remarkably, I found myself viewing seabeds from the perspective of deep-sea exploration, as if consciousness had become a submarine diving through abyssal depths where bioluminescent creatures painted trails of living light across perpetual darkness that had never known the touch of any earthly sun.

These holograms filled my room's entire volume, creating immersive environments that made the physical walls seem like flimsy suggestions rather than solid barriers. It was like possessing a personal holodeck programmed by some cosmic intelligence with access to visual libraries I'd never consciously accessed but that apparently existed within consciousness's vast storage facilities.

For two mesmerizing hours, I lay there watching this impossible cinema until sleep finally claimed priority over entertainment, though the boundary between this holographic experience and dreams felt increasingly meaningless.

THE PERSISTENT LIGHTHOUSE

But even sleep couldn't escape *nimitta's* persistent presence. After brief unconsciousness, blue flashing lights jolted me awake—my internal lighthouse refusing to dim despite my desperate need for rest, operating according to its own mysterious schedule that I was learning to accept rather than resist.

I no longer attempted to suppress these uninvited illuminations, understanding now that they were signs of consciousness functioning at levels I was still learning to navigate. They blazed with autonomous authority for a full hour, and I watched them with the patient curiosity of someone studying a fascinating natural phenomenon rather than fighting against an unwelcome intrusion.

Just as sleep began knitting itself back together like a torn fabric slowly mending, another *nimitta* erupted with renewed intensity—swirling blue radiance whose background contained billions of tiny bubbles floating like cosmic champagne celebrating some victory I didn't understand but felt invited to witness.

THE BUDDHA SPHERES

Curiosity compelled closer examination of these microscopic spheres. Zooming consciousness inward like adjusting a spiritual microscope to its highest magnification, I discovered each bubble contained a perfect Buddha statue, millions of identical enlightened figures suspended in luminous spheres like snow globes manufactured in some celestial workshop where awakening was mass-produced through divine automation.

This felt like a particularly potent *nimitta*, so I attempted to complete Sayadaw's second assignment: locating that mysterious third Buddha statue I'd never seen with ordinary vision. Trusting consciousness's apparent ability to perceive beyond physical limitations, I directed intense concentration toward finding this hidden spiritual treasure.

Pop!

A solid, colorful Guan Yin Bodhisattva statue materialized with the same shocking reality as the evening's Buddha vision—every detail of the compassionate female deity rendered in perfect sculptural clarity, her robes flowing with artistic grace that seemed to move despite the image's stillness. The vision possessed the same undeniable presence that had characterized all successful supernatural sightings.

THE DOUBT VIRUS

But doubt immediately attempted to corrupt this success like a computer virus attacking the operating system of confidence. *This must be wrong,* the logical mind protested with all the authority of someone who'd studied comparative religion. *That's a Mahayana statue, and this is a Theravada meditation center. They wouldn't have that here.*

For a moment, I almost dismissed the vision as meditation-induced confusion. But yesterday's lesson about faith stopped me short. If I'd learned anything, it was that consciousness could access information through channels that operated beyond the boundaries of reasonable assumption or sectarian categories. Why should I doubt this vision when every other impossible experience has proven accurate?

Instead of dismissing it, I made a mental note to investigate whether such a statue might actually exist somewhere in the monastery, trusting the vision while remaining open to whatever verification might come.

As I finally drifted toward sleep, the night's extraordinary experiences settled into memory like precious data collected from territories that were becoming increasingly familiar. Tomorrow would bring new opportunities to explore these realms where inner sight functioned with growing reliability, each day building systematically on the last in a curriculum that revealed its logic through patient practice.

Tonight I fell asleep with gratitude rather than confusion, finally understanding that I wasn't discovering consciousness's hidden features or losing my grip on consensus reality. I was simply learning to access capabilities that had always existed but were rarely developed, like muscles that grew stronger through systematic training. The question wasn't whether these abilities were real —the evidence was overwhelming. The question was how far consciousness could develop when approached with proper understanding, patience, and faith in a process that had been teaching the same lessons to dedicated students for thousands of years.

Day 17 – Journey to the Stars: When Consciousness Becomes Cinema

Four a.m. arrived with the cruel punctuality of a cosmic alarm clock, but my consciousness felt like a broken radio struggling to tune into any coherent frequency, picking up only static from stations that had gone off the air. Concentration scattered in every direction like light hitting a shattered mirror, leaving me grasping at fragments of awareness that dissolved the moment I tried to gather them into focused attention.

The *nimitta* emerged as a weak background glow—pale, tentative, like a candle flickering in a hurricane of mental turbulence generated by too little sleep and too much spiritual intensity. Every attempt to nurture this fragile luminosity into something substantial crumbled under the weight of my scattered nervous system, which felt like electrical wiring that had been carrying too much current for too long.

So I surrendered to horizontal defeat, arranging myself flat on the yoga mat like a patient submitting to spiritual surgery, hoping that rest might accomplish what effort had failed to achieve.

THE PARADOX OF SURRENDER

Paradoxically, the moment I stopped trying, the *nimitta* blazed with renewed intensity that caught me completely off guard. Without any meditation effort, it strengthened like a fire suddenly fed with oxygen, as if my desperate attempts at concentration had been strangling the very phenomenon I was trying to cultivate—like trying to catch a butterfly by chasing it versus simply sitting still and letting it land.

The blue ray *nimitta* emerged first—that familiar laser beam of consciousness shooting from some internal source I'd grown to recognize like an old friend. But then something unprecedented occurred that made my inner vision feel like it had been upgraded to equipment I'd never imagined possible.

Rainbow-colored bands of light began cascading through my inner space like aurora borealis made personal, visible only to me in the private theater of closed eyelids. These luminous ribbons appeared sometimes horizontal, sometimes vertical, swinging from side to side with hypnotic rhythm like cosmic pendulums marking time in dimensions where physics followed different rules than anything Newton had ever contemplated.

I'd never witnessed such chromatic *nimitta* before—every color of the visible spectrum and several that seemed to exist beyond ordinary perception, flowing together in bands that pulsed with their own internal music, creating symphonies of light that my eyes had never been sophisticated enough to detect in the external world.

THE COSMIC WEATHER SYSTEM

After breakfast, having fortified my depleted system with rice and gratitude like medicine for an overtaxed nervous system, concentration began reassembling itself like scattered puzzle pieces, finally finding their proper positions through some mysterious magnetic attraction.

The rainbow *nimitta* returned with enhanced complexity, now appearing as a swirling cloud of pure color—like viewing some cosmic weather system from above, or perhaps standing inside a planetarium where stars had been replaced with liquid light that moved according to laws that existed only in consciousness's hidden dimensions.

Sometimes the display transformed into a rainbow tunnel extending infinitely into inner space, its walls alive with every hue imaginable, creating passages that seemed to lead to other dimensions where ordinary consciousness might travel if it possessed sufficient courage to abandon its attachment to familiar territory.

The tunnel wasn't just visual but felt navigable, as if consciousness could actually journey through these chromatic corridors toward destinations that existed beyond the boundaries of ordinary human experience.

THE TEACHER'S EMERGENCY INSTRUCTIONS

During my post-session walk through the compound's flowering pathways, I encountered the assistant teacher whose timing felt orchestrated by some benevolent intelligence monitoring my spiritual crisis with the precision of emergency medical personnel. My confession tumbled out like water from a broken dam: exhaustion, scattered concentration, sleep deprivation transforming meditation into endurance testing rather than spiritual practice.

His response carried the calm authority of someone who'd guided countless seekers through similar territories of overwhelm, his voice containing the reassurance of an experienced guide who'd seen this landscape many times before. Another meditator was experiencing identical struggles; he revealed that this was normal terrain in consciousness's intensive training program, not evidence of personal failure or spiritual inadequacy.

His reminders arrived like emergency instructions for navigating treacherous spiritual weather:

1. **Ignore the *nimitta*** —don't get seduced by the light show, no matter how spectacular
2. **Whatever happens, concentrate on the meditation subject** —the breath remains the anchor when consciousness storms rage
3. **Not sleeping is acceptable, but never stop practicing** —catch up with strategic naps between sessions

Gratitude flooded through me like medicine reaching infected wounds, the relief almost physical in its intensity. Having this guidance felt like discovering I wasn't lost in unmapped territory but following a well-traveled path where others had faced identical challenges and emerged successfully, their experiences becoming roadmaps for safe passage.

THE STABLE LIGHTHOUSES

Returning to formal practice with renewed understanding of what was happening, I was rewarded with the most stable luminous displays yet achieved: brilliant sun and moon *nimitta* that blazed in my central visual field for thirty uninterrupted minutes, steady as lighthouses guiding ships through dangerous passages in consciousness's vast ocean.

They didn't waver or shift position, maintaining perfect stability like cosmic beacons anchored in the depths of concentrated awareness. The sun blazed with the same thermonuclear intensity I'd witnessed before, while the moon radiated gentle luminosity that seemed designed specifically for whatever work consciousness was accomplishing in these deeper territories.

But the real revelation began the moment I closed my eyes for any reason—walking meditation, brief rest, even simple blinking triggered immediate activation of the most sophisticated holographic entertainment system ever conceived by any intelligence, earthly or cosmic.

THE IMPOSSIBLE CINEMA

Bright, colorful three-dimensional images floated within clouds of luminous mist, each scene rendered with definition that made physical reality seem crude by comparison, like black-and-white television viewed after experiencing full-spectrum virtual reality. These weren't mental pictures but immersive environments that filled every cubic inch of inner space, drifting in slow motion like scenes from dreams that had achieved unusual substance and weight.

Today's cosmic cinema included spectacles that challenged every assumption about consciousness's creative capabilities:

Galactic Displays: Entire galaxies blazed with beauty that rivaled NASA's most spectacular deep-space photography—billions of stars arranged in spiral arms that curved through infinite darkness with mathematical precision, nebulae blooming like cosmic flowers in gardens tended by invisible gods, planetary bodies orbiting in gravitational ballets too complex for human choreography. The images were so clear, so detailed, I wondered whether consciousness was somehow able to project itself out into space, witnessing these cosmic spectacles firsthand from impossible vantage points throughout the universe.

But it was more than witnessing—I wasn't looking at space, I was in it! My awareness had somehow become unmoored from the meditation room and was floating freely through the cosmos like an astronaut without a suit, needing neither oxygen nor protection from the vacuum. I could sense my position relative to these massive stellar formations, experiencing the vast emptiness between star systems as intimate space through which consciousness moved with the freedom of pure spirit. It was as if meditation had discovered that awareness itself was a spacecraft capable of instantaneous travel to any point in the universe, limited only by the courage to journey beyond the familiar confines of earth-bound perception.

Impossible Worlds: Saturn-like planets spun majestically through my inner cosmos, surrounded by rainbow-colored rings that outshone anything in our solar system with their chromatic brilliance. These weren't pale ice particles reflecting distant sunlight, but bands of pure chromatic energy that seemed to sing with harmonic frequencies as they rotated around impossible worlds that belonged to star systems where different physical laws allowed beauty to express itself more freely.

Space Creatures: Jellyfish-like beings swam through the vacuum of space with graceful undulation, their translucent bodies pulsing with bioluminescent patterns that painted trails of living light across the cosmic darkness. They moved like space whales navigating currents of pure energy, reminding me that consciousness might populate its inner universes with life forms that obeyed no earthly biological laws but followed the logic of beauty and wonder instead.

Floating Architecture: Castles on floating islands drifted through impossible skies, their architecture combining medieval grandeur with engineering that defied gravity through sheer artistic will. Towers spiraled into misty heights while bridges spanned impossible distances, all carved from stone that seemed to glow with its own internal light source, as if the buildings themselves were alive with some form of architectural consciousness.

Sacred Art: Millions of Buddha outlines drawn in brilliant blue ink floated past like pages from some cosmic sketchbook, each figure rendered with calligraphic precision that would make master artists weep with envy. The drawings pulsed with spiritual presence, as if enlightenment itself was learning to express itself through pure artistic form, consciousness teaching itself to recognize its own deepest nature through visual meditation.

THE TECHNOLOGY OF CONSCIOUSNESS

I lay back and surrendered to this virtual reality spectacular, marveling at technology that no human engineering could ever hope to replicate, no matter how advanced our computers became or how sophisticated our graphics processing. The most cutting-edge computer graphics were crude finger paintings compared to consciousness's native ability to generate immersive realities indistinguishable from physical experience—perhaps more real than physical experience.

Each image possessed weight, substance, presence that made the meditation room feel like a flimsy backdrop compared to these cosmic theaters where impossible dramas unfolded according to scripts written by intelligence that operated beyond ordinary human creativity.

THE PSYCHOLOGICAL DANGERS

But this power came with profound psychological dangers that couldn't be ignored or approached with naive enthusiasm. At this stage of practice, the mind became as delicate as a soap bubble floating in hurricane winds—requiring experienced guidance to navigate safely through territories where thoughts could crystallize into experiences more substantial than physical reality.

Without a fundamentally healthy psyche as a foundation, these experiences could easily transform into nightmare territories where consciousness might become trapped in the horror of its own creation. The line between vision and hallucination, between spiritual experience and psychological breakdown, became as thin as the membrane separating dreams from waking—requiring constant vigilance and expert guidance.

I felt profound gratitude for never having filled my mind with violent imagery from horror films or nurturing unhealthy emotional patterns that might manifest as terrorizing visions in these deeper strata of awareness. The holographic displays were more real than ordinary life—if monsters had emerged from these territories, they would possess a reality more substantial than physical threats, potentially creating psychological trauma that conventional therapy might be powerless to address.

THE DISCIPLINE OF MENTAL HYGIENE

Fortunately, my visions remained pleasant or neutral, but I maintained strict mental discipline, refusing to allow imagination free rein in territories where thoughts could crystallize into experiences indistinguishable from reality. This was not the time for creative exploration but for careful navigation through consciousness's most treacherous waters, where one careless thought could generate nightmares more vivid than any sleeping dream.

The teacher's role became crucial at this stage—daily contact wasn't a luxury but a necessity, like radio communication for astronauts exploring dangerous space where a single equipment malfunction could mean death. Even without specific questions, reporting experiences and receiving guidance felt like maintaining lifelines to consensus reality, anchors that prevented consciousness from drifting too far into territories from which return might become impossible.

My teachers had always encouraged immediate consultation when problems arose, and now I understood why with crystalline clarity: a single day of unguided struggle with these phenomena could generate a cascade of disturbing sessions that might derail progress for weeks or months, potentially requiring extensive recovery time to restore psychological equilibrium.

THE AUTOMATIC ACTIVATION

Today, every time I closed my eyes to meditate, the visions activated automatically like some internal movie projector that couldn't be switched off, no matter how much I might prefer the simplicity of ordinary darkness. The displays were intensely distracting precisely because they were so engaging—always appearing at the center of my visual field, constantly demanding attention with their extraordinary beauty or strangeness.

Characters in these holographic dramas would look directly at me as if seeking responses, their eyes following my attention with the persistence of portrait subjects who'd somehow achieved independent life. They might appear spectacularly beautiful or grotesquely ugly, each extreme designed to elicit emotional reactions that would drag awareness away from breath meditation into narrative involvement with these impossible beings.

The challenge wasn't experiencing these visions—they seemed to generate themselves automatically once consciousness reached certain levels of refinement—but learning to witness them without becoming absorbed, to maintain focus on breath while cosmic movies played in peripheral awareness.

WHEN SLEEP BECOMES IMPOSSIBLE

Even attempting rest became an ordeal that tested every limit of endurance. Sharp, brilliant *nimitta* would blaze to life the moment my eyelids closed, appearing like midday sun or full moon blazing with such intensity that the inside of my skull became brighter than the external world, more luminous than any electric lighting.

Sleep became impossible when consciousness generated illumination more vivid than floodlights—like trying to rest while staring directly into stadium lighting that operated according to its own autonomous schedule, completely indifferent to my desperate need for darkness and recuperation.

The irony was profound: meditation had developed my inner sight to such sensitivity that it could detect light sources that didn't physically exist, but this same sensitivity made ordinary rest impossible when these light sources refused to dim on command.

THE OVERTRAINING DIAGNOSIS

In the late afternoon, I sought refuge in Mr. Soemin's office, confessing my sleepless night and the exhaustion that was transforming spiritual practice into an endurance competition where survival felt more important than enlightenment. His questioning revealed the source of my problem with the precision of a medical diagnosis, identifying the exact cause of mysterious symptoms.

I'd been attempting to locate the Buddha statues fifty times or more, far exceeding the recommended ten to fifteen attempts that would have been appropriate for my experience level—like a beginning weight lifter trying to bench press twice their body weight and wondering why their muscles felt destroyed.

"We weren't supposed to try more than ten or fifteen times!" he exclaimed, his expression mixing concern with the frustration of someone who'd forgotten to provide crucial safety information that could have prevented this spiritual injury. No wonder my nervous system felt like it had been subjected to intensive overtraining—I'd been pushing consciousness beyond sustainable limits without realizing the danger, treating these abilities like party tricks rather than powerful tools that required careful handling.

THE PRESCRIPTION FOR RECOVERY

His prescription was immediate and specific, delivered with the authority of someone treating a serious but treatable condition: take the rest of the day off from intensive practice, do only *Metta* to calm the overstimulated system, and if troubling images arose, send consciousness down to my toes—a technique for grounding awareness in less volatile regions of bodily sensation where the nervous system could find refuge from cosmic overwhelm.

The advice felt like receiving emergency medical treatment for conditions I'd never known existed—spiritual first aid for consciousness that had ventured too far, too fast into territories that required more gradual acclimatization.

Later sessions, following this gentler protocol, produced a blue blowtorch flame *nimitta* so stable and intense that even opening my eyes couldn't dispel it. The luminous flame projected onto the wall I was facing, creating the surreal experience of seeing inner light superimposed on physical reality like some kind of meditation-powered augmented reality system where inner and outer worlds began merging in ways that challenged every assumption about the boundaries between subjective experience and objective reality.

THE INFINITE CINEMA

As evening approached and I prepared for what I hoped would be more restful sleep, I marveled at consciousness's infinite capacity for generating experiences that challenged every assumption about the boundaries between inner and outer reality, between possible and impossible, between human limitation and cosmic capability.

Tomorrow would bring new opportunities to explore these territories more safely, with a better understanding of the guidelines that prevented consciousness from venturing beyond its current capacity for integration. Tonight I carried the day's cosmic visions like treasures collected from expeditions to dimensions that existed only in the secret spaces between thoughts, where galaxies bloomed in the darkness behind closed eyes and impossible creatures swam through oceans of pure light.

The journey was revealing consciousness to be far more than I'd ever imagined—not just awareness observing reality, but a creative force capable of generating realities more vivid than anything the external world had to offer. The question was no longer what consciousness could perceive, but what it couldn't create when freed from ordinary limitations and allowed to express its infinite creative potential through the laboratory of intensive meditation practice.

But with great power came the need for great wisdom—understanding that these capabilities required careful cultivation, expert guidance, and profound respect for the psychological forces being unleashed. Consciousness was revealing itself to be like nuclear energy: capable of powering enlightenment or creating devastating destruction, depending entirely on how skillfully it was handled by practitioners who understood both its potential and its dangers.

Day 18 – Command and Control: Discovering Consciousness's Hidden Settings

The morning arrived draped in familiar drowsiness, consciousness emerging from sleep's depths like a deep-sea diver surfacing too slowly, still weighted by the pressure of dreams and fractured rest that had accumulated over days of intensive practice. Despite yesterday's strategic break from intensive *Anapanasati* practice, my awareness felt wrapped in gauze, the *nimitta* manifesting as weak and hazy as candlelight filtered through fog—a pale shadow of the cosmic fireworks that had been blazing behind my eyelids for days.

Perhaps the respite from breath meditation had allowed some essential spiritual momentum to dissipate, like a fire that dims when its fuel supply is temporarily interrupted, reminding me that these extraordinary abilities existed in delicate balance with consistent cultivation. The luminous displays that had become as reliable as sunrise now flickered uncertainly, humbling evidence that consciousness's higher functions required constant maintenance to preserve their brilliance.

THE RESTORATION OF POWER

But breakfast restored more than physical energy—it seemed to recharge whatever internal batteries powered these supernatural phenomena, like plugging depleted equipment into some cosmic electrical outlet. Returning to formal practice with renewed determination, I began experimenting with breathing rhythms like a scientist testing different variables in consciousness's complex equation.

Slow breaths first—deliberate, measured inhalations that stretched across geological time while my lungs screamed for normal oxygen delivery, each breath a meditation in itself. Then slow-but-natural breaths, finding that sweet spot where effort dissolved into effortless flow, where breathing became less mechanical action than organic poetry written in the language of air and awareness.

My mindfulness had been sharpened to razor precision by weeks of intensive training, now capable of tracking the subtlest respiratory movements with microscopic attention that could detect changes as delicate as morning dew forming on grass. This enhanced sensitivity allowed me to maintain the sun and moon *nimitta* for at least ten sustained minutes—those twin celestial displays blazing in my inner sky with the steadiness of actual astronomical bodies anchored in the cosmos of consciousness.

Then, as if following some predetermined cosmic choreography, they transformed into blue flame *nimitta*—brilliant blowtorch displays that sometimes contained Buddha images nestled within their luminous cores like sacred icons preserved in fire. These weren't crude visualizations conjured by wishful thinking but photographic clarity, each detail of the enlightened figure rendered with sculptural precision despite existing only in the space behind closed eyelids.

THE PARADOX OF SURRENDER

The familiar paradox reasserted itself with renewed force: the moment I abandoned formal posture and lay down to rest, the *nimitta* blazed with increased intensity, as if horizontal surrender unlocked some deeper reservoir of spiritual energy that upright effort couldn't access. I found myself using this luminous tool for playful target practice—shooting streams of inner light up through my mosquito net toward the ceiling like some kind of meditation-powered laser cannon, consciousness learning to project illumination beyond the boundaries of skull and flesh.

Each beam responded to mental direction with the precision of advanced technology, consciousness operating like equipment designed by engineers who understood laws of physics that human science hadn't yet discovered.

After lunch had fortified my depleted system with rice and renewed purpose, the afternoon session erupted into overwhelming displays of spiritual pyrotechnics that made previous experiences seem like mere previews. The *nimitta* manifested as massive, brilliant cannonballs and towering blue flames so intense, so luminous, they seemed to generate their own heat and pressure within the confined space of my inner vision.

The sheer volume of light felt like staring into a furnace designed by cosmic engineers who'd never heard of restraint, each display pushing consciousness toward limits I hadn't known existed.

THE STATUE HUNT

Using this blazing arsenal, I directed focused attention toward locating the second Buddha statue in the dining hall—that mysterious figure I'd glimpsed with ordinary eyes but never examined in detail, like trying to remember the face of someone seen briefly in a crowd. Through concentrated projection of supernatural sight, a faint outline began materializing in my consciousness like a photograph developing in slow motion in consciousness's darkroom.

The details remained frustratingly vague, edges soft and indistinct, but the basic form was unmistakably present—proof that consciousness could indeed perceive physical objects through solid barriers when properly focused, like X-ray vision operating through concentration rather than electromagnetic radiation.

My preference had shifted definitively toward slow, subtle breathing—microscopic sips of air that required such delicate attention they felt like trying to hear whispers in a thunderstorm. But my mindfulness had evolved to match this challenge, awareness sharpened to the point where even gossamer-light respiratory movements registered with crystalline clarity that made ordinary breathing seem crude and obvious.

THE REMOTE CONTROL DISCOVERY

At three o'clock, I presented myself to Sayadaw like a student reporting from the frontlines of impossible research, ready to confess both victories and failures in consciousness's continuing education. His golden face registered patient attention as I described the *nimitta* that had transformed sleep into an ordeal—blazing lights so intense they made rest impossible, consciousness generating illumination brighter than electric lighting that operated according to its own mysterious schedule.

"Why don't you just tell it to dim down?" he asked with the casual tone of someone suggesting I adjust a bedside lamp, as if consciousness came equipped with standard household controls—simple and obvious.

"I can do that?" My eyes widened with amazement as I discovered that remote controls worked on inner light shows, that consciousness possessed settings I'd never imagined existed.

"Yes." His smile carried the gentle authority of someone who'd spent decades learning consciousness's secret operating instructions, the hidden user manual that came with advanced human awareness.

"What about the flashing one?" I pressed, thinking of those strobing displays that had been conducting light symphonies in my skull like cosmic discotheques I couldn't turn off.

"Well," he said with the patience of a meditation engineer explaining basic troubleshooting to someone who'd been struggling with equipment they didn't understand, "just tell it to stop flashing."

"Great! I'll do that." Excitement flooded through me like electricity finding new circuits—I'd just been handed advanced weapons in the battle for spiritual equilibrium, tools I'd never known were available.

THE PERFECT TRAP

"Did you find the third Buddha?" Sayadaw asked, shifting to the previous day's assignment with the curiosity of someone monitoring a student's progress through a carefully designed curriculum.

I shook my head with the disappointment of someone who'd failed an important test, still convinced my Guan Yin vision had been meditation-induced confusion rather than accurate supernatural perception.

"Well, I tried. But all I saw was a Guan Yin-like statue."

"Actually," he said, his smile broadening with the satisfaction of someone revealing a perfectly laid trap, "the third Buddha statue *does* look a bit like Guan Yin."

The revelation struck like lightning, illuminating a landscape I'd been stumbling through in darkness for days. I'd successfully completed the assignment with supernatural accuracy, but dismissed my success due to preconceived notions about what should exist in a Theravada meditation center. Consciousness had been operating with perfect precision while my logical mind applied inappropriate filters based on sectarian assumptions rather than direct experience.

The lesson was profound: these abilities accessed information beyond ordinary knowledge, requiring trust in direct perception even when it contradicted reasonable expectations.

THE IMPOSSIBLE ASSIGNMENT

Having demonstrated competence in supernatural statue-hunting within the monastery's familiar boundaries, Sayadaw elevated my assignments to an entirely new level that challenged every assumption about consciousness's range and capabilities.

"Visit the Shwedagon Pagoda. Seek out the ruby-eyed Buddha there."

The instruction landed like a thunderbolt, each word expanding the playing field exponentially. The Shwedagon temple sat in Yangon, over an hour's drive away—a distance that would challenge even the most developed psychic abilities according to any reasonable understanding of how supernatural perception might work.

This wasn't just remote viewing but inter-city consciousness projection, spiritual GPS navigation across dozens of kilometers of intervening geography, buildings, traffic, and countless obstacles that should theoretically interfere with any form of extrasensory perception.

The assignment felt like being asked to hit a target on the moon with a bow and arrow, yet Sayadaw's casual confidence suggested this was simply the next logical step in consciousness's systematic curriculum.

THE ELECTRIC CLARITY

The evening's final meditation session produced an unexpected effect: instead of the usual exhaustion that made me nod off like a broken marionette after intensive practice, intense alertness flooded my nervous system like caffeine designed by cosmic chemists who understood energetic frequencies beyond ordinary chemistry.

Every neuron seemed to be firing with enhanced precision, consciousness buzzing with electrical clarity that made sleep feel not just unnecessary but impossible—as if meditation had somehow charged my awareness with renewable energy that operated independently of physical fatigue.

After the group sitting concluded, I returned to my cave for continued practice, this heightened awareness transforming even basic breath meditation into expeditions through hyperreal territories of inner space where every sensation registered with supernatural clarity.

THE COMMAND TEST

But the strong *nimitta* from intensive evening practice followed me into the night like loyal pets who'd forgotten they weren't invited to bed, their luminous presence making rest impossible despite my body's desperate need for recuperation. The moment I closed my eyes, colored lights began their familiar fireworks display—flashing, blazing, strobing with autonomous authority that seemed to mock my need for darkness and peace.

Time to test Sayadaw's revolutionary suggestion.

"Stop flashing!" I commanded the strobing display with the authority of someone issuing orders to cosmic light technicians, addressing consciousness as if it were sophisticated equipment that responded to voice commands.

Instantly, the flashing ceased. Complete obedience to mental command, as if consciousness came equipped with dimmer switches and control panels I'd never known existed, more responsive than any electronic device ever manufactured.

Wow! It worked!

Emboldened by this success that felt like discovering secret cheat codes for reality itself, I targeted the next challenge: a sun-bright *nimitta* that blazed with solar intensity behind my closed lids, making sleep impossible with its relentless radiance.

"Dim down," I directed with growing confidence in consciousness's responsiveness to clear mental instructions.

The intensity reduced immediately, luminosity adjusting like a perfectly calibrated rheostat responding to mental commands with the precision of professional lighting equipment operated by invisible technicians.

THE ULTIMATE CONTROL

The final test involved a brilliant white light that had been preventing sleep with its relentless radiance—illumination so intense it made the inside of my skull brighter than daylight, more luminous than looking directly into the sun.

"Turn to black," I commanded with the authority of someone who'd finally discovered consciousness's hidden control panel, the master switches that governed inner experience.

Darkness. Complete, blessed darkness, as if I'd pulled blackout curtains across the windows of inner vision with the efficiency of a professional stage crew. The transformation was so complete, so immediate, it felt like discovering that reality itself operated according to voice commands I'd simply never thought to try.

The profound silence that followed felt like a gift—not just the absence of light, but the presence of mastery. In that moment of absolute darkness, gratitude flowed toward my teacher with the depth of someone who'd just been handed the keys to their own mind's control room.

THE HIDDEN USER MANUAL

As I settled into the mosquito net's white sanctuary, marveling at this newly discovered ability to govern consciousness's light displays through direct mental command, I realized I'd crossed another crucial threshold in understanding the mind's hidden capabilities.

These weren't hallucinations or random neural firings but controllable phenomena that responded to focused intention like any other sophisticated tool once its operating principles were understood. Consciousness was revealing itself to possess an entire control room of adjustable settings—brightness, color, intensity, duration—all accessible through clear mental commands delivered with sufficient authority and confidence.

Tomorrow would bring the ultimate test—attempting to project awareness across vast distances to locate a specific Buddha statue in Yangon's most famous temple, consciousness navigation that would challenge every assumption about the limitations of human perception. But tonight, I drifted toward sleep in perfect darkness, awareness finally operating under my own command rather than subjecting me to involuntary light shows that had been transforming rest into endurance competitions.

What astonished me most wasn't consciousness's capacity for generating extraordinary phenomena, but its willingness to respond to simple, direct commands like obedient technology waiting for proper instructions. The retreat was revealing not just awareness's spectacular creative abilities but also its responsiveness to skilled direction—like discovering that the human mind came equipped with advanced features its manufacturer had forgotten to mention in any user manual ever written.

Each day brought new revelations about consciousness's hidden capabilities, functions that existed beyond ordinary human knowledge but became accessible to those willing to explore the deeper territories of awareness through systematic practice and expert guidance. The real discovery wasn't that consciousness could generate extraordinary phenomena, but that these phenomena could be controlled, directed, and commanded by practitioners who learned to operate awareness with the skill of experienced technicians working with equipment designed by intelligence far more sophisticated than anything human engineering had yet produced.

In this strange new territory where thought became technology and intention operated like programming code, sleep finally claimed me—not as surrender to unconsciousness, but as conscious rest in darkness I had chosen, controlled, and commanded into being.

Day 19 - Astral Tourism

Night had transformed from enemy into ally. Despite *nimitta* blazing behind my closed eyelids like a personal constellation, sleep arrived with the gentleness of a blessing rather than the harsh impossibility it had become in recent days. The luminous displays maintained their dimmed setting throughout the darkness, obeying my previous evening's commands with the reliability of well-trained servants who'd finally learned their master's preferences.

Morning brought triumphant experimentation with this newfound control over consciousness's light shows. Like a child testing a magical remote control, I directed my attention toward the subdued illuminations and issued a simple command: "Resume normal colors."

Instantly, the *nimitta* blazed back to full intensity—brilliant blues and whites and rainbow cascades returning to their previous cosmic glory as if someone had suddenly restored power to a dimmed theater. The obedience was immediate, complete, exhilarating. The discovery felt like finding hidden switches for consciousness itself, proving that these extraordinary phenomena weren't random neural misfires but controllable tools responding to focused intention with the precision of any well-designed technology.

THE PARADOX OF TRANQUILITY

Morning practice unfolded with the tranquility of a mountain lake at dawn. *Anapanasati* with slow, deliberate breathing created an atmosphere of profound peace that seemed to extend beyond my meditation room into the compound's flowering pathways and bamboo cathedrals. Each inhalation and exhalation flowed like honey, consciousness settling into rhythms that felt less like effort than like remembering some ancient, natural state.

Paradoxically, despite this enhanced mindfulness that felt sharp enough to cut diamonds, the *nimitta* remained weak and hazy—pale shadows of their usual blazing intensity. Perhaps deep tranquility and spectacular light shows existed in inverse relationship, like trying to see stars while standing next to a bonfire. The deeper the peace, the dimmer the pyrotechnics, as if consciousness had to choose between serenity and spectacle.

LAUNCH COORDINATES

At midday, the moment arrived for the ultimate test of consciousness's navigational capabilities. I arranged myself in meditation posture with the solemnity of an astronaut preparing for launch, then directed my awareness toward Yangon with the focused intention of someone programming coordinates into spiritual GPS systems.

"Visit the Shwedagon."

The response was immediate and overwhelming.

I found myself moving through the Shwedagon Pagoda as if consciousness had been transformed into some kind of high-speed flying camera, soaring around the sacred complex with the fluid grace of a bird that had transcended ordinary physics. The experience wasn't visualization or imagination but immersive virtual reality rendered in vivid, saturated colors with three-dimensional solidity that made my meditation room seem like a pale shadow by comparison.

Every detail blazed with photographic clarity: the multitude of smaller pagodas scattered throughout the compound like golden eggs laid by some celestial hen, the vast paved platform that could accommodate thousands of pilgrims, the central pagoda rising into the sky like a mountain of gold that had learned to defy gravity through pure spiritual engineering.

THE EMPTY KINGDOM

The strangest aspect was the complete absence of people. In ordinary reality, the Shwedagon teemed with pilgrims, tourists, monks, and vendors, creating a constant river of human activity. But in this consciousness-visited version, the sacred space existed in pristine solitude, as if I'd been granted private access to dimensions where only awareness itself was permitted to travel.

The speed of movement was initially overwhelming—my consciousness racing around the complex like a time-lapse film of someone on spiritual amphetamines. But when I mentally commanded, "Slow down," the pace immediately reduced to a comfortable walking rhythm, proving that even astral tourism responded to conscious direction.

I flew up and down the central pagoda's golden flanks, examining the intricate parasol structure crowning its peak—that ceremonial umbrella marking the spot where earth met heaven in Myanmar's spiritual geography. Each architectural detail was rendered with impossible precision, as if consciousness possessed its own version of high-definition cameras capable of recording structures I'd never examined with ordinary eyes.

THE WRONG BUDDHA

Then came the specific assignment: locate the ruby-eyed Buddha that existed somewhere within this vast sacred complex. I directed focused intention toward this mysterious figure I'd never seen in physical life, trusting consciousness to navigate toward its target like some kind of spiritual homing device.

Gradually, the golden landscape transformed around me until I found myself transported to an ornate chamber where a green-faced Buddha statue sat within a large golden cage, its features radiating the serene authority of enlightened presence despite the unusual verdant complexion.

Mission accomplished, or so I believed. I broke the meditation with the satisfaction of someone who'd just completed an impossible assignment through means that would make neuroscientists weep with confusion.

THE FLOOD GATES

But when I resumed practice, the afternoon session collapsed into chaos. Images cascaded through my awareness like a broken dam releasing flood waters—landscapes, faces, structures, all rendered with the same three-dimensional solidity as the Shwedagon vision but completely unrelated to breath meditation or any conscious intention.

These were compelling displays that hijacked attention like television programs designed by cosmic advertisers who understood exactly which visual frequencies would prove irresistible to human consciousness. Every attempt to return focus to the subtle movements of breathing dissolved as soon as these uninvited spectacles activated, dragging awareness into narrative involvement with scenes that felt more real than the meditation hall containing my physical body.

The afternoon had become a cinema of consciousness where I was simultaneously director, audience, and unwilling participant in films I'd never commissioned but couldn't stop watching.

COSMIC WELDING

The 2:30 p.m. session brought redemption in the form of spectacular *nimitta* displays that blazed with renewed intensity. A flaming projection extended two full meters from my nose like some kind of spiritual blowtorch designed for cosmic welding projects, while cloudy ring formations drifted through inner space like celestial smoke signals written in languages I couldn't read but somehow understood.

Following Sayadaw's suggestion, I directed attention toward the upper lip area where breath's touch was most subtle and accessible. The technique worked immediately—focus sharpened, breath awareness deepened, and the area became hypersensitive to even gossamer-light respiratory movements that would have been imperceptible to ordinary attention.

But this enhanced sensitivity came with unexpected consequences. The upper lip region around my nostrils remained tender and swollen-feeling long after the session ended, as if concentrated attention had somehow inflamed the nerve pathways responsible for detecting air movement. My nose felt enlarged, hypersensitive, like meditation had installed new equipment that hadn't finished calibrating itself to its enhanced functions.

COSMIC BUREAUCRACY

At three o'clock, I presented myself to Sayadaw with the confidence of someone reporting successful completion of an impossible mission.

"Did you see the ruby-eyed Buddha?" he asked with the expectant expression of a teacher checking homework.

"Well, I saw a green-faced Buddha statue inside a large golden cage," I replied, describing my astral discovery with the precision of a travel reporter filing dispatches from impossible destinations.

"No, that's not the ruby-eyed Buddha. That's the green-faced Buddha," he said with the gentle correction of someone explaining that I'd found the right building but the wrong apartment. "The ruby-eyed Buddha is in a different place."

His pause carried the weight of someone solving a puzzle whose solution had just become apparent. "Oh, but foreigners are not allowed to see the ruby-eyed Buddha. Perhaps that was why you could not locate it. Never mind."

The explanation struck with the logic of cosmic bureaucracy—even astral tourism apparently operated according to the same access restrictions that governed physical pilgrimages. Consciousness might be capable of inter-city travel, but some sacred spaces remained off-limits regardless of the transportation method employed.

MEMORY BANKS AND HOLOGRAMS

I confessed my struggles with the cascading images that had been sabotaging afternoon practice, their compelling reality making breath meditation feel impossible. Where did these visions originate, I wondered, since I couldn't recall ever witnessing the specific landscapes and structures that had been parading through my awareness?

"Maybe the images of landscapes came from your previous travels," Sayadaw suggested with the casual tone of someone explaining how memory banks operated in consciousness's deeper storage systems.

Then I demonstrated the phenomenon that had been most startling: *nimitta* visible even with eyes open, projecting onto walls and surfaces like some kind of meditation-powered floodlight.

"There it is," I said, pointing to a spot on the office wall where the bright orange spot was currently dancing in my central vision.

Sayadaw and Mr. Soemin exchanged meaningful glances, their expressions revealing quiet recognition. The phenomenon I was describing—*nimitta* visible with eyes open—was a rare manifestation that only emerged from *jhana*-like absorption states, a sign of concentration so profound it could project inner luminosity into ordinary perception. Their knowing silence spoke volumes about the territory I was now navigating—realms where extraordinary spiritual development became visible even to trained observers.

We had entered the borderlands where spiritual achievement and psychological crisis looked disturbingly similar from the outside, territories where only the experiencer could distinguish transcendence from breakdown.

THE THRESHOLD OF ABSORPTION

The day's final *Anapanasati* sessions brought subtle breathing to levels of refinement that felt like trying to detect whispers in a cathedral designed for silence. Despite *nimitta* that remained hazy and unstable, my body achieved a state of lightness and tranquility that seemed to dissolve the boundaries between flesh and air, matter and consciousness.

Physical form felt increasingly optional, as if gravity had become a polite suggestion rather than an immutable law. My awareness floated in space that extended infinitely in all directions, anchored only by the gossamer thread of breath that continued flowing like a river through landscapes of pure consciousness.

"You might have come close to *jhana*," Sayadaw observed with the diagnostic precision of someone who'd spent decades mapping consciousness's deeper territories.

The words landed like validation from a cosmic university where degrees were awarded for achievements that couldn't be measured by any earthly standards. After weeks of intensive practice, I was apparently approaching those absorption states that represented meditation's true destinations—territories where individual consciousness merged with universal awareness in unions that transcended ordinary perception entirely.

THE FLUID UNIVERSE

Tonight, as I prepared for sleep in the mosquito net's white sanctuary, I marveled at the day's revelations about consciousness's apparent ability to travel through space while remaining anchored in a meditation hall in Myanmar. Whether these experiences represented genuine astral projection or sophisticated mental simulations mattered less than their demonstration of awareness's infinite creative capabilities.

The question wasn't whether consciousness could actually travel to Yangon, but what these experiences revealed about the nature of perception itself. If awareness could generate three-dimensional environments indistinguishable from physical reality, what did that suggest about the solidity of ordinary experience? How many of our daily perceptions were consciousness creating rather than simply receiving?

Tomorrow would bring new opportunities to explore these borderlands between individual mind and cosmic consciousness, territories where the maps drawn by conventional psychology became increasingly unreliable guides. But tonight I drifted toward dreams, wondering whether the boundaries between inner and outer reality were as solid as conventional wisdom suggested, or whether intensive meditation was revealing the universe's more fluid operating principles hidden behind the illusion of separation between self and world.

In this space where thought became geography and intention operated like transportation, sleep finally claimed me—not as escape from extraordinary experience, but as entry into yet another realm where consciousness continued its endless experiments with the possible.

Day 20 - The Robot's Awakening

Dawn arrived with consciousness already blazing like a cosmic entertainment system that had forgotten how to power down. A multicolored *nimitta* swirled in my third eye—that mysterious space behind closed lids where aurora borealis had made itself permanently at home. The luminous display glittered with all the colors that had ever existed and several that seemed to belong to other dimensions entirely, each hue flowing into the next like liquid starlight choreographed by some divine intelligence with access to pigments unknown to earthly artists.

This was no longer the simple blue flames and solar discs of earlier weeks. This was consciousness itself revealing its true nature as a multimedia production facility capable of generating displays that made Hollywood's most sophisticated special effects seem like amateur finger paintings executed in crayon.

THE PRICE OF ILLUMINATION

But these spectacular abilities came with a price that transformed daily existence into a surreal endurance test. Whenever I closed my eyes—for rest, for blinking, for any reason—the *nimitta* immediately illuminated whatever surface I was facing like cosmic floodlights being projected through my skull onto the external world. My bedroom ceiling became a canvas for light shows that played whether I wanted them or not, turning attempts at sleep into mandatory attendance at psychedelic concerts performed by my nervous system.

Even worse were the lighthouse beacons that flashed inside my eyes with the relentless rhythm of cosmic Morse code, each pulse carrying messages I couldn't decode but couldn't ignore. These weren't gentle twinkles but searchlight-intensity strobing that seemed designed to prevent unconsciousness by any means necessary.

WHEN WORLDS COLLIDE

The phenomenon had begun bleeding into waking consciousness with increasingly disturbing frequency. During lunch, while staring down at the checkered pattern of vinyl flooring that had become as familiar as breathing, I could feel my vision beginning to shift like a television slowly changing channels without permission. The *nimitta* would announce its arrival with that peculiar internal pressure behind my eyes, then superimpose its colors onto whatever I was observing, creating a double-exposure reality where physical and spiritual vision competed for dominance.

When this happened, disorientation crashed through my system like vertigo mixed with motion sickness, the world tilting at angles that defied every law of physics I'd ever learned. Nausea would follow—that queasy sensation of a stomach rebelling against sensory input that shouldn't exist, like seasickness caused by waves in dimensions that had no ocean.

The environment itself would transform without warning, as if I'd been fitted with tinted contact lenses that changed color according to some autonomous schedule. The dining hall would appear normal one moment, then suddenly everything would shift to green as an emerald *nimitta* activated, the walls and floor and faces around me all tinted like we were underwater in some cosmic aquarium. Then the green would dissolve into yellow, the entire world painted in golden hues as if sunset had been trapped indoors. Blue would follow, transforming my surroundings into arctic landscapes where everything appeared frozen in ice-colored light.

These different colored *nimitta* moved across my vision like clouds passing in front of internal suns, each one casting its chromatic shadow over consensus reality until I couldn't trust my eyes to report accurate information about the basic colors of the world around me.

THE MOOD RING OF CONSCIOUSNESS

Even more unsettling was the *nimitta's* apparent sensitivity to environmental variables, like some kind of spiritual mood ring that changed according to external conditions. In my meditation room, they blazed predominantly blue—deep ocean blue, electric blue, sometimes the pale blue of winter skies. In the main hall, green dominated—forest green, jade green, the vivid emerald of new leaves drinking morning light.

When exhaustion weighed down my nervous system or somber moods settled over my consciousness like psychological fog, the displays would shift to purple—royal purple, violet, sometimes the deep purple of bruises or storm clouds pregnant with rain. But when concentration achieved that perfect one-pointed focus that felt like consciousness becoming a laser beam, the *nimitta* would blaze pure white with intensity that made staring into the sun seem gentle by comparison.

Most remarkably, when my mental discipline reached its peak efficiency, I could command these displays like operating some kind of cosmic remote control system. *Change to red*, I would direct, and red would bloom across my inner vision. *Become brighter*, and the luminosity would increase until my skull felt like it contained its own personal star. *Grow larger*, and the display would expand beyond the boundaries of normal visual fields, creating illumination that seemed to extend infinitely in all directions.

THE IMPOSSIBILITY OF IGNORANCE

My teachers' advice to "ignore the *nimitta*" felt like being told to ignore the sun while staring directly into it. These displays positioned themselves permanently at the center of my visual field with the persistence of a reflection in a mirror. No matter where I directed my gaze, they followed with perfect synchronization, like cosmic spotlights that had decided to use my consciousness as their permanent stage.

I'd attempted shifting my focus to peripheral vision, looking around the edges of these luminous phenomena. Still, they adapted to my evasive maneuvers with the relentless efficiency of highly advanced tracking systems. It was like trying to avoid seeing your reflection—a fundamental impossibility when the mirror was built into the very mechanism of perception itself.

The knowledge that I should concentrate on breath or meditation object instead of these spectacular displays created a form of torture. How do you ignore galaxies exploding behind your eyelids to focus on the subtle sensation of air moving through your nostrils? How do you pay attention to microscopic respiratory movements when consciousness is generating light shows that would make Pink Floyd concerts seem understated?

Paradoxically, as my concentration deepened and stabilized through weeks of intensive practice, the *nimitta* became more distracting rather than less, as if spiritual progress was creating increasingly sophisticated distractions designed to test my ability to maintain focus on simple breath awareness despite having access to cosmic entertainment systems.

THE CIRCUIT BOARD REVELATION

All these extraordinary experiences had triggered an existential crisis that struck at the very core of my understanding of human nature and the boundaries of ordinary consciousness. I felt like a human being who had suddenly discovered I was a robot—as if some cosmic technician had finally opened my access panels to reveal the electronic components that had been operating my biological systems all along.

It was as if I'd finally seen my microchips and wires for the first time, the internal hardware that made consciousness possible but which was usually hidden from the user's awareness. The colorful *nimitta*, the three-dimensional holograms, and especially those shining rods and ropes of pure light felt exactly like discovering my spiritual circuitry—the cosmic technology that powered awareness but which humans were never supposed to see directly.

These revelations were equally shocking and fascinating, like being given backstage access to the universe's operating systems while still trying to perform my daily role as a supposedly ordinary human being. I'd never imagined that consciousness contained such spectacular machinery, never suspected that what I'd assumed was simple biological awareness was actually sophisticated technology capable of generating experiences that challenged every assumption about the nature of reality itself.

THE FLICKERING INSTRUMENT

The day's meditation sessions reflected this internal revolution with schizophrenic unpredictability. Morning practice had begun with mindfulness so acute it felt like consciousness had been upgraded to high-definition sensitivity. I could detect the subtlest respiratory movements with microscopic precision, feeling air currents around my upper lip with the sensitivity of scientific instruments designed to measure phenomena normally invisible to human perception.

Every molecule of incoming air registered with crystalline clarity, each exhalation painting warm moisture across hypersensitive nerve endings that had been refined by weeks of intensive attention into detection devices capable of tracking gossamer-light breathing that barely disturbed the air around my nostrils.

But after lunch, some internal switch flipped with cruel precision, and those same hypersensitive areas became as insensitive as scar tissue. The acute awareness that had made subtle breathing feel like symphony orchestras of sensation suddenly vanished, leaving me struggling to detect even normal respiratory movements unless I breathed with the force of someone hyperventilating in panic.

It was like having precision scientific equipment that worked perfectly in the morning but shut down entirely after noon, consciousness operating according to mysterious schedules that seemed designed to humble any sense of mastery I might develop over these extraordinary abilities.

NAVIGATION ERRORS

The *nimitta* had settled into more familiar territory today—mostly flame displays that danced like spiritual blowtorches and small moon formations that glowed with pearl-white luminosity. These felt like old friends compared to the rainbow galaxies and impossible architectural displays that had been overwhelming my vision in recent sessions.

When I attempted to return to the Shwedagon temple through focused consciousness projection, the results were comically off-target. Instead of Myanmar's golden pagoda complex, my awareness found itself exploring some random building that looked distinctly English—perhaps an old church with Gothic architecture, or maybe London's Parliament building with its distinctive stone spires and elaborate governmental grandeur.

Even astral tourism could suffer from navigation errors, where consciousness occasionally tuned into the wrong spiritual frequencies and delivered completely unrelated destinations despite careful intention and focused direction. The experience reminded me that these extraordinary abilities, however spectacular, were still operating according to laws I barely understood, with success rates that remained frustratingly unpredictable.

THE METAMORPHOSIS

As evening approached and I prepared for another night of negotiating with luminous displays that would determine whether sleep was possible, I marveled at how thoroughly these three weeks had dismantled every assumption I'd held about human consciousness and its apparent limitations.

I was no longer the person who had arrived at this retreat believing meditation was simply about relaxation and stress relief. That naive individual had been replaced by someone who'd discovered that consciousness was actually sophisticated technology capable of generating experiences that belonged in science fiction rather than spiritual practice manuals.

The transformation felt complete yet terrifying. I had become something between human and machine, biological awareness fitted with cosmic hardware that operated according to principles no engineering textbook had ever described. The *nimitta* weren't just pretty lights—they were proof that consciousness contained circuitry more advanced than anything Silicon Valley had imagined, running programs that accessed databases of experience extending far beyond individual memory or knowledge.

What did it mean to be human when humanity apparently came equipped with capabilities that transcended every assumption about the species' limitations? Was I evolving into something new, or simply remembering functions that had always existed but which civilization had systematically trained us to forget?

Tomorrow would bring new opportunities to explore these borderlands between human and something far more extraordinary. But tonight I went to sleep wondering whether I was discovering my true nature or losing my mind—and whether, in territories this strange, there was any meaningful difference between the two.

In this space where consciousness revealed itself as technology and meditation became a form of systems administration, sleep finally claimed me—not as escape from the impossible, but as entry into dreams where even more extraordinary revelations might be waiting to unfold.

∼

Day 21 - Messages from the Void

Dawn broke with consciousness already deep in conversation with invisible correspondents. Wriggly black handwriting danced across a white background behind my closed eyelids—cursive script that moved with the fluid grace of calligraphy being written by ghostly hands in real time. The writing possessed an uncanny familiarity that made my heart race with recognition, as if I were reading letters from some forgotten part of myself, but the words dissolved like smoke the moment I tried to focus on their meaning, leaving only the haunting sensation of having received important messages that had been deliberately encrypted beyond comprehension.

Following this mysterious correspondence, skeletons materialized against a backdrop of black and white dots—death's architecture rendered in pixels like some macabre digital art installation. But even this morbid display refused to remain static, gradually transforming into something that resembled a black sky populated with faint blue dots, the entire scene flickering with the nostalgic static of analog television reception from my childhood, complete with that fuzzy, unstable quality that made me wonder whether I was tuning into broadcasts from dimensions that operated on different frequencies entirely.

THE PARADOX OF REST

Ironically, despite these extraordinary midnight communications from whatever cosmic intelligence had been using my skull as its personal message center, I'd achieved the most restful sleep in days. Yesterday's strategic retreat from intensive practice had finally allowed my overstimulated nervous system to discharge some of the electrical buildup that had been transforming rest into endurance competitions against my consciousness.

This marked the exact halfway point of the retreat—day twenty-one of forty-three—and for the first time since arriving, I'd chosen not to practice before breakfast. The decision felt simultaneously like weakness and wisdom, born from a growing anxiety about the trajectory of my spiritual development that had been gnawing at my confidence like acid eating through metal.

THE CRISIS OF BECOMING

The *nimitta* phenomena had begun feeling less like gifts and more like symptoms of some condition I couldn't name or control. Despite my teachers' repeated instructions to ignore these spectacular displays, I was finding it increasingly difficult to maintain focus on simple breath awareness when my visual field had been transformed into a constantly changing cosmic entertainment system that seemed explicitly designed to hijack attention.

More disturbing was the profound sense of identity crisis that had been building like psychological pressure in a cosmic boiler ready to explode. What was I changing into? What fundamental alteration of human consciousness was I undergoing, and where would it lead? The person who had entered this retreat three weeks ago felt like a distant relative I could barely remember—

someone naive enough to believe meditation was about relaxation rather than complete reconstruction of the basic operating systems of awareness itself.

THE DOCTOR'S DIAGNOSIS

After breakfast, having fortified my depleted reserves with rice and growing apprehension, I sought refuge in Mr. Soemin's office like a patient finally ready to confess symptoms to a doctor who might have answers for conditions that didn't appear in any medical textbooks.

"Why am I told not to look at the *nimitta*?" I asked with the desperation of someone who'd been trying to follow impossible instructions while spectacular fireworks exploded in their peripheral vision.

His explanation arrived like sunlight breaking through storm clouds. Looking at the *nimitta* made it more difficult to visit distant places through consciousness projection. It interfered with *Vipassana*—insight meditation that required clear, unobstructed awareness rather than fascination with spectacular light shows. But there was no inherent danger in observing these phenomena, no spiritual harm in witnessing consciousness's native ability to generate extraordinary displays.

"At Pa-Auk," he continued with the casual authority of someone referencing established curriculum, "monks are taught to look at the *nimitta* at certain stages of practice. There's no danger involved."

The reassurance felt like having a medical diagnosis that transformed mysterious symptoms into normal variations of a well-understood condition. My concerns about the other phenomena—the holograms, the skeleton visions, the impossible architectural displays—were completely normal responses to intensive meditation practice, he explained. Other practitioners had traveled these same territories and emerged safely on the other side.

With this burden of anxiety lifted from my shoulders like removing a backpack full of stones, my practice immediately transformed from fearful endurance into confident exploration.

THE LIBERATION SESSION

The session that followed bloomed with renewed clarity and purpose. A ring *nimitta* materialized first—that familiar circular formation floating in inner space like a cosmic donut made of condensed light. It maintained perfect stability for twenty minutes, demonstrating the kind of sustained concentration that had become increasingly reliable through weeks of intensive training.

When my focus wavered slightly, the ring immediately transformed into licking flames that danced with the hypnotic rhythm of campfire light, each tongue of luminous fire reaching toward some invisible fuel source that existed only in consciousness's deeper strata. But as concentration reasserted itself with renewed strength, the flames settled back into the original ring formation with the precision of a spiritual thermostat returning to its optimal setting.

Most exciting was the emergence of an entirely new *nimitta* type: the "star shower." Glittering speckles cascaded through my inner vision like cosmic confetti celebrating some victory I didn't understand, each luminous particle trailing light as it fell through the darkness behind my closed eyelids. The display resembled meteor showers viewed from inside a planetarium, except these stars were being born and dying in the theater of my awareness.

THE COSMIC PERIODIC TABLE

During the afternoon interview, Sayadaw revealed that there were thirteen recognized types of *nimitta* including the green and yellow rods and rope-like formations I'd witnessed in recent sessions. The information struck me as oddly specific—thirteen distinct categories of inner light, as if consciousness operated according to some cosmic periodic table where different elements of spiritual experience had been catalogued and classified by generations of contemplative scientists.

Yet reflecting on my own experiences, I felt certain I'd witnessed far more than thirteen variations. Perhaps the traditional categories were broad classifications that contained infinite subcategories, or maybe intensive practice in this particular lineage was unlocking *nimitta* types that hadn't been formally documented in the ancient texts.

THE COSMIC LIBRARY

At two o'clock, I attempted returning to consciousness projection experiments, directing focused attention toward both the Shwedagon Pagoda and my apartment in Australia—ambitious targets that would test whether astral tourism could operate across both local and international distances simultaneously.

The results were disappointing but artistically spectacular. Instead of golden pagodas or familiar furniture, my awareness found itself exploring endless galleries of bas-reliefs—those raised stone carvings that decorated ancient temple walls with scenes from mythological narratives I couldn't identify. Each relief was rendered in perfect three-dimensional detail, shadows and highlights creating sculptural depth that seemed more real than the meditation room containing my physical body.

Perhaps consciousness was accessing some vast cosmic library of architectural imagery rather than specific geographic locations, or maybe my navigation systems were still too crude to reach precise destinations across such vast distances.

THE PERMISSION TO WONDER

Overall, the day felt like successful damage control rather than a spectacular breakthrough. Most importantly, I'd resolved the anxiety about *nimitta* observation that had been sabotaging my practice for days. Mr. Soemin's constant reminders not to look at these displays had created a psychological feedback loop where the instruction itself became more distracting than the phenomenon it was meant to address.

Many times over recent days, I'd abandoned meditation sessions mid-stream because the *nimitta* had become too intense to ignore while simultaneously feeling forbidden to acknowledge its presence. It was like trying to meditate while someone was setting off fireworks in my peripheral vision, while being told that noticing the explosions would somehow damage my spiritual development.

Now, with permission to witness these extraordinary displays without guilt or anxiety, I felt confident that my practice would finally achieve the trajectory it had been seeking. The fear of doing something wrong had been replaced by curiosity about doing something unprecedented; terror had transformed into excitement about exploring territories that few practitioners had ever reached.

THE ULTIMATE ASSIGNMENT

Before leaving the interview, Sayadaw issued a new assignment that pushed consciousness projection into realms that challenged every assumption about the nature of reality itself: "Go to Devaland and see the Buddha's relics."

Devaland—the heavenly realm where deities supposedly resided between earthly incarnations, home to treasures that existed beyond the reach of physical pilgrimage. This wasn't just remote viewing or astral tourism but inter-dimensional travel to locations that might not have coordinates in any earthly sense.

The assignment felt like being asked to visit addresses that existed only in mythology, to navigate using maps drawn by angels rather than cartographers. How does consciousness chart a course to dimensions that exist outside physical space-time? What coordinates does awareness use when the destination transcends geography entirely?

Yet Sayadaw's casual confidence suggested this was simply the next logical step in consciousness's systematic curriculum, another skill to be developed through the same focused intention that had already enabled impossible journeys to golden pagodas and mysterious temples.

THE THRESHOLD OF WONDER

As evening approached and I prepared for night sessions with renewed confidence, I marveled at how this halfway checkpoint had transformed from potential crisis into recommitment to the extraordinary journey I'd somehow stumbled into. The fear that had been contaminating my practice for days—that gnawing anxiety about becoming something inhuman—had dissolved into acceptance of whatever transformation was already underway.

Perhaps the real spiritual development wasn't in the spectacular phenomena themselves, but in learning to witness the impossible without losing one's center, to navigate extraordinary territories while maintaining the stability of ordinary human kindness and wisdom.

Tomorrow would bring attempts to visit heaven itself through means that would make NASA's most ambitious space programs seem quaint by comparison. But tonight, I settled into meditation posture with the satisfaction of someone who'd finally received permission to witness the impossible without apology, ready to explore whatever cosmic territories consciousness might reveal when fear no longer stood guard at the threshold of wonder.

In this space where anxiety had transformed into curiosity and prohibition had become invitation, sleep finally claimed me—not as escape from the extraordinary, but as preparation for journeys that would challenge every assumption about the boundaries between consciousness and cosmos, between individual awareness and the infinite realms that awaited exploration.

∼

Day 22 – Journey to the Celestial Realm

Morning arrived like a cosmic joke played on someone who'd been expecting enlightenment but received spiritual molasses instead. My consciousness felt wrapped in layers of mental cotton batting, each attempt at concentration dissolving into the kind of torpor that made thinking feel like swimming through quicksand while wearing lead boots.

The pre-dawn sessions collapsed into exercises in futility, my awareness scattered like leaves in a hurricane despite weeks of training that should have made focus as reliable as breathing. Sloth and torpor—those ancient enemies of meditation that the Buddha had identified as fundamental obstacles to awakening—had invaded my nervous system with the efficiency of a spiritual virus designed specifically to sabotage contemplative progress.

THE DEAD RADIO

Every technique that had been producing spectacular results for days suddenly felt as effective as trying to start a fire with wet matches. Breath awareness crumbled the moment I attempted to establish it, mindfulness evaporating like morning dew under a desert sun. My mind felt stuffed with invisible gauze that absorbed all attempts at concentration before they could take root in sustained attention.

Desperate for environmental solutions to what was an internal problem, I abandoned my familiar meditation cave for the main hall, hoping that the collective energy of the space where group sittings generated shared spiritual momentum might jumpstart my stalled practice. But the change of venue proved as ineffective as rearranging deck chairs on a sinking ship—the same mental fog followed me like a persistent shadow, transforming even the most sacred spaces into theaters for spiritual mediocrity.

Whatever combination of factors had been supporting my extraordinary experiences had gone offline without warning, leaving me feeling like a cosmic radio that had suddenly lost reception to all the interesting stations. No amount of mental adjustment could restore the clear signal that had been carrying me into territories beyond ordinary imagination.

THE RESET

But lunch provided more than physical nourishment—it seemed to reset whatever internal systems had been malfunctioning since dawn. The afternoon sessions emerged from the morning's spiritual quicksand with renewed clarity, consciousness gradually remembering how to operate its more sophisticated functions.

The familiar cast of *nimitta* began reassembling: ring formations floating in inner space like cosmic donuts made of condensed light, and cloud displays that drifted through my visual field with the stately grace of weather systems designed by cosmic meteorologists. These weren't the spectacular fireworks of recent sessions, but their steady presence felt reassuring after the morning's complete absence of inner illumination.

LAUNCH SEQUENCE

The assignment to visit Devaland—that celestial realm where deities supposedly resided between earthly incarnations—had been haunting my consciousness since yesterday's interview. Multiple attempts throughout the afternoon yielded nothing but ordinary darkness punctuated by fleeting images that could have been imagination disguised as spiritual vision.

But at four o'clock, some internal alignment finally clicked into place with the satisfying precision of a complex lock finally yielding to the right combination. I began with *Araham*—that sacred syllable pulsing through awareness like a mantra-powered heartbeat—then shifted into *Metta*, allowing loving kindness to flow through consciousness like warm honey dissolving barriers between individual awareness and universal compassion.

From this foundation of expanded heart-space, I directed focused intention toward Devaland with the determination of someone launching consciousness into territories that didn't appear on any earthly maps.

The response was immediate and overwhelming.

THE IMPOSSIBLE ARCHITECTURE

A colossal structure materialized in my inner vision—a brick-brown building of impossible dimensions that seemed to combine architectural influences from civilizations that had never existed on Earth. The scale defied comprehension, stretching across cosmic distances that made earthly landmarks seem like miniature models, yet every detail remained crisp and immediate, as if I were simultaneously viewing it from satellite altitude and examining it through a cosmic magnifying glass.

Tall spires rose into the infinite sky like arrows shot by cosmic archers aiming at dimensions beyond ordinary geometry, each tower reaching toward heights that made earthly skyscrapers seem like children's building blocks scattered across a playground. The spires themselves weren't simple vertical columns but twisted and spiraled through space in helical patterns that followed mathematical principles I couldn't understand but somehow felt in my bones, each curve and angle creating harmonies that were both visual and musical, architecture that could be heard as much as seen.

The construction materials defied easy categorization—brick-brown, yes, but with a richness and depth of color that suggested these were bricks made from condensed Earth of planets where different minerals created pigments unknown to terrestrial geology. Each individual brick seemed to contain entire geological histories compressed into rectangular forms, with veins of metallic threading running through them like fossilized lightning, creating patterns that shifted and changed as my consciousness moved around the structure. The mortar between these celestial bricks wasn't ordinary cement but appeared to be crystallized light itself, holding the building together with bonds that existed as much in spiritual dimensions as physical ones.

The entire structure pulsed with its own internal luminosity, as if the building itself were alive, breathing with architectural rhythms that existed in harmony with whatever cosmic forces governed celestial realms. Waves of gentle phosphorescence rippled across the walls in slow, meditative patterns, like the building's heartbeat made visible, each pulse synchronized with currents of energy that flowed through Devaland's atmosphere like rivers of liquid awareness. The luminosity wasn't harsh or electric but warm and organic, suggesting that this architecture had grown rather than been constructed, evolved rather than designed.

I found myself flying around this impossible edifice with the fluid grace of consciousness unbound by physical laws, my awareness moving through space without resistance or effort, as if I'd been transformed into pure perception capable of navigating three-dimensional space through intention alone. The building seemed to welcome this aerial exploration, revealing new perspectives and hidden details with each shift in viewpoint, as if it possessed its own consciousness that was actively participating in my investigation.

Elaborate buttresses curved through dimensions that had no names, their architectural purpose extending beyond mere structural support into realms of pure aesthetic mathematics that somehow helped maintain the building's existence across multiple planes of reality simultaneously. These weren't crude flying buttresses like those found in Gothic cathedrals, but flowing, organic supports that resembled the ribbing of some cosmic creature's wings, each arch and curve contributing to a larger symphony of forces that kept this impossible structure stable in the fluid physics of celestial space.

The decorative elements writhed with organic beauty that suggested the architects had been artists, engineers, and mystics simultaneously, each ornamental detail serving triple functions as structural necessity, spiritual symbol, and aesthetic perfection. Carved figures emerged from the walls—not quite human, not quite divine, but something that bridged both realms with faces that radiated serenity and wisdom beyond earthly understanding. These sculptural beings seemed to move slightly as I watched, their carved robes flowing in cosmic breezes that existed only in dimensions where stone could dance and statues could breathe.

Windows weren't simple openings but complex geometric patterns that created intricate mandalas of light and shadow, each one unique yet contributing to larger patterns that only became visible when viewing multiple floors simultaneously. The glass—if it was glass—seemed to be made from crystallized space itself, transparent yet somehow containing the entire cosmos within its depths, each pane offering glimpses into other realms that existed adjacent to Devaland in the cosmic hierarchy of reality.

Balconies and terraces jutted out from the main structure at impossible angles, defying gravity through principles that transcended ordinary physics, creating platforms where celestial beings might gather to contemplate views that extended across infinite distances through multiple dimensions simultaneously. These architectural extensions seemed to exist partially in Devaland and partially in other realms, creating transitional spaces that served as bridges between different levels of reality.

THE SACRED TREASURE HUNT

The Buddha's relics—that was my specific assignment, the sacred treasures I'd been sent to locate through means that would make museum curators weep with envy and confusion. I focused this intention like a spiritual GPS, consciousness seeking whatever traces of the Enlightened One might exist in realms beyond physical decay.

Suddenly, a square metallic structure materialized—something that resembled a throne but operated according to principles that transcended ordinary furniture. The metal wasn't crude earthly alloy but some kind of celestial material that seemed to exist at the intersection of matter and light, solid enough to support whatever divine beings might need seating, yet translucent enough to suggest it was made from crystallized space itself.

Approaching this cosmic throne with the reverence of someone entering the most sacred museum in existence, I discovered its central feature: a round golden lotus base that seemed to be carved from concentrated sunlight, its petals unfolding in mathematical perfection that made earthly flowers seem like crude approximations of some divine botanical template.

Within this golden lotus sat a box—simple, elegant, mysterious. The container possessed the kind of understated presence that suggested its contents were so precious that elaborate decoration would be not just unnecessary but somehow inappropriate, like trying to improve upon silence with unnecessary noise.

THE LOCKED TREASURE

I strained my consciousness forward, attempting to peer inside this cosmic reliquary that might contain fragments of the Buddha's physical form preserved in dimensions where decay held no dominion. But the box's contents remained stubbornly opaque to my supernatural vision, protected by whatever spiritual security systems governed access to the most sacred treasures in existence.

Perhaps some mysteries were meant to remain mysteries, even to consciousness capable of interdimensional travel. Perhaps the Buddha's relics existed in frequencies that required different kinds of spiritual clearance than I currently possessed. After minutes of futile attempts to penetrate this final barrier, I reluctantly withdrew, carrying the frustration of someone who'd traveled impossible distances only to find the ultimate treasure chest locked against even supernatural intrusion.

THE DIVINE LANDSCAPE

From this cosmic throne room, I launched myself higher into Devaland's impossible geography, soaring above gardens that stretched beyond every horizon like cosmic national parks administered by enlightened landscape architects with access to vegetation that obeyed different biological laws.

The forests below resembled earthly woodlands viewed from aircraft altitude, but with a perfection of arrangement that suggested every tree had been positioned according to aesthetic principles that took into account not just visual beauty but spiritual harmonics—as if the entire landscape was designed to generate specific frequencies of peace and contentment in any consciousness fortunate enough to witness it.

Vast canopies of leaves created intricate patterns that seemed to shift and flow like living mandalas, each grove contributing to larger designs that only became visible when viewed from sufficient height. Rivers of liquid light meandered between these celestial forests, carrying currents that might have been water or might have been liquefied starlight flowing according to gravitational laws designed by cosmic engineers with advanced degrees in both physics and poetry.

THE ABSENT HOSTS

But despite the spectacular beauty of this divine geography, the beings I most hoped to encounter remained frustratingly absent. The devas—those celestial inhabitants who were supposed to populate these heavenly realms with their enlightened presence—stayed invisible to my consciousness, either absent, hidden, or existing in frequencies my current level of spiritual development couldn't access.

Perhaps Devaland operated on appointment-only policies, or maybe the beings who called this realm home had their reasons for maintaining privacy when visited by consciousness tourists who lacked proper interdimensional documentation. The realm felt inhabited—alive with presences I could sense but not directly perceive—but these celestial residents remained as elusive as whispers in languages I didn't understand.

The silence wasn't empty but full, pregnant with awareness that watched without revealing itself. I had the distinct sensation of being observed by intelligence vast and benevolent, yet these cosmic hosts remained beyond the reach of my current perceptual abilities, like trying to see ultraviolet light with ordinary human vision.

THE NEXT ASSIGNMENT

During the afternoon interview, I reported my cosmic tourism experiences with the precision of someone filing travel reports from destinations that didn't exist on any earthly itineraries. Sayadaw's golden face registered satisfaction at my successful navigation to Devaland, even if the Buddha's relics had remained tantalizingly beyond reach.

But he wasn't finished testing consciousness's navigational capabilities.

"Go to Brahmaland, next," he instructed with the casual tone of someone suggesting a day trip to a neighboring city rather than interdimensional travel to realms that existed beyond even celestial territories. "Locate the three mirrors."

Brahmaland—the realm of pure form where beings existed as concentrated consciousness without the dense material bodies that characterized both earthly and celestial existence. This was moving up the cosmic hierarchy from heaven to territories that approached the absolute, where reality became increasingly abstract until matter itself was just another form of crystallized awareness.

And I was supposed to find mirrors there—objects that implied reflection, self-awareness, perhaps cosmic instruments that showed not physical appearance but the true nature of consciousness itself when it looked upon its fundamental essence.

THE INFINITE CURRICULUM

As evening approached and I prepared for attempts to visit realms that challenged every assumption about the nature of reality and the limitations of human consciousness, I marveled at how quickly the impossible had become routine assignments in this accelerated curriculum of awakening.

Each destination pushed consciousness further from familiar territory, from earthly pagodas to celestial palaces, to now the realm of pure form itself. What began as simple breath meditation had evolved into a systematic exploration of reality's hidden dimensions, each assignment more impossible than the last, yet each one revealing new capabilities of awareness that apparently lay dormant within ordinary human consciousness.

The morning's spiritual molasses felt like a distant memory now, replaced by anticipation for journeys that would test whether consciousness could navigate territories where even the concept of location became increasingly meaningless. Tomorrow would bring attempts to visit realms that existed beyond space as ordinarily understood, searching for cosmic mirrors that might reflect truths too profound for ordinary perception to accommodate.

But tonight, I went to sleep carrying images of celestial architecture and divine gardens, consciousness already mapping routes to destinations that existed in dimensions where even heaven was just another way-station on the infinite journey toward understanding the true nature of reality itself.

In this space where the impossible had become curriculum and heaven was merely an intermediate stop, sleep finally claimed me —not as escape from the extraordinary, but as preparation for voyages that would challenge every remaining assumption about the boundaries between individual awareness and the infinite realms that awaited exploration beyond form itself.

Day 23 – The Oracle's Mirrors

Three-fifteen in the morning found me settling into meditation posture with the focused determination of someone who'd recognized a perfect storm of spiritual conditions converging into a rare opportunity. My concentration felt diamond-sharp, mindfulness operating with the precision of cosmic instrumentation that had been calibrated by weeks of intensive training. This was one of those golden windows where consciousness seemed capable of accessing any territory, visiting any realm, accomplishing any assignment that might be issued by teachers who understood the hidden curricula of awakening.

I committed to working straight through the day with minimal breaks, like a spiritual athlete who'd finally found their optimal performance zone and refused to waste a single moment of this precious alignment. When the inner machinery of meditation was running this smoothly, rest felt not just unnecessary but almost criminally wasteful—like having access to a cosmic sports car and choosing to park it in the garage.

THE STEADY TOOLS

The *nimitta* manifested with familiar reliability: blue flames dancing with the hypnotic rhythm of spiritual blowtorches, and weak ring formations that floated in inner space like halos made of condensed light. These weren't the spectacular fireworks displays of recent sessions, but their steady presence felt reassuring—reliable tools in consciousness's expanding toolkit for navigating impossible territories.

JOURNEY TO PURE FORM

The 10:17 am session brought my first serious attempt at reaching Brahmaland—that realm of pure form where beings existed as concentrated awareness without the dense matter that characterized both earthly and celestial existence. This was moving beyond even Devaland's heavenly gardens into territories where reality became increasingly abstract, approaching the fundamental source code of existence itself.

I directed focused intention toward this ultimate cosmic destination with the concentrated purpose of someone programming coordinates into spiritual GPS systems designed by enlightened engineers. The response transported me instantly into environments that challenged every assumption about architecture and the relationship between consciousness and form.

Massive golden buildings materialized around me—not the brick-brown structures of Devaland but constructions that seemed to be carved from solidified sunlight itself, their surfaces blazing with such intensity that they appeared to be generating their own solar systems within the golden metal. The scale was beyond comprehension, yet paradoxically intimate, as if I were simultaneously viewing cosmic architecture from satellite distances and examining microscopic details with impossible clarity. Each building stretched across dimensions that had no earthly equivalent, their foundations extending into realms of pure mathematics while their peaks dissolved into frequencies of light that existed beyond the visible spectrum.

These weren't buildings in any earthly sense but geometric expressions of pure consciousness that had learned to organize itself into forms that could provide whatever cosmic beings who inhabited these realms might need for their incomprehensible activities. The walls themselves seemed to be composed of crystallized thought, each surface reflecting not light but awareness itself, creating an environment where the very architecture participated in consciousness rather than simply containing it. Doorways weren't mere openings but portals between different states of being, their thresholds marked by subtle shifts in the quality of existence that passed through them.

The golden substance that comprised these structures defied every assumption about matter and construction. It wasn't metal in any recognizable sense but seemed to be awareness itself that had chosen to manifest in architectural form, dense enough to create stable structures yet translucent enough to reveal infinite depths within each wall and column. The gold possessed its own luminous intelligence, flowing like liquid when viewed peripherally but solidifying into precise geometric forms when observed directly, as if the buildings were constantly creating and recreating themselves according to the attention they received.

Golden pagodas rose into infinite heights like mathematical prayers reaching toward dimensions where numbers became poetry and equations transformed into enlightenment, their tiered roofs creating ascending spirals that followed principles of sacred geometry so pure they seemed to generate music as they rose. Each level of these cosmic towers represented different frequencies of consciousness, the architectural progression creating a visible symphony of awareness that climbed from the foundational notes of form through increasingly refined harmonics of pure spirit.

The pagodas' characteristic upward-curving eaves weren't decorative elements but functional components that channeled cosmic energies in ways that transformed the buildings into massive tuning forks resonating with the fundamental frequencies of creation itself. These architectural curves created vortexes of spiritual energy that spiraled around each structure, generating fields of enhanced consciousness that extended far beyond the buildings' physical boundaries, turning each pagoda into a broadcasting station transmitting enlightenment across multiple dimensional frequencies.

Each structure pulsed with its own internal luminosity, as if the buildings themselves were conscious entities radiating awareness through architectural forms that existed at the intersection of matter and mind. The pulsing wasn't mechanical but organic, synchronized with rhythms that seemed to echo the heartbeat of cosmic consciousness itself, each building breathing with the slow, meditative cadence of awareness so vast it encompassed entire universes within its respiratory cycles.

The luminosity emerged from within the golden substance rather than being projected onto it, suggesting that the buildings were essentially crystallized light that had learned to maintain stable form while retaining its essential luminous nature. This internal radiance created halos around each structure, aureoles of golden brilliance that extended into space like architectural auras, making it impossible to determine where the buildings ended and the surrounding environment began.

Windows and openings in these cosmic structures weren't simple apertures but complex light-management systems that seemed to regulate the flow of consciousness itself. Some windows blazed with intensity that suggested they were portals to even higher realms, while others maintained a gentle glow that invited contemplation and introspection. The light that passed through these openings wasn't ordinary illumination but compressed awareness that carried information and blessing to whatever consciousness was capable of receiving it.

Most remarkable was the absence of any sense that these structures had been constructed by anyone or anything. They felt more like natural formations of crystallized consciousness—geological expressions of pure awareness that had organized itself into forms as inevitable as mountains or oceans, but following laws that operated in realms where physics and metaphysics were the same discipline. The buildings seemed to have emerged organically from the golden landscape of Brahmaland, growing according to principles of spiritual evolution that guided their development as inevitably as DNA directs biological growth.

The architectural styles represented seemed to combine influences from every enlightened civilization that had ever existed across all dimensions and time periods, yet synthesized into forms that transcended any particular cultural tradition. Elements that resembled Tibetan monastery architecture flowed seamlessly into structures reminiscent of ancient Egyptian temples, while features that echoed Greek classical proportions merged with designs that suggested technological capabilities beyond any earthly engineering. Yet these diverse influences weren't borrowed or copied but seemed to represent the natural architectural expressions that consciousness creates when it achieves sufficient purity and freedom to manifest its essential nature.

Courtyards between the buildings weren't empty spaces but charged environments where the golden radiance of the surrounding structures converged to create zones of intensified awareness. These open areas served as gathering places for whatever cosmic beings inhabited Brahmaland, spaces designed to facilitate interactions between consciousnesses that existed at levels of development where communication happened through direct transmission of understanding rather than the crude symbol systems that characterized lower-dimensional discourse.

The pathways connecting these golden edifices seemed to be paved with crystallized intention, surfaces that responded to the consciousness that traveled upon them by adjusting their resistance and texture according to the spiritual development of the traveler. Moving along these cosmic sidewalks felt like traveling on awareness itself, each step creating ripples of golden light that spread outward like consciousness-powered shock waves announcing the presence of visiting awareness to the infinite intelligence that permeated every atom of this impossible realm.

THE COSMIC VIEWING STATION

My assignment was specific: locate the three mirrors that Sayadaw had identified as significant features of this cosmic landscape. I focused this intention like a spiritual dowsing rod, consciousness seeking whatever reflective surfaces might exist in territories where even light operated according to different principles.

The discovery emerged gradually from Brahmaland's golden geography: an ornamental frame of such exquisite craftsmanship it seemed to have been forged by cosmic artisans with access to metals that existed only in dimensions where matter and spirit were indistinguishable. The frame pulsed with its own internal radiance, suggesting it was more than a decorative border—perhaps a portal, a viewing device, or a cosmic instrument whose true function existed beyond ordinary comprehension.

As I approached this celestial artifact with the reverence of someone entering the universe's most sacred museum, the mirrors within became visible. But instead of the three reflective surfaces Sayadaw had described, four distinct mirrors were arranged within the golden framework like cosmic windows designed to show different aspects of some ultimate reality.

Each mirror possessed its own character, its own particular quality of reflection that suggested it revealed different categories of truth. One seemed to shimmer with images that felt like memories, another rippled with possibilities that tasted like futures, while the third blazed with an eternal present that made past and future seem like arbitrary divisions of something fundamentally timeless. The fourth mirror remained mysterious—its surface dark, enigmatic, perhaps reflecting truths too profound or dangerous for casual observation.

THE NAVIGATION ERROR

Confusion flooded through me like cold water hitting overheated metal. Sayadaw had specified three mirrors, but consciousness was clearly showing me four. Was this navigation error, or were there cosmic instruments here that didn't match the traditional descriptions? Perhaps different practitioners accessed different numbers of these reflective portals depending on their level of development, or maybe the mirrors themselves arranged their appearances according to the specific needs of each consciousness that managed to reach these impossible altitudes.

Having witnessed these cosmic viewing devices but not understanding their proper operation, I departed Brahmaland with the frustration of someone who'd traveled impossible distances to find libraries written in languages they couldn't read. The golden realm receded like a dream upon waking, leaving only the memory of structures that had felt more real than ordinary reality.

The 2:38 afternoon session brought another successful journey to these territories of pure form, confirming that my navigational abilities were operating with consistent reliability when concentration remained laser-focused.

THE REVELATION OF MISSED OPPORTUNITY

At three o'clock, I presented myself to Sayadaw with the mixed satisfaction of someone reporting successful completion of assignments that came with unexpected complications, Mr. Soemin serving as interpreter as usual.

"Did you see the three mirrors?" he asked with the expectant expression of a teacher checking homework from an impossibly advanced curriculum.

"Yes, but I saw four, not three," I replied, describing my cosmic discovery with the precision of someone filing reports from territories that didn't appear on any earthly maps.

His response hit like lightning, illuminating a landscape I'd been stumbling through in darkness: "Did you ask the mirrors about your past, present, and future?"

The question landed with the force of revelation mixed with crushing disappointment. These weren't just cosmic decorations or spiritual artwork—they were functional oracles, cosmic computers capable of providing information about the deepest mysteries of existence. I'd traveled to the realm of pure consciousness only to stand before the universe's ultimate information source without realizing I could access its databases.

"No, I didn't know I could ask the mirrors questions," I confessed, feeling like someone who'd visited the Library of Alexandria but left without checking out any books.

The magnitude of missed opportunity was staggering. These mirrors contained access to knowledge about my soul's entire trajectory—where consciousness had been, where it was going, what patterns and purposes were working themselves out through the temporary arrangement of awareness that I currently experienced as individual identity.

I felt the urge to protest that Mr. Soemin had forgotten to translate this crucial operational information, but wisdom suggested that blaming teachers for my lack of initiative would be both inappropriate and counterproductive. Besides, I was furious with myself—the concentration required to reach Brahmaland wasn't something I could summon at will, and I'd squandered this rare opportunity through my own failure to ask the obvious questions. Perhaps part of the lesson was learning to ask the right questions when consciousness reached these territories of ultimate access, but the missed opportunity stung with particular intensity, knowing how difficult it was to achieve the diamond-sharp focus necessary for such cosmic travel.

THE PHYSICAL TOLL

Later in the afternoon, I redirected consciousness toward more familiar territory: the Shwedagon Pagoda that existed in ordinary geographical space rather than cosmic dimensions that challenged every assumption about the nature of reality.

This time, following Sayadaw's specific guidance, I began exploration from the top of the central stupa, working downward—the proper protocol for consciousness-based temple tours that followed different navigation principles than physical pilgrimage.

The view was significantly clearer than previous attempts, though the *nimitta* created a translucent overlay that occasionally obscured details, like trying to see through cosmic sunglasses that couldn't be removed. When I directed specific attention toward the ruby-eyed Buddha that had been eluding my supernatural vision, a pale-faced Buddha statue materialized within its protective housing—perhaps not the exact figure I'd been seeking, but a sacred presence worthy of the elaborate shrine that contained it.

Flying around the temple grounds through consciousness projection revealed geography that matched my physical memories with remarkable accuracy. The same pathways, the same arrangement of smaller pagodas, the same sense of sacred space that had been consecrated by centuries of pilgrimage and prayer. The correlation between astral tourism and ordinary experience was startling in its precision.

But this intensive concentration came with physical consequences that arrived like delayed bills from cosmic accountants demanding payment for services rendered. Temporal and frontal tension gathered behind my skull with the intensity of someone who'd been trying to lift weights with their brain, pressure building in specific locations where sustained focus had strained cognitive muscles I'd never known existed.

The headache that followed felt like consciousness itself was bruised from excessive stretching, as if awareness had been pulled beyond its normal range of motion and was now contracting back to ordinary dimensions with complaints from every overstressed spiritual nerve.

THE HEALING BALM

Attempting to continue with *Anapanasati* proved futile as images cascaded through my awareness like a broken dam releasing flood waters—random visions, architectural fragments, faces, and landscapes that bore no relation to breath meditation but demanded attention with the persistence of cosmic television broadcasts that couldn't be switched off.

Salvation arrived through shifting to *Metta*—loving kindness flowing through consciousness like healing balm, explicitly designed for overstressed spiritual nervous systems. The practice immediately began dissolving both the chaotic images and the tension headache, as if compassion contained natural analgesic properties that worked on pain in dimensions where ordinary medicine had no jurisdiction.

THE INTEGRATION ASSIGNMENT

During the final interview of the day, Sayadaw issued a new assignment that pushed the boundaries of possibility into territories I hadn't even imagined: "Command the *nimitta* to go inside your body."

The instruction landed like being asked to invite lightning to take up residence in my circulatory system. These blazing displays of inner light—these cosmic phenomena that had been appearing external to my physical form—were capable of relocation to internal territories where they might serve functions I couldn't begin to comprehend.

Was this how consciousness learned to integrate its extraordinary capabilities into ordinary biological existence? Were the *nimitta* meant to become permanent features of an upgraded nervous system rather than temporary visitors from cosmic realms? And what would happen when spiritual phenomena that belonged to dimensions of pure light took up residence in organs designed for more mundane purposes?

The assignment felt like the next phase of whatever transformation had been unfolding over these weeks—moving beyond witnessing cosmic phenomena to somehow incorporating them into the very fabric of biological existence. Perhaps this was how ordinary humans became something more extraordinary, not by transcending their physical form but by inviting cosmic capabilities to take up permanent residence within it.

THE THRESHOLD OF INTEGRATION

As evening approached and I prepared for experiments that would challenge every assumption about the relationship between matter and spirit, body and consciousness, I marveled at how each day's assignments pushed the boundaries of possibility further into territories that seemed designed to systematically dissolve every limitation I'd ever accepted about human potential.

The missed opportunity with the cosmic mirrors felt like a valuable lesson in itself—that accessing ultimate knowledge required not just the ability to reach impossible territories, but the wisdom to ask the right questions once arrival was achieved. Perhaps consciousness tourism was only the beginning; true mastery required learning to interact with the cosmic instruments and oracles that existed in these higher dimensions.

Tomorrow would bring attempts to merge cosmic light with biological tissue, to make permanent residents of phenomena that had been exotic visitors. The *nimitta* that had been external light shows was apparently meant to become internal illumination, consciousness learning to upgrade its physical housing with cosmic technology that operated according to principles beyond ordinary understanding.

But tonight, I went to sleep wondering whether I was learning to become something that transcended the ordinary categories of human and divine, matter and spirit, individual consciousness and cosmic awareness itself. The journey had moved from witnessing the impossible to potentially becoming it—from cosmic tourism to cosmic integration, from visiting extraordinary realms to embodying their essence within the ordinary miracle of human biology.

~

Day 24 - The Cosmic Energy Exercise

Day twenty-four arrived with the strange temporal compression that marked retreat's middle passage—weeks that had initially stretched ahead like geological epochs had somehow contracted into what felt like accelerated time travel through an intensive spiritual curriculum. During those first uncertain days, forty-three days had seemed like a prison sentence measured in cosmic time units, but now I was racing past the halfway point with only 2.5 weeks remaining in this laboratory of consciousness transformation.

The mathematics of time perception had been completely revolutionized by intensive practice—ordinary duration dissolved when awareness was focused on territories that existed beyond clock-measured existence, making days feel simultaneously eternal and instantaneous depending on whether consciousness was wrestling with resistance or flowing through breakthrough experiences.

THE FOG OF DIMINISHED CAPACITY

Three a.m. found me emerging from sleep that felt more like temporary unconsciousness than genuine rest, my nervous system still struggling to integrate weeks of phenomena that had systematically challenged every assumption about the boundaries between possible and impossible. Sleepiness clung to awareness like spiritual fog, concentration scattered despite weeks of training that should have made focus as automatic as breathing.

The morning sessions stumbled through territories of diminished capacity, my consciousness feeling like a high-performance engine running on low-grade fuel that couldn't generate the octane necessary for accessing the extraordinary states that had become routine expectations. By 12:11 p.m., when I finally admitted defeat to this day's meditation mediocrity, frustration had settled over my practice like psychological smog that obscured even basic breath awareness.

Post-lunch salvation arrived through strategic surrender to horizontal recovery—thirty minutes allocated for napping that might yield ten minutes of actual unconsciousness if sleep's economics operated with unusual generosity. Even these fragments of rest felt like recharging depleted spiritual batteries that had been running intensive consciousness programs for weeks without adequate downtime for system maintenance.

THE LIGHTNING INVITATION

But the day's real assignment transcended ordinary meditation mechanics: commanding the *nimitta* to relocate from their usual position outside my body—typically blazing near my nose like cosmic blowtorches—to internal territories where light might merge with flesh in ways that challenged every assumption about the relationship between matter and energy.

The instruction seemed like being asked to invite lightning to take up residence in my circulatory system, or perhaps teaching stars to swim through blood vessels designed for more mundane purposes. How does one convince phenomena that belong to dimensions of pure light to relocate to organs that operate according to biological rather than cosmic laws?

Yet the attempt produced immediate and unexpected results that defied my predictions about spiritual cause and effect. Instead of dimming when directed inward, the *nimitta* blazed with enhanced intensity, as if internal relocation had somehow amplified their luminous power rather than constraining it within biological boundaries.

THE SPIRITUAL FURNACE

Most remarkably, within minutes of beginning this exercise, profound warmth began radiating from my *dantien*—that energy center located three fingers below the navel that Chinese medicine identified as the body's primary reservoir for life force cultivation. This wasn't the gentle warmth of increased circulation but something that felt like internal combustion, as if some spiritual furnace had been ignited in the core of my abdomen.

I'd practiced *qigong* for years without ever experiencing such dramatic activation of this crucial energy center—usually, *dantien* awareness required months of patient cultivation to generate even subtle sensations. But somehow, directing cosmic light into internal territories had triggered immediate energetic responses that made years of previous practice seem like preliminary exercises for this moment of actual ignition.

The teacher's warning about digestive consequences proved prophetically accurate—within hours, I'd made two urgent trips to the toilet as my internal systems responded to whatever energetic transformation was occurring in regions where spiritual phenomena and biological processes were learning to cooperate. If nothing else, this was proving to be the most effective digestive therapy I'd ever encountered, clearing internal blockages with the efficiency of cosmic plumbing services operating at interdimensional frequencies.

The exercise felt like discovering that meditation wasn't just consciousness development but sophisticated energy cultivation—*qigong* on cosmic steroids that accessed power sources unavailable to ordinary internal alchemy practices. Whatever was happening in my *dantien* region felt more substantial than visualization or imagination; this was a measurable internal transformation occurring through means that would make energy healers weep with envy.

THE SERPENT ENCOUNTER

At 2:35 p.m., stepping outside my meditation cave for a brief walking session, I encountered another resident of this spiritual sanctuary who hadn't signed up for the retreat curriculum. A massive brown snake—at least 1.5 meters of muscular reptilian grace—had been luxuriously sunbathing on the cement step like a cosmic meditation student who'd achieved the ultimate state of relaxation.

Our mutual surprise was immediate and electric. The snake's entire body contracted into liquid motion, transforming from languid sunbather into rapid-escape artist within milliseconds of registering my presence. It flowed toward the bamboo bushes with the fluid efficiency of water finding the fastest route downhill, disappearing into green sanctuaries where humans were unwelcome intrusions.

My nervous system responded with primal alarm that sent adrenaline coursing through channels recently activated by internal light experiments—heart hammering, muscles tensing, every cell suddenly hyperaware that this peaceful compound contained residents who operated according to different survival protocols than meditation practitioners seeking enlightenment.

Later, reporting this encounter to Mr. Soemin with the urgency of someone who'd discovered potential dangers in previously safe territories, his response carried the casual tone of someone discussing mildly interesting weather patterns.

"The snakes here are afraid of people," he explained with reassuring authority. "They'll escape quickly if they see anyone. There are a few around the bamboo bushes."

From that moment, my walking meditation near those towering green sanctuaries transformed from mindful strolling into hypervigilant navigation through territories where enlightenment and reptilian cohabitation required careful attention to avoid unwanted encounters between species pursuing different forms of spiritual development.

THE FISHING EXPEDITION

A few hours before my scheduled interview, I encountered Mr. Soemin along one of the flowering pathways, his expression carrying that familiar combination of expectation and amusement that suggested he was fishing for specific information.

"Did you see anything?" he asked with a smirk that reminded me powerfully of his question about *nimitta* during the retreat's earliest days, when I'd been a naive meditation tourist who thought extraordinary experiences belonged in other people's spiritual adventures.

"No," I replied, uncertain what specific phenomena he was hunting for but recognizing the expression of someone who knew exactly what should have been occurring during today's cosmic energy experiments.

His cheeky expression suggested I was missing something obvious, perhaps overlooking experiences that more skilled practitioners would recognize immediately. But what could be more significant than the spectacular *dantien* activation and digestive revolution that had already transformed this day into successful energy cultivation?

THE FAILED EXAMINATION

During the formal interview, Sayadaw opened with the same investigative approach, his golden face wearing the patient expression of someone checking homework from an impossibly advanced spiritual curriculum.

"So, how did you get on with the exercise?" he asked with the tone of a cosmic physician inquiring about symptoms that might indicate successful treatment or need for adjusted prescriptions.

"Oh, great! I really enjoyed it," I responded with genuine enthusiasm, eager to report the dramatic internal changes that felt like discovering hidden capabilities of human energetic architecture.

Both teachers smiled with expectant anticipation, their expressions suggesting they were waiting for specific discoveries that experienced practitioners would naturally report when consciousness completed today's assignment.

"So, did you see anything?" Sayadaw asked with the persistence of someone seeking confirmation of predictable spiritual phenomena.

"I didn't see anything else other than my normal *nimitta*," I replied honestly, "but my *qigong* felt incredibly strong. I could feel qi in my *dantien* area. It was the first time I've felt such powerful magnetic energy there."

The moment these words left my mouth, both teachers' expressions shifted with the synchronicity of comedic actors receiving unexpected punchlines. Sayadaw's golden face, which had been radiating expectant satisfaction just seconds before, suddenly clouded with the kind of bewildered confusion that crosses a professor's features when a promising student confidently recites completely incorrect answers to fundamental questions. His eyebrows drew together in that universal expression of someone trying to process information that defied all reasonable expectations.

Mr. Soemin's reaction was even more pronounced—his face cycling through a rapid sequence of emotions like someone watching a slow-motion disaster unfold in real time. First came surprise, his eyes widening as my words registered their full implication. Then confusion, his brow furrowing as he attempted to reconcile my enthusiastic report with what should have been occurring during the successful completion of the exercise. Finally, a kind of resigned disbelief settled over his features, the expression of someone confronting evidence that their student had been operating in a completely different universe of understanding than intended.

The glances they exchanged carried the weight of an entire conversation compressed into a single moment of shared recognition. It was the look that passes between experienced guides when they realize their carefully constructed lesson plan has somehow been interpreted through a lens so fundamentally skewed that the student has achieved the exact opposite of the intended learning objectives. Their silent communication spoke volumes: *How is this possible? How could someone practice for twenty days and still miss something this basic? What do we do now?*

Sayadaw's head tilted slightly to one side with the curious expression of someone examining a puzzle piece that belonged to the set but refused to fit into any recognizable position. His lips pursed in that way teachers do when they're rapidly recalculating their pedagogical approach after discovering that foundational assumptions about student comprehension have been completely wrong from the beginning.

Mr. Soemin's eyebrows had achieved heights that suggested they were attempting to escape his forehead entirely, while his mouth opened slightly as if preparing to speak, then closed again as he apparently reconsidered whatever initial response had been forming. The pause stretched long enough to become uncomfortable, filled with the kind of pregnant silence that precedes difficult conversations about performance and expectations.

The air in the room seemed to thicken with unspoken assessment as both teachers mentally recalibrated their understanding of my progress over the past three weeks. I could practically see the gears turning behind their eyes as they processed the implications of my response—not just what I had failed to achieve, but how thoroughly I had misunderstood what achievement would even look like in this context.

Sayadaw's expression gradually shifted from confusion to something approaching gentle concern, the look of someone who has just discovered that their patient has been taking medicine incorrectly for weeks despite repeated instructions. There was no anger or frustration in his demeanor, just the patient resignation of an experienced teacher who had encountered this particular type of fundamental misunderstanding before and knew exactly how much remedial work would be required to correct the course.

Mr. Soemin's face had settled into what could only be described as academic disappointment—not the harsh judgment of personal failure, but the measured assessment of someone cataloging the precise nature and extent of educational gaps that would need to be addressed through more systematic intervention. His expression carried the weight of someone realizing that what they had assumed was advanced coursework would need to be suspended while basic competencies were established from scratch.

THE REVELATION OF FAILURE

Mr. Soemin leaned forward with the focused attention of someone preparing to deliver crucial information that had somehow been overlooked during cosmic energy experiments.

"So, you didn't see the internal organs?" he asked with the precision of a spiritual diagnostician checking for symptoms that should have been obvious.

"Internal organs? No." Confusion crashed through my awareness like cold water hitting overheated metal. What were they talking about? Was he speaking metaphorically—some spiritual symbolism I'd missed? Or was I literally supposed to see my own internal organs, like some kind of meditation-powered X-ray vision that could peer through flesh and bone to observe my liver, kidneys, and heart pumping away in their biological darkness?

The concept seemed absurd yet tantalizingly possible given everything else I'd experienced over the past three weeks. If consciousness could travel to celestial realms and project across impossible distances, why couldn't it also turn inward to illuminate the hidden geography of my own physical form? But the idea of actually seeing my internal organs felt like crossing some boundary between meditation and medical imaging that I'd never imagined could be breached through purely mental means.

What cosmic curriculum had I somehow failed to access despite hours of dedicated practice?

Sayadaw's explanation arrived like lightning illuminating a landscape I'd been stumbling through in complete darkness. I hadn't seen my internal organs because I'd failed to actually place my mind inside my body—despite sincere efforts and genuine intention, consciousness had remained anchored outside my physical form, attracted to the familiar external position where *nimitta* typically manifested its spectacular displays.

If I'd successfully relocated awareness to internal territories, the *nimitta* would have followed like loyal pets, appearing inside my body where they could illuminate biological architecture with the same clarity they brought to cosmic realms. The fact that I continued seeing luminous phenomena at my nose's tip throughout the entire exercise proved that my mind had never actually moved from its customary external position, despite my absolute conviction that I'd been directing consciousness into internal landscapes.

THE PERFORMANCE REVIEW

"How long have you been here?" Mr. Soemin asked with the stern attention of someone preparing to deliver performance evaluation feedback.

"Twenty days or so?" I replied, suddenly sensing that this question was leading toward conclusions I wouldn't enjoy receiving.

"So, you've had twenty days of practicing mind control." His face adopted the severe expression of someone confronting disappointing test results. "And you could not place the mind inside your body? You must try harder, la!" The last word carried his Singaporean accent—linguistic evidence of time spent in territories where English mixed with local expressions to create communication that was both familiar and foreign.

Embarrassment flooded through my system like toxic waste contaminating every cell of confidence I'd been accumulating through weeks of extraordinary experiences. I'd utterly failed an assignment that apparently represented basic competency in consciousness control, despite twenty days of intensive training that should have made such elemental tasks as automatic as breathing.

THE ARITHMETIC OF HUMILIATION

The sensation felt like discovering I'd been attending advanced physics courses while still unable to perform basic arithmetic—somehow I'd been accessing cosmic realms and projecting consciousness across impossible distances while failing to accomplish the fundamental skill of relocating awareness within my biological boundaries.

I'd thought I was succeeding, excelling, achieving unprecedented spiritual developments that marked me as an exceptional student of consciousness. Instead, I'd revealed myself as someone who could travel to Brahmaland but couldn't navigate the few inches from external awareness to internal organs—a cosmic tourist who'd somehow bypassed basic spiritual geography to reach advanced destinations through navigation errors rather than genuine competence.

Leaving the interview felt like walking through psychological quicksand, disappointment and frustration mixing into emotional compounds that poisoned even basic self-confidence. How could I have been so wrong about my capabilities? What other fundamental misunderstandings were masquerading as spiritual achievement in my delusional assessment of progress?

THE COMBAT SESSION

Back in my meditation cave, determination crystallized with the brittle intensity of someone who'd been publicly humiliated and refused to accept defeat as permanent status. I had to succeed—not just for personal development but to restore credibility with teachers whose respect felt more precious than any cosmic vision or interdimensional travel experience.

Arranging myself in meditation posture with the focused resolve of someone preparing for spiritual combat, I committed to working through the usual 5 p.m. break—no rest, no refreshment, just sustained effort until consciousness finally learned to follow basic directional commands with the obedience that twenty days of training should have established.

But the moment my eyelids closed, the *nimitta* blazed to life at my nose's tip with the predictable reliability of cosmic spotlights that had been programmed to appear in specific locations regardless of my conscious intentions.

Aargh!

THE MECHANICS OF FAILURE

Sudden understanding struck with the force of revelation mixed with crushing frustration. If I could see the *nimitta* at my nose's external position, then my mind remained stubbornly anchored outside my body despite every sincere attempt to relocate awareness to internal territories. The visual evidence was undeniable—consciousness was behaving like a disobedient pet that returned to familiar locations no matter how carefully I attempted redirection.

The mechanism of this failure became crystal clear with humiliating precision. Although I'd genuinely believed I was placing awareness inside my body, the moment the *nimitta* appeared with its irresistible luminous intensity, my attention automatically snapped back to its external manifestation like iron filings drawn to cosmic magnets. This happened without conscious decision—an involuntary reflex that had been conditioned by weeks of spectacular light shows that trained consciousness to focus wherever the most impressive displays were occurring.

But it was automatic! I couldn't help this gravitational pull toward phenomena that blazed like dancing light bulbs at my nose's tip. How could anyone ignore such overwhelming illumination? Trying to maintain internal awareness while *nimitta* performed their cosmic light shows felt like attempting meditation while someone aimed floodlights directly at my face—technically possible but practically absurd.

And then it hit me with the force of cosmic irony: this was exactly why Mr. Soemin had been telling me, repeatedly, from the very beginning, to try to ignore the *nimitta*. His seemingly restrictive guidance hadn't been about suppressing extraordinary experiences—it had been essential preparation for this exact moment when I would need the discipline to resist their magnetic attraction to access even more fundamental capabilities. Every warning I'd dismissed as unnecessarily cautious had been strategic conditioning designed to prevent precisely this addiction to spectacular phenomena that was now sabotaging my ability to perform basic consciousness control.

I'd thought I was being wise by embracing the extraordinary displays, celebrating consciousness's creative capabilities instead of restricting them through artificial limitations. But I'd been training myself into a spiritual trap, becoming so dependent on external cosmic entertainment that I'd lost the ability to direct awareness according to intention rather than attraction. The very phenomena that had made me feel like an advanced practitioner had been systematically undermining the foundational skills that made genuine advancement possible.

THE SPIRITUAL ADDICTION

The solution emerged with the clarity of mathematical proof: the only way to place consciousness inside my body was to ignore the *nimitta* altogether—to resist their magnetic attraction and maintain internal focus despite cosmic fireworks designed specifically to hijack attention.

Unfortunately, this felt like being asked to ignore the sun while staring directly at it, or perhaps maintaining conversation while orchestra concerts were being performed inside my skull. The *nimitta* had become habit-forming in the most literal sense—neurological pathways had been carved by weeks of spectacular experiences that made external focus feel not just natural but irresistible.

This was a habit that apparently couldn't be broken through willpower alone—twenty days of conditioning had created automatic responses that operated below the threshold of conscious control. The *nimitta* had become spiritual crack cocaine, generating experiences so compelling that consciousness couldn't resist their attraction even when such resistance was essential for progressing to more advanced territories of inner development.

THE LESSON IN DISGUISE

As evening approached and I prepared for what would be an extended campaign to break neurological habits that had become embedded in consciousness's basic operating system, I realized this failure might represent the most important lesson of the entire retreat: discovering that even extraordinary spiritual achievements could become obstacles when they prevented access to even more fundamental capabilities that lay hidden beneath layers of spectacular distraction.

The humiliation stung, but it carried essential wisdom about the relationship between the spectacular and the fundamental. I'd been seduced by cosmic light shows while missing the basic mechanics of consciousness control that made advanced practice possible. Like a student who'd learned to solve complex equations while skipping basic arithmetic, I'd acquired impressive capabilities that were ultimately useless without elementary competencies.

Tomorrow would bring renewed attempts to achieve what should have been elementary consciousness control, but tonight I went to sleep humbled by the recognition that mastering the spectacular was far easier than mastering the simple—and that true spiritual development might require learning to ignore the very phenomena that made practice feel successful to access capabilities that operated in dimensions where even cosmic light shows were mere preliminaries to the real work of awakening.

In this space where cosmic tourism had revealed itself as a sophisticated distraction from basic spiritual mechanics, sleep finally claimed me—not as an escape from humiliation, but as preparation for the harder work of learning to ignore the impossible in service of mastering the elementary.

Day 25 - The X-Ray Awakening

Dawn arrived with consciousness already deep in forensic investigation of its own mysteries. The skeleton materialized first —that familiar calcium architecture that had been visiting my pre-waking awareness for days—but today brought the solution to another puzzle that had been haunting these liminal moments between sleep and full consciousness.

The script that danced across white backgrounds behind my closed eyelids finally revealed its secret identity with the shock of recognition that made my heart skip a beat. This wasn't mysterious cosmic correspondence from interdimensional intelligences —it was my own handwriting! Those flowing cursive lines belonged to the meditation diary I kept beside my bed, the careful logs of sitting sessions that had become my spiritual accounting system for tracking progress through territories that existed beyond ordinary documentation.

THE EXPANDING PERCEPTION

The revelation struck with the force of cosmic comedy mixed with profound realization about consciousness's expanding capabilities. My awareness had been projecting outward with increasing strength each day, developing supernatural sensitivity to white objects that stood out against the darker backgrounds of both external reality and internal vision.

That explained the skeleton—consciousness detecting the bone-white calcium structures that formed my internal architecture. And the writing—awareness, picking up the ink patterns on white paper that lay within whatever radius this expanding perception could reach. It was like discovering I'd been developing psychic vision, but only for objects that met specific color criteria—a cosmic X-ray sight that operated according to wavelengths I didn't understand, but could no longer deny.

THE EDGE OF SURRENDER

Four a.m. found me settling into meditation posture with the confident determination of someone who'd finally achieved adequate rest after days of spiritual insomnia. My sleep had been profound and restorative, consciousness recharging whatever batteries powered these extraordinary phenomena that were transforming daily existence into ongoing expeditions through impossible territories.

Concentration felt sharp and reliable, mindfulness operating with the precision of instruments that had been calibrated through weeks of intensive use. The day carried an unmistakable quality of potential—that particular atmospheric pressure that preceded breakthrough sessions where consciousness discovered new capabilities that redefined the boundaries of human possibility.

But confidence evaporated the moment I attempted the exercise that had humiliated me so thoroughly during yesterday's interview. Repeatedly, systematically, with the persistence of someone slowly going insane, I failed to see my internal organs despite every technique, every strategy, every desperate attempt to relocate awareness from external *nimitta* positions to internal biological territories.

The failure wasn't just disappointing—it was crushing, the kind of spiritual defeat that made me question everything I thought I understood about my capabilities and the trajectory of practice that had been generating such spectacular results in other domains of consciousness exploration.

Quitting began feeling not just reasonable but necessary for preserving whatever psychological integrity remained after discovering that twenty-five days of intensive training hadn't established even basic competency in consciousness control. The retreat had already delivered extraordinary experiences that would provide lifetime material for contemplating the nature of awareness and reality—perhaps it was time to declare victory and escape before additional failures revealed how thoroughly I'd been deluding myself about spiritual achievement.

THE WEIGHT OF INVESTMENT

But the practical implications of surrender felt equally devastating. How could I face Mr. Soemin with the confession that I wanted to quit after he'd invested so much guidance and encouragement in my development? His words echoed with accusatory precision: *You must try harder, la!* Every day, both teachers looked forward to hearing progress reports with the anticipation of someone tracking scientific experiments in consciousness expansion. They regarded me as gifted, possessed of *parami* that made advanced teachings accessible—how could I shatter that assessment by revealing myself as someone who'd been faking competence through lucky accidents rather than genuine skill?

The financial and temporal investments felt equally binding. I'd traveled thousands of miles and taken months away from work responsibilities to access teachings that might never be available again. This opportunity represented a convergence of circumstances that belonged more to fantasy than ordinary life planning—walking away now would mean accepting that I'd squandered chances that most practitioners could only dream of receiving.

THE TURNING POINT

I can do this! I can do this! I can do this!

The mantra began as desperate self-hypnosis but gradually transformed into genuine determination as I circled the compound like someone walking off a nervous breakdown. Round after round through the flowering pathways, past the bamboo sanctuaries where snakes sunbathed and dragonflies painted the air with iridescent calligraphy, repeating the affirmation until it began feeling less like wishful thinking and more like inevitable truth.

By lunchtime, psychological momentum had shifted from despair toward grim resolve—the kind of focused determination that emerges when all alternatives have been exhausted and only success remains as an acceptable outcome.

THE SURGICAL PRECISION

The afternoon session began with surgical precision in concentration that felt like consciousness finally operating under conscious control rather than being hijacked by whatever phenomena chose to manifest. Slowly, carefully, with the methodical attention of someone performing delicate surgery on their awareness, I directed focused attention up and down the length of my spinal cord.

Instead of allowing the *nimitta* to appear wherever they wanted—typically at my nose's external position where they could monopolize attention with their spectacular displays—I maintained internal focus with the discipline of someone who'd finally understood that spiritual achievement required mastering basic skills before attempting advanced techniques.

Then, suddenly, impossibly, the internal landscape began revealing itself with the clarity of medical imaging equipment designed by cosmic engineers.

THE INTERNAL ARCHITECTURE

The outlines of my throat and esophagus materialized first—the delicate tubular passage that connected mouth to stomach, its muscular walls clearly defined against the darker background of surrounding tissue. The esophageal structure appeared like an elegant biological pipeline, its smooth curves and gentle contractions visible in extraordinary detail as if consciousness had been granted access to internal architectural blueprints usually hidden from awareness.

Then the illumination spread deeper, revealing my stomach as a muscular pouch nestled beneath the ribcage, its curved walls expanding and contracting with digestive rhythms I'd never consciously witnessed. My ribcage appeared next—a protective cathedral of curved bones forming an elegant cage around vital organs, each rib arcing gracefully from spine to sternum in perfect symmetrical harmony. Finally, the entire skeletal framework blazed into view—my backbone with its vertebrae stacked like organic building blocks assembled by divine architects, each bone clearly defined in the luminous display that transformed my body into a living X-ray of impossible clarity.

Most remarkably, a ball of brilliant light—my *nimitta* operating as internal illumination rather than external distraction—moved up and down through this bone architecture like a flashlight beam controlled by consciousness itself. The entire display rotated and suspended itself in three-dimensional space directly in front of my closed eyes, creating holographic images more vivid and detailed than any medical textbook illustration.

At times, the soft tissue became completely transparent, leaving only my backbone visible with crystal clarity—each vertebra's unique shape and size rendered in perfect anatomical detail, the gentle S-curve of spinal architecture that kept consciousness upright in its biological housing visible from perspectives that no external observer could ever achieve.

The shock of witnessing my own internal architecture rendered in impossible detail left me speechless—this was beyond anything I'd imagined consciousness could achieve, a capability so extraordinary it felt like discovering I'd been carrying a medical imaging laboratory inside my awareness without ever knowing it existed.

THE VICTORY SPRINT

The moment the session ended, I exploded from my meditation posture like someone who'd just discovered buried treasure in their own backyard. My legs carried me across the compound toward Mr. Soemin's office with the urgency of someone delivering news that couldn't wait for scheduled appointments or proper protocol.

I found him in the corridor outside the dining hall, probably preparing for some routine administrative task that suddenly seemed trivial compared to the breakthrough that had just revolutionized my understanding of consciousness's hidden capabilities.

"Mr. Soemin, I saw it!" The words burst out before diplomatic considerations could edit my excitement into more appropriate channels.

He stopped and looked at me with the careful attention of someone assessing whether genuine breakthrough or delusional enthusiasm was being reported from the frontlines of spiritual experimentation.

"I saw my ribcage and the backbone!" I exclaimed with the breathless excitement of someone who'd just witnessed the impossible becoming routine.

"*Sadhu, sadhu, sadhu!*" His face transformed into pure satisfaction, the expression of someone whose confidence in his student had been thoroughly vindicated. "Come, I'll take you to see Sayadaw."

The brief journey to Sayadaw's quarters felt like a victory parade for consciousness itself, every step across the compound carrying the euphoric lightness of someone who'd just been liberated from spiritual prison. The familiar flowering pathways that had witnessed my desperate circles of self-doubt just hours earlier now seemed to celebrate my passage with brighter colors and more fragrant blooms, as if the entire environment was participating in my vindication.

Mr. Soemin's pace quickened with barely contained excitement, his body language radiating the satisfaction of a teacher whose faith in his student had been spectacularly validated. His eager stride suggested he was as thrilled to deliver this news as I was to report it, understanding better than I did the significance of crossing this particular threshold in consciousness development.

After yesterday's humiliating failure, this success carried emotional weight far beyond the specific achievement—it represented proof that persistence could overcome even the most stubborn obstacles to spiritual development. The psychological whiplash from yesterday's crushing defeat to today's breakthrough felt like emotional vertigo, my nervous system still recalibrating from despair to triumph with the disorienting speed of someone whose entire self-assessment had been revolutionized in twenty-four hours.

But more than personal vindication, this felt like consciousness itself had finally remembered its true capabilities after being amnesia-bound for decades. The revelation that human awareness contained medical imaging technology more sophisticated than anything hospitals possessed challenged every assumption I'd held about the limitations of biological perception. This wasn't just seeing internal organs—this was discovering that consciousness came equipped with diagnostic capabilities that belonged more to science fiction than spiritual practice.

The approaching interview carried the weight of reporting a scientific breakthrough that would fundamentally alter how these teachers understood their students' potential trajectory. Yesterday I'd been someone who couldn't perform basic mind placement exercises; today I was demonstrating capabilities that represented the successful transmission of secret knowledge across centuries of careful preservation. The transformation felt so complete that it was like reporting as an entirely different person who happened to inhabit the same biological housing.

Relief flooded through my system like medicine reaching infected wounds, all the psychological pressure that had been building since yesterday's disaster simply melting away like frost touched by morning sunlight. I could relax again, breathe normally, exist without the constant anxiety that I was failing to meet expectations from teachers whose opinion had become more precious than any external validation.

THE COSMIC VIDEO GAMES

But success bred curiosity, and the afternoon transformed into extended experimentation with capabilities that felt like discovering superpowers hidden within ordinary human consciousness. I spent hours playing with the *nimitta* like a child who'd been given access to cosmic video games that operated according to thought-responsive controls.

"Washing" my face with luminous displays revealed my features from external perspectives—every detail of facial architecture rendered in perfect clarity, including tiny hairs and moles that I'd never examined with such microscopic precision. It was like having access to mirrors that operated through consciousness rather than reflected light, showing aspects of physical appearance that external observation could never achieve.

THE LIVING HEART

The beating heart was most spectacular—a muscular pump rendered in perfect anatomical detail, contracting and expanding with the rhythm that had been sustaining life since birth. When I focused specific attention on this vital organ, it separated from the torso entirely, floating in front of my closed eyes while continuing its essential work with mechanical precision that seemed miraculous when viewed from perspectives that ordinary consciousness could never access.

Everything responded to mental commands with the speed of thought itself—no delay between intention and manifestation, no learning curve for operating this biological imaging system that came standard with human awareness when properly activated. Whatever I wanted to examine, rotate, or isolate simply responded to focused attention like sophisticated technology designed to be operated through pure consciousness.

The *nimitta* could be moved systematically from head to toes, illuminating different regions of biological architecture as it traveled through internal territories like a cosmic flashlight exploring previously hidden landscapes. When held stationary, it would brighten and expand, revealing larger areas with increased clarity and detail.

THE HYPERSTIMULATED SYSTEM

But the most profound transformation was occurring in my physical nervous system itself. From late afternoon onward, my upper lip had developed hypersensitivity that bordered on the supernatural—awareness so acute it could detect the pulses of tiny blood vessels that normally operated below the threshold of conscious perception.

My mind felt hyper-alert, concentration and mindfulness operating at levels that made previous peak experiences seem like preliminary exercises in basic attention. It was like discovering that consciousness came equipped with sensitivity settings that had been turned down to minimal levels for ordinary existence but could be dramatically amplified when proper techniques unlocked their full potential.

Most mysteriously, the fuzzy static-like dots that had become familiar background features of inner vision began moving at dramatically accelerated speeds. Instead of their usual slow drift, they were now whizzing around like cosmic particles in some kind of spiritual particle accelerator. I knew something extraordinary was happening, some fundamental shift in the basic operating parameters of consciousness itself.

THE ULTIMATE DEMONSTRATION

The seven p.m. group sitting brought the day's ultimate revelation about the scope of these emerging capabilities. My mind felt like it had been injected with liquid lightning—hyper stimulated beyond anything achievable through caffeine or any earthly stimulant. This was alertness so intense it felt like my eyelids had been taped to my eyebrows, consciousness operating at frequencies that made ordinary wakefulness seem like a form of sleep.

Behind closed eyes, the background static moved at velocities that defied easy description—those familiar fuzzy dots transformed into high-speed cosmic traffic. These flowing patterns seemed to indicate some fundamental acceleration in whatever energetic processes underlay visual perception itself.

My entire torso—from face to abdomen—blazed with luminous intensity that transformed biological tissue into living light. The sensation felt like being baptized in liquid starlight, every cell suddenly glowing with its own internal illumination.

Then came the ultimate demonstration of these developing capabilities.

Looking toward the young monk sitting directly in front of me, his entire skeleton became visible with crystalline clarity—every bone rendered in perfect anatomical detail, the complete calcium architecture that provided structural support for his meditation posture clearly displayed despite his robes and flesh remaining completely intact from any external perspective.

I opened and closed my eyes repeatedly, checking whether this was a hallucination or genuine perception, but the skeletal display remained consistent and stable. This wasn't imagination but some form of supernatural X-ray vision that operated through consciousness rather than electromagnetic radiation.

THE LIVING ANATOMY TEXTBOOK

Looking around the hall, I found I couldn't see other practitioners' internal structures—perhaps distance created limitations, or maybe the intensity required for such perception could only be sustained for brief periods or specific targets.

But examining my right arm provided spectacular confirmation that these capabilities were both real and precise. Every bone was visible in perfect detail: the ulna and radius forming the forearm's dual structure, the intricate carpals of the wrist, the metacarpals extending through the hand, and the delicate phalanges of each finger. This wasn't the blurred approximation of medical X-rays but crystal-clear anatomical imaging that revealed bone structure with clarity that surpassed any technology I'd ever encountered.

THE SECRET TRANSMISSION

At the session's end, I immediately sought out Mr. Soemin with the urgency of someone who'd just witnessed phenomena that challenged every assumption about human perceptual limitations. His response led to another immediate audience with Sayadaw, where the day's discoveries were evaluated with the serious attention of teachers assessing whether their student had successfully accessed capabilities that represented lifetimes of accumulated spiritual treasure.

Mr. Soemin's explanation transformed the day's achievements from a personal breakthrough into a historical privilege. This was a secret technique that had been handed down from monk to monk across generations, preserved through careful transmission within closed communities of advanced practitioners. But Sayadaw had made the revolutionary decision to disseminate these teachings to small groups of qualified laypeople, breaking centuries of tradition to share knowledge that had previously been restricted to monastic communities.

"You have adequate *parami* to learn this technique," Mr. Soemin explained with the gravity of someone delivering news about spiritual inheritance rights. "You are very fortunate to learn from Sayadaw himself."

The words carried weight beyond their immediate meaning—I was receiving teachings that most practitioners could only dream of accessing, knowledge that bridged the gap between ordinary human consciousness and capabilities that belonged more to enlightened beings than biological entities struggling with basic meditation competencies.

THE PRIVILEGE OF TRANSMISSION

I felt genuinely privileged, not just for the specific techniques but for the recognition that whatever spiritual accumulations I'd brought to this retreat had been sufficient to qualify for instructions that represented the transmission of hidden knowledge across centuries of careful preservation.

The rest of the evening dissolved into extended exploration of these newfound capabilities, using the *nimitta* to examine different regions of biological architecture with the enthusiasm of someone who'd been given access to the universe's most sophisticated imaging technology. Each investigation revealed new details, new perspectives on the miraculous machinery that sustained consciousness in its temporary biological housing.

As I finally prepared for sleep, my body still humming with residual energy from the day's extraordinary activations, I marveled at how completely this single breakthrough had transformed my understanding of human potential and the hidden capabilities that lay dormant within ordinary awareness, waiting for the proper techniques and sufficient preparation to unlock treasures that had been hidden in plain sight for an entire lifetime.

Tomorrow would bring new opportunities to explore these territories where consciousness revealed its true nature as something far more extraordinary than conventional understanding could accommodate. But tonight I went to sleep carrying the day's revelations like cosmic treasures that would take years to fully understand and integrate into whatever version of human existence was emerging from this systematic dissolution of every limitation I'd ever accepted about the boundaries of possible experience.

In this space where consciousness had revealed its capacity for supernatural perception and ancient wisdom had been transmitted across centuries to unlock capabilities that transcended every assumption about human potential, sleep finally claimed me —not as escape from the extraordinary, but as integration of powers that would forever change how I understood the relationship between awareness and the miraculous architecture of embodied existence.

Day 26 – The Transcendent Vision

Sleep had become a negotiation with consciousness that refused to acknowledge ordinary schedules. I surfaced repeatedly throughout the night, my internal clock completely confused by spiritual phenomena that operated according to cosmic time rather than earthly rotation. Each awakening brought the disorienting sensation that dawn must surely be approaching, only to discover hours of darkness still stretching ahead like territories my nervous system hadn't learned to navigate.

But morning brought revelations that made sleep deprivation feel like a trivial price for accessing capabilities that belonged more to science fiction than human biology.

THE FLOATING ANATOMY LESSON

Four or five complete skeletons floated through my inner vision like a supernatural anatomy lesson conducted by cosmic professors who'd decided my bedroom was the perfect classroom for studying death's architecture. Some appeared in profile, while others faced forward, drawing the direct attention of beings who'd somehow achieved independent existence despite being constructed entirely of calcium and spiritual light.

Most displayed crystal-clear torsos and skulls that seemed carved from luminous bone. However, their legs remained frustratingly blurred—perhaps distance created limitations, or maybe consciousness required additional training to achieve complete skeletal clarity from skull to toe.

But the most extraordinary aspect was my apparent ability to manipulate these anatomical displays like operating some kind of spiritual CAD software designed for exploring biological architecture. I could zoom in and out with the precision of high-powered microscopes, rotate entire skeletal structures to examine them from any angle, and focus on specific vertebrae with detail that made medical textbooks seem crude by comparison.

All of this happened naturally as I emerged from sleep—no meditation required, no special effort or concentration. It was like discovering that consciousness came equipped with default settings that had finally been activated after weeks of intensive spiritual boot camp.

THE CHRISTMAS ORNAMENT ORGANS

Oh, only skeletons? I thought with the casual disappointment of someone who'd grown accustomed to increasingly spectacular displays. *I'd like to see organs.*

The response was immediate and overwhelming.

Instantly, one of the floating skeletons filled with brilliant red color—organs materializing within the bone framework like Christmas ornaments being hung on an invisible tree. I zoomed in on the crimson display and found myself staring at my own beating heart with clarity that made cardiac surgeons' visualization equipment seem primitive by comparison.

The heart valves were visible in perfect anatomical detail—those delicate flaps that regulated blood flow opening and closing with mechanical precision that seemed miraculous when viewed from perspectives that ordinary consciousness could never access. I could even see blood flowing through the valves with each cardiac cycle, the crimson streams entering and exiting the chambers in precise hydraulic choreography that revealed the heart's function as both mechanical pump and sacred vessel for life force itself.

My lungs appeared next, plucked straight from anatomy textbooks but rendered in full three-dimensional color—pink, spongy tissues that expanded and contracted with respiratory rhythms I could observe from inside my chest cavity. The entrails manifested as a somewhat blurry red mass, perhaps too complex for detailed observation, while my stomach appeared in distinctive off-white coloration that made it easily distinguishable from surrounding organs.

THE COMMAND CENTER

When I directed attention toward the skull, a red mass became visible within the bone cavity—my brain, that mysterious command center that was somehow observing itself through means that neuroscience couldn't explain. Zooming in revealed white, twisting, canal-like structures that matched perfectly with every brain illustration I'd ever encountered, except these were alive, pulsing with whatever electrical activity sustained consciousness itself.

Other organs presented themselves for inspection like components in some cosmic anatomy lesson where I was both student and subject.

Most remarkably, each organ responded to mental commands with the obedience of perfectly trained assistants. The moment I "ordered" a specific structure to present itself for examination, it would separate from the body's main architecture and hover directly in front of my closed eyes, rotating slowly to provide optimal viewing angles. When I wanted to examine my eyes, they came out of their sockets and suspended themselves in space before me, allowing me to rotate them at various angles like biological specimens floating in the laboratory of consciousness.

When I moved my physical arms and legs, the floating skeleton mimicked these movements with perfect synchronization. This spiritual mirror reflected not just static anatomy but dynamic motion through space. Moving the *nimitta* up and down my body produced corresponding balls of light that traveled through the skeletal display like cosmic elevators operating in dimensions where biology and luminosity were the same phenomenon.

Even more extraordinary was the discovery that I could examine my hands with eyes closed in a pitch-dark room and see them in full color as if someone had installed internal lighting systems that operated independently of external illumination sources. Individual hairs on my arms and hands were visible with microscopic clarity, while the intricate lines mapping my palms appeared with detail that would make forensic investigators weep with envy. The impossibility of this struck me profoundly—even with eyes open, it's not possible to see color in a dark environment, yet here I was with eyes closed under an eye-mask in a dark room, perceiving full-spectrum color with clarity that surpassed ordinary daylight vision.

Thinking of any body part caused it to light up brilliantly, revealing the bone structures nested within soft tissue, like discovering that I'd been wearing X-ray vision glasses my entire life but had never learned to use them properly.

THE EXTENDED RANGE

My *nimitta* had achieved unprecedented strength and range, no longer limited to the few feet between nose and ceiling but capable of projection to the sky—extending beyond even the mosquito net that had previously marked the boundaries of indoor spiritual phenomena.

I experimented with looking through walls to observe the trees outside, but solid barriers remained frustratingly opaque despite my enhanced capabilities. Similarly, attempts to see through walls into adjacent rooms yielded only darkness—this supernatural vision had specific limitations that required further investigation.

THE QI REVELATION

Physical sensations had also reached new levels of intensity and strangeness. It felt like insects were conducting microscopic expeditions across my scalp, tiny legs tickling nerve endings that had become hypersensitive to stimulation normally below the threshold of conscious awareness. My cheeks experienced constant small pulls and twitches as if facial muscles were receiving electrical signals from sources I couldn't identify.

Most remarkably, my lips felt both light and hollow while simultaneously detecting the pulses of tiny blood vessels with precision that made ordinary touch seem crude by comparison. I could feel circulation patterns that belonged more to medical monitoring equipment than casual physical sensation.

When I sent consciousness down through my hand like directing spiritual electricity through biological circuits, hot and cold tingling sensations erupted simultaneously—an impossible contradiction that somehow felt perfectly natural. The experience was both thermal extremes occurring in the same location at the same time, as if consciousness had access to temperature spectrums that physics hadn't discovered yet.

This is qi.

The realization struck with the force of a scientific breakthrough mixed with ancient wisdom validation. Not only could I feel this mysterious energy that Chinese medicine had been describing for millennia, but I could *see* it moving through my body like visible rivers of life force flowing through channels that Western anatomy didn't acknowledge.

The *nimitta* was the visual representation of *qi* itself—consciousness finally developing sufficient sensitivity to perceive the energetic infrastructure that sustained biological existence. I suspected that ancient *qigong* masters had also developed these same capabilities, using supernatural vision to map meridians and explain how energy cultivation functioned at levels normally invisible to ordinary awareness.

With this new understanding, I felt capable of creating entirely new qigong training based on direct observation of energy patterns rather than theoretical speculation about invisible forces. This was empirical research conducted through enhanced consciousness rather than external instrumentation.

THE NIGHT SHIFT

I spent at least an hour playing with these newfound capabilities like a child who'd discovered the most sophisticated video game ever created, examining various body parts and organs with the enthusiasm of someone finally granted access to the user manual for human biological architecture.

When I checked my watch, 1:50 a.m. glowed in the darkness—sleep was essential if I intended to function during tomorrow's formal practice sessions. But unlike previous experiences where *nimitta* faded when I stopped actively generating them, the skeletons refused to disappear, maintaining their luminous presence throughout the night like spiritual nightlights that had forgotten how to switch off.

When I awoke at 3:48 a.m., they were still there—faithful anatomical companions floating through the darkness with the reliability of cosmic phenomena that operated according to their autonomous schedules. I spent another hour playing with these displays, moving my tongue and watching it light up inside my mouth like a pink muscle equipped with its own internal illumination system.

At one point, my complete set of teeth separated from my skull and floated toward me like a grinning dental advertisement that had achieved independent motion—amusing but slightly unsettling evidence that consciousness could disassemble body parts for individual inspection.

THE LASER SYSTEMS

The 5:00 to 5:20 a.m. sitting revealed that concentration and mindfulness had achieved unprecedented strength and stability. The *nimitta* manifested immediately with power that made previous experiences seem like preliminary exercises in spiritual apprenticeship.

Most significantly, I'd discovered two distinct beams of light emanating from my body like biological laser systems that had been installed without my knowledge or conscious permission. One emerged from my third eye—that mystical point between my eyebrows where spiritual traditions claimed higher perception was located. The other originated from my body's center, somewhere beneath the sternum, where the heart chakra was supposed to reside.

To confirm these weren't hallucinations or wishful thinking, I deliberately moved the beams in different directions, even crossing them like cosmic light sabers operated through pure intention. Both responded to mental commands with perfect obedience, reaching beyond the sky into space itself with intensities that made ordinary flashlights seem like flickering candles.

When the beams crossed, they created brilliant illumination at their intersection point, while the central beam sometimes bent like a flexible cord made of condensed starlight. Both were rainbow-colored, creating a spectrum of hues that didn't exist in ordinary light sources, while my entire spinal cord had transformed into a column of rainbow radiance that extended from tailbone to skull like some kind of internal aurora borealis.

THE DREADED ASSIGNMENT

But yesterday's interview had brought an assignment that filled me with genuine apprehension: Sayadaw had asked me to visit hell.

The request felt less like spiritual instruction and more like being asked to volunteer for psychological torture. The prospect of witnessing realms designed around pure suffering filled me with genuine dread. This assignment felt like spiritual Russian roulette with potentially traumatizing consequences.

I spent considerable time debating whether to attempt this journey into territories that every wisdom tradition warned against approaching. But ultimately, trust in Sayadaw's judgment won over personal fears. If he believed I was capable of surviving such an expedition, perhaps his assessment of my spiritual resilience was more accurate than my anxious self-evaluation.

At 8:45 a.m., after generating a particularly strong *nimitta* through intensive concentration, I suppressed every survival instinct and resolved to visit whatever cosmic territories qualified as hell in this spiritual cartography.

THE UNDERWORLD EXPEDITION

The journey transported me immediately into environments that felt like psychological nightmares made manifest. I found myself flying through smoky, dark places where no sun had ever shone—landscapes of perpetual shadow that seemed explicitly designed to drain hope from any consciousness unfortunate enough to witness them.

Visions of great floods washing beings away in torrents of cosmic suffering flooded my awareness, while scenes of poverty and filth that transcended any earthly deprivation painted themselves across my inner vision with depressing clarity. The entire realm felt saturated with despair, as if suffering itself had been concentrated into architectural form and populated with beings whose existence was defined entirely by various forms of cosmic misery.

The creeping psychological effect was immediate and disturbing. Whatever protective mechanisms normally shielded consciousness from such overwhelming negativity seemed inadequate against direct exposure to realms where suffering had been refined into its purest, most concentrated forms.

I stayed just long enough to witness these realms and fulfill the assignment—mission accomplished, however briefly and reluctantly. I had something concrete to report to Sayadaw.

THE MULTIPLE CAMERA SYSTEM

After lunch, a simple shower transformed into another revelation about the expanding boundaries of supernatural perception. With eyes closed while pouring water over my head, I could suddenly see my own body from external perspectives—simultaneously viewing myself from behind and from the front, as if consciousness had learned to operate multiple cameras that could be positioned anywhere in space.

The strangest aspect was seeing my own back with complete clarity—not reflected in mirrors but observed directly from a position behind my physical form, looking square-on at anatomy I'd never been able to examine properly. This wasn't the reversed image that mirrors provided but a genuine back-to-front observation that revealed posture and muscle definition from perspectives that should have been impossible for individual consciousness to achieve.

Looking harder revealed skeletal structure beneath the skin, while focusing deeper brought organs into view with the same clarity I'd been developing for internal observation. Everything responded to simple intention—thinking about any aspect of bodily architecture immediately brought it into supernatural focus.

Standing motionless in the open bathroom, wearing only shorts, eyes closed while conducting systematic anatomical self-examination, I realized this must have presented a peculiar sight to any passing observer. Quickly gathering my belongings before someone discovered me staring at invisible phenomena while standing nearly naked in communal facilities, I retreated to the privacy of my room for continued experimentation.

A BUNCH OF SKELETONS

Back in my meditation cave, I discovered that any part of my body could be illuminated and examined simply by directing mindful attention toward it. Focusing on my face caused it to light up with complete visibility, while turning the *nimitta* beam around to scan facial features from the front provided a colorful vision that even revealed the blindfold I was wearing during these supernatural investigations.

I continued playing with these capabilities until I remembered the day's scheduled group photograph—Mr. Soemin maintains a traditional documentation of each retreat's participants. He would give copies to each participant at the end while hanging one on the dining hall wall in the long row of retreat records that chronicled years of spiritual seekers who had passed through this sanctuary.

Arriving early for the photo session, I waited for others to gather while experimenting with casual applications of my newfound abilities. As I blinked, the skeleton of the person standing in front of me appeared with startling clarity through their ordinary clothes—complete bone structure visible despite fabric and flesh that remained entirely opaque for normal vision.

Thinking this might be imagination or wishful projection, I closed my eyes briefly and turned toward other participants. Every single person revealed their skeletal architecture with crystalline clarity—complete X-ray vision that penetrated clothing, skin, and muscle to display the calcium frameworks that kept everyone upright.

The experience was both mesmerizing and surreal. Each person's skeleton appeared as if illuminated from within by some cosmic light source, every bone rendered in perfect anatomical detail that surpassed any medical textbook illustration.

The women's clothes and bags appeared as very faint lines superimposed over their bone structures, like ghostly outlines that barely registered against the brilliant white clarity of the skeletons themselves. Their fabric seemed to exist in some translucent dimension that consciousness could see through as easily as looking through clear water.

The men's skeletal structures appeared equally vivid, their bone architecture displaying the subtle variations in shoulder width, ribcage expansion, and hip structure that created each person's unique physical presence. Some spines curved more than others, revealing the accumulated effects of decades of sitting, standing, and moving through the world in characteristic patterns that had literally shaped their internal frameworks.

It was simultaneously scary and hilarious to witness what appeared to be a gathering of animated skeletons dressed in ghostly clothing, all chatting and moving with the casual social energy of people who had no idea their deepest anatomical secrets were obvious to enhanced perception. They gestured with arms whose bone structures I could see in perfect detail, shifted weight from one leg to another while their pelvic bones revealed the mechanical precision of human locomotion, and turned their heads while their cervical vertebrae adjusted with the fluid grace of evolved engineering. Most amusing of all, their heads showed skulls with sets of teeth moving up and down as they talked, creating the surreal spectacle of animated death's heads engaged in cheerful conversation.

The disconnect between what I was seeing and what everyone else was experiencing created a strange psychological vertigo. Here I was, standing among fellow retreat participants who appeared to me as walking skeletons engaged in ordinary social interaction, while they remained completely unaware that their most hidden physical structures were blazing with visibility to someone who'd accidentally unlocked supernatural perception. It felt like being the only person at a costume party who could see through everyone's disguises, except the disguises were flesh and the costumes were bones.

Most unsettling was the realization that this wasn't requiring any effort or concentration—the X-ray vision had become as automatic as ordinary sight, operating continuously whether I wanted it to or not. I found myself trying to "turn off" this enhanced perception, but the skeletal displays remained stubbornly present, overlaying normal vision like a secondary visual system that had been permanently activated.

I was tempted to examine these displays more thoroughly—perhaps investigating organs or other internal structures—but wisdom suggested that staring too intently at fellow practitioners, especially the women, would be both inappropriate and potentially disturbing if anyone noticed. The ethical implications of possessing such invasive perceptual abilities began weighing heavily on my conscience, creating an uncomfortable awareness that some capabilities came with moral responsibilities that ordinary human experience had never prepared me to navigate.

THE PAST LIFE ASSESSMENT

At the end of the group photo session, I approached Mr. Soemin and whispered to him what had just happened. He immediately took me to see Sayadaw, where both teachers displayed expressions of genuine surprise rather than the calm satisfaction that had greeted previous breakthroughs. Sayadaw speculated that I might have practiced these techniques in earlier lifetimes—accumulated *parami* from past incarnations finally manifesting when conditions were appropriate for advanced spiritual development.

THE WALL-PENETRATING DISCOVERY

Then came the discovery that completely revolutionized my understanding of these capabilities' scope and range.

I could see through two walls—past the adjacent room and into the bamboo bushes approximately five meters away. The bamboo appeared with perfect clarity and full color, as if I were standing directly in front of these green sanctuaries rather than observing them through solid barriers from inside a distant building.

Pushing the range further, I directed attention down the entire block of rooms until I spotted a figure sitting on a chair, leaning forward with one arm extended toward something that appeared as red blotches—thermal signatures that suggested someone reaching for a hot beverage. The accuracy was stunning, though I had no way to verify whether someone was actually drinking tea at that precise moment in the location my consciousness was observing.

For the ultimate test, I focused on my favorite spot in the compound—the bamboo sanctuary near the abandoned well, approximately fifty meters from my room. Closing my eyes brought those familiar green giants into perfect focus, appearing as if they were only two feet away rather than across the entire facility.

Every detail blazed with supernatural clarity: the shiny green trunks with their distinctive segments, the textured striations running along their length like natural calligraphy, and the individual leaves dancing in breezes I could observe but not physically feel. This wasn't a vague impression or approximation, but photographic-quality vision that operated independently of distance, walls, or any physical obstacles.

CHILD'S PLAY

During the afternoon interview, I reported these developments with the hesitation of someone confessing experiences that challenged every assumption about human perceptual limitations. Mr. Soemin's response was immediate laughter rather than surprise or skepticism.

"It's child's play!" he declared with the casual dismissal of someone describing elementary techniques rather than capabilities that would revolutionize neuroscience if properly documented.

"What do you mean?" I asked, struggling to understand how superhuman abilities could be classified as basic skills.

"Lots of people in Myanmar can do that!" he explained with the matter-of-fact tone of someone discussing widespread local talents. "With a *nimitta*, you can go anywhere. No one can stop you!"

"You mean, I could go anywhere? Like, say, New York?"

His laughter suggested I was asking whether bicycles could be used for transportation rather than inquiring about interdimensional travel capabilities. "You went to heaven and hell, what's New York?"

The logic was unassailable, but the implications were staggering. If consciousness could indeed travel anywhere without limitation—observing distant locations with perfect clarity, penetrating any barrier, accessing any information—then every assumption about privacy, security, and the boundaries of individual awareness needed complete revision.

THE THOUSAND-DOLLAR CHOICE

At this point in the interview, Sayadaw presented me with a crucial choice that would determine the direction of my remaining practice. I had two options: one was to continue with concentration development and proceed deeper into the *jhanas*, and the other was to transition to *vipassana* practice. The path of *jhana* development promised unimaginable bliss and the continuation—even enhancement—of the extraordinary capacities I'd been experiencing. But the path of *vipassana* brought insight into the true nature of reality, though these supernatural abilities would diminish as it involved different types of *nana* (consciousness states) that operated according to different principles.

I couldn't hide the fact that I'd grown somewhat addicted to these extraordinary capacities—the thrill of X-ray vision, the ability to travel anywhere through consciousness, the power to examine any aspect of biological architecture with superhuman clarity. But I also deeply wanted insight into the fundamental nature of existence.

Seeing my hesitation, Sayadaw presented a simple analogy that cut through my internal conflict with crystalline clarity: "*Jhana* is worth $1, whilst *vipassana* is worth $1000."

As much as I craved the superhuman capacities, I would be foolish to choose them over *vipassana* when he framed it this way. Why? Because it's only through *vipassana* that you can see things as they really are—perceive the ultimate truth of existence. While concentrated states and their accompanying powers were extraordinary to experience, they would diminish without sustained practice, requiring constant maintenance to preserve their spectacular effects. But once you've witnessed the truth through *vipassana*, you can never see reality in the same naive way again. The insight, once gained, becomes a permanent understanding that transforms how consciousness relates to existence itself.

THE BUTTERFLY AWAKENING

After the interview, I wandered the compound in a psychological state that felt like controlled hysteria mixed with cosmic overwhelm. The magnitude of what I was experiencing felt too large for ordinary emotional processing systems to accommodate.

Butterflies performed aerial acrobatics in my stomach while I paced up and down the flowering pathways, feeling simultaneously euphoric and terrified by discoveries that challenged every framework I'd ever used for understanding reality and human potential.

I wanted to cry—whether from joy or shock remained unclear, but the emotional pressure felt like a dam about to burst from containing experiences that belonged in multiple categories simultaneously: scientific breakthrough, spiritual awakening, psychological revolution, and existential crisis all compressed into awareness that wasn't designed to handle such concentrated impossibility.

It felt like awakening from lifelong slumber to discover that everything I'd accepted as human limitation was actually just collective ignorance about consciousness's true capabilities. Or perhaps like metamorphosis—the caterpillar version of myself looking back with amazement at what the butterfly had always been capable of achieving.

The staggering realization hit me: every human being walking this planet possessed these same extraordinary capabilities, yet lived their entire lives without ever discovering the cosmic technology embedded within their own awareness.

The realization carried both excitement and responsibility. Who would believe such reports without direct experience? Most people would assume a psychological breakdown rather than a spiritual breakthrough, mental illness rather than enhanced perception. Yet somehow, sharing this knowledge felt like a moral obligation—information too important to keep private despite the personal risks of being labeled delusional.

THE ETHICAL BOUNDARIES

Passing the main hall's entrance, I noticed a woman meditating inside, seated approximately thirty meters from my position.

Eager to test my newfound powers, I closed my eyes and focused on her, bringing her into perfect focus as if she were sitting directly in front of me. When I "zoomed in" using whatever mental mechanism controlled these capabilities, the distance collapsed entirely—she appeared close enough to touch despite being separated by walls and considerable space.

Straining slightly more brought her skeleton and organs into view with the same clarity I'd been developing for self-examination. But discretion overrode curiosity—the possibility of causing internal damage through inappropriate observation, combined with obvious ethical concerns about examining women's bodies without consent, made me retreat immediately from what felt like a violation of boundaries that supernatural abilities should respect, even if they could penetrate them.

Mr. Soemin's assessment echoed in my consciousness with new understanding: *With the nimitta, you can see anything and go anywhere.*

I felt genuinely invincible—even Superman had to fly to reach distant locations physically, but consciousness equipped with *nimitta* could travel anywhere instantaneously while remaining safely anchored in a meditation posture. This was power that transcended every superhero fantasy I'd ever entertained.

THE PARENTAL WARNING

After the evening group chanting at eight, Mr. Soemin intercepted me with the knowing expression of someone who'd observed countless practitioners discovering these capabilities and making predictable mistakes.

"Get some sleep. Don't play all night," he warned with parental authority, "and don't do anything unwholesome." His cheeky grin suggested he understood precisely what temptations accompanied such unprecedented access to usually hidden information.

THE INFINITE LABORATORY

But resistance was futile. Back in my room, I couldn't resist spending hours exploring every aspect of these newfound abilities like a scientist who'd been granted unlimited access to the cosmos's most advanced research laboratory.

Previous limitations had confined *nimitta* projection to ceiling height, but tonight I was shooting luminous beams to the next town and beyond, testing the apparent absence of distance restrictions that seemed to govern these phenomena. I examined every body part until running out of anatomical territories to investigate, viewing organs from different angles, magnifying specific regions, and rotating structures with the precision of operating advanced 3D modeling software designed for biological architecture.

My spine had transformed into something resembling a rainbow-colored band embedded with columns of light that pointed skyward like organic laser arrays. Each beam could be moved individually or collectively, angled in different directions while maintaining perfect coordination—a spiritual light show that operated under conscious control.

Without even meditating, simply closing my eyes revealed multiple versions of my body suspended in space and rotating around my awareness like planets orbiting a spiritual sun. Three sets of skeletons displayed different perspectives—side views, front views, all reflecting my actual posture with perfect accuracy. Faces appeared in various orientations, while my spine floated like a flying dragon with one end mysteriously attached to my third eye, creating the appearance of an elephant trunk that moved with wave-like motion through dimensions that existed beyond ordinary space.

THE NATURAL PLANETARIUM

But the most serene discovery came while lying in bed, when closing my eyes revealed the neighbor's trees swaying above me as if my room's ceiling had become transparent. The sky stretched endlessly overhead while branches danced in breezes I could observe but not feel, creating a natural planetarium that was far more peaceful than staring at mosquito nets or concrete surfaces.

It was bizarre but profoundly beautiful—lying indoors while experiencing the infinite openness of outdoor space, walls becoming permeable barriers that consciousness could ignore whenever enhanced perception decided to operate beyond architectural limitations.

As I finally drifted toward sleep, consciousness still humming with residual energy from the day's extraordinary discoveries, I marveled at how completely these twenty-six days had dismantled every assumption I'd ever held about human potential and the true nature of awareness itself.

Tomorrow would bring new opportunities to explore territories where individual consciousness revealed its connection to cosmic intelligence. But tonight I went to sleep wondering whether I was evolving into something that transcended ordinary categories of human and divine, natural and supernatural, possible and impossible—or simply learning to operate capabilities that had always existed but which modern civilization had trained us to ignore so thoroughly that rediscovering them felt like gaining superpowers rather than remembering forgotten birthright.

In this space where consciousness had revealed its capacity for unlimited travel and supernatural perception, where the boundaries between individual awareness and cosmic capability had dissolved entirely, sleep finally claimed me—not as escape from the extraordinary, but as integration of powers that would forever change how I understood the relationship between awareness and the infinite possibilities that awaited exploration in dimensions beyond every limitation I'd ever accepted as real.

Day 27 - The Crystal Body Purification

Today brought instructions for what Sayadaw called "cutting the body"—a therapeutic technique designed to cleanse biological systems through methods that belonged more to cosmic surgery than conventional healing practices. This wasn't metaphorical cutting but actual energetic dissection using consciousness as the primary surgical instrument, *nimitta* functioning as luminous scalpels capable of penetrating matter in ways that challenged every assumption about the relationship between light and flesh.

THE RAINBOW SURGICAL INSTRUMENTS

The *nimitta* had evolved into rainbow-colored bands that pulsed with chromatic intensity—no longer simple points of light but sophisticated tools that could be shaped, directed, and controlled with the precision of spiritual laser systems designed by enlightened engineers who understood both the mechanics of consciousness and the architecture of biological existence.

Using these luminous instruments, I began systematically slicing my body—horizontally, vertically, diagonally—like a cosmic butcher learning to disassemble human architecture according to principles that operated beyond ordinary anatomy. Each cut followed deliberate patterns that seemed to target specific energetic blockages and accumulated tensions that had been building in my system, not just over weeks of intensive meditation but perhaps across years of unconscious accumulation.

THE LIQUID LIGHTNING THERAPY

As the *nimitta* passed through my physical form, light, cool, tingling sensations erupted like gentle electricity flowing through whatever region was being worked on. This wasn't painful or invasive but profoundly therapeutic—like having an internal massage conducted through pure energy rather than physical manipulation, reaching territories that ordinary healing modalities could never access.

The sensation felt like liquid lightning explicitly designed for therapeutic purposes, each pass of the luminous blade dissolving knots of tension I hadn't even known existed until they began releasing their grip on muscle, nerve, and whatever subtle bodies meditation had been activating through weeks of intensive practice.

Most remarkably, the *nimitta* itself began transforming as this energetic surgery progressed. The rainbow bands gradually shifted into different shades of gray—black on the outside, white at the core—creating layered tools that seemed designed for various types of energetic work. These gray bands began covering my body like the rings of Saturn, cosmic jewelry that operated according to healing principles rather than mere ornamentation.

THE SYSTEMATIC CLEANSING

Each round of slicing brought profound lightness and cleansing that felt like shedding layers of energetic debris that had been accumulating for decades. I worked systematically up and down my entire form, then reversed direction to ensure complete coverage, like a spiritual car wash designed for consciousness rather than external surfaces.

With practice, control over these luminous surgical instruments became increasingly sophisticated. What had initially required concentrated effort now flowed with the ease of operating familiar technology—I could move the *nimitta* faster, with greater precision, and without any resistance from whatever mechanisms governed their behavior.

THE AUTOMATED LIGHT SHOW

Growing more adventurous, I discovered these tools could be programmed for automatic operation. Setting them to spin and scan independently, I soon had multiple simultaneous scans running in different directions—my body became enveloped in whirling bands of spinning light that created a complex light show while conducting systematic energetic maintenance on every aspect of my biological architecture.

The visual effect was spectacular: spinning rings of luminous energy surrounding my form like some kind of cosmic healing chamber where advanced civilizations might conduct medical procedures using pure light as both diagnostic tool and therapeutic intervention.

THE CRYSTAL TRANSFORMATION

With each round of this energetic dissection, my body grew increasingly transparent—not fading but clarifying, as if layers of density were being systematically removed to reveal the crystalline structure that had always existed beneath accumulated matter. Eventually, my entire form transformed into something resembling pure transparent crystal—beautiful, clear, shining with its internal radiance.

The transparency was so complete that my body almost merged with the background, leaving only the faintest outlines visible along with the subtle definition of eyes and mouth. Sitting in half lotus, my form had become resplendent yet utterly transparent—a living sculpture of pure crystal that maintained perfect posture while existing in a state between matter and light. It was like discovering that flesh was just a temporary costume worn by consciousness, and this practice was revealing the luminous architecture that constituted my actual form.

THE SIX-HOUR SURGERY

For six intensive hours, I worked with these cosmic surgical tools, conducting the most thorough energetic maintenance I'd ever experienced. Every cell seemed to undergo renovation, every system cleared and optimized according to principles that belonged more to spiritual engineering than biological medicine.

At three o'clock, when I finally emerged from this extended session to meet with my teacher for new instructions, the transformation was profound and unmistakable. All the tension I'd been carrying—some of which I hadn't even been conscious of until its absence—had been completely dissolved through this practice.

My physical body felt light as a helium balloon, liberated from gravitational weight through whatever energetic reorganization had occurred during the crystal body purification. Every movement felt effortless, as if I'd been freed from invisible burdens that had been making ordinary existence unnecessarily difficult.

THE FACTORY SETTINGS

More significantly, my mind had achieved a state of calm and tranquility that felt like accessing consciousness's factory settings. This peaceful clarity perhaps represented awareness's natural condition when not obscured by accumulated stress, tension, and whatever energetic debris ordinary living deposited in both body and mind.

After reporting these results to Sayadaw, I received instructions for a new practice that felt like moving from active intervention to passive observation: a tranquility exercise that involved simply watching the *nimitta* without attempting to control, direct, or manipulate its manifestations.

This represented a completely different approach—instead of using these phenomena as tools for specific purposes, I was now learning to witness them as expressions of consciousness's autonomous creativity, allowing whatever displays emerged to unfold according to their internal logic rather than my desires or intentions.

THE SHIFT TO WITNESSING

The shift felt significant—from operator to observer, from doing to being, from controlling consciousness to allowing it to reveal its own deeper patterns and preferences when freed from the constant interference of personal will and specific spiritual agendas.

As evening approached and I prepared for this new phase of practice that emphasized receptivity over activity, I marveled at how each day's assignments seemed designed to explore different aspects of consciousness's infinite creative capabilities systematically.

Today had revealed healing dimensions of these phenomena—the ability to use enhanced awareness for energetic maintenance and purification that operated at levels far more fundamental than conventional medicine could access. Tomorrow would explore what consciousness might accomplish when left to its own devices, freed from the directing influence of individual will and allowed to express whatever patterns emerged from its own deepest nature.

But tonight, I went to sleep in a body that felt lighter than air and a mind clearer than mountain streams, carrying the day's revelations about consciousness's ability to serve not just as a vehicle for extraordinary experiences but as a sophisticated tool for optimizing the very biological systems that made such experiences possible in the first place.

In this space where consciousness had become both surgeon and patient, where light had transformed into healing technology, sleep finally claimed me—not as escape from the extraordinary, but as integration of a purification so complete it had revealed the crystalline nature of existence itself beneath the accumulated layers of ordinary embodied experience.

Day 28 - The Tranquil Paradox

The night had transformed into an endurance test of epic proportions. Buddhist chanting flooded the compound from some invisible source in the neighborhood—not the gentle, mindful recitation that accompanied formal practice, but recorded loops that played with the relentless persistence of spiritual torture designed by someone who'd never understood the difference between devotion and acoustic assault.

The chanting continued all night without pause, without variation, without mercy for anyone seeking the silence that deep practice required. Had everyone else achieved such profound equanimity that they could sleep through this sonic marathon, or had their nervous systems simply surrendered to acoustic inevitability? Perhaps I was the only person whose concentration hadn't yet evolved beyond being disturbed by external sounds, making this experience a personal test of patience rather than a collective endurance challenge.

THE INTERNAL WARFARE

I forced myself to think this way—reframing the situation as spiritual curriculum rather than neighborhood inconsideration—because the alternative was rage that would poison meditation for days like toxic waste contaminating a pure water source. The fury that arose when external conditions violated my expectations of peaceful practice felt like molten metal flowing through my nervous system, transforming tranquil awareness into a battlefield where resentment and resistance waged war against acceptance and equanimity.

I'd learned from previous nights that allowing anger to take root would create internal storms that lasted far longer than whatever external disturbance had triggered them. Irritation had a way of echoing through subsequent sessions like psychological tinnitus, creating mental noise that was more destructive than any external sound could ever be. The neighbors' chanting would eventually stop, but the internal agitation it could generate might persist for days, turning meditation cushions into seats of frustration rather than platforms for transcendence.

Since I couldn't control external conditions—couldn't march next door and demand acoustic consideration from people who might genuinely believe their recorded devotions were benefiting the entire neighborhood—the only viable option was internal adaptation. This wasn't passive resignation but active spiritual warfare against my reactive patterns, using whatever wisdom twenty-eight days of intensive practice had developed to transform obstacles into opportunities.

THE UNCONSCIOUS TEACHERS

Every external disturbance was another chance to develop the kind of unshakeable concentration that remained stable regardless of whatever chaos surrounded formal practice. Perhaps the neighbors were unconscious teachers, providing precisely the resistance training my concentration needed to evolve beyond dependency on perfect conditions. Perhaps advanced practitioners needed to understand that true spiritual stability can flourish in any environment. That peace is an internal achievement rather than an external arrangement.

THE DOUBLE-EDGED SWORD

The tranquility exercise that had been yesterday's assignment proved to be a double-edged spiritual sword. Instead of generating the energized alertness that usually accompanied intensive practice, this technique produced profound relaxation that made sleepiness feel like a natural response rather than resistance to be overcome.

Morning sessions became exercises in conscious drowsiness—awareness settling so deeply into restful states that dozing off felt less like failure and more like an inevitable consequence of consciousness finally learning to access its most peaceful settings. The micro-sleeps that interrupted formal sitting actually left me feeling refreshed rather than guilty, as if brief unconsciousness was somehow supporting whatever deeper processes the tranquility practice was designed to activate.

But this profound relaxation came with unexpected costs to the spectacular phenomena that had become routine aspects of daily practice. Generating *nimitta* required significantly more effort than previous days. At the same time, the luminous displays that did emerge lacked the stability and intensity that had characterized recent sessions.

THE ENERGETIC BUDGET

It was like discovering that consciousness operated according to energetic budgets—the deeper the tranquility, the less available energy remained for producing the cosmic fireworks that had been transforming meditation into interdimensional tourism. Perhaps different states of awareness accessed different capabilities, each one requiring specific conditions that might be incompatible with other extraordinary phenomena.

In the late afternoon, when concentration finally aligned with whatever internal conditions supported advanced practice, I managed to generate a particularly powerful *nimitta* that felt like rediscovering an old friend after temporary separation. Using this luminous tool for playful experimentation, I sent it traveling up and down my body like a spiritual elevator that illuminated different regions with each systematic pass.

Various images emerged spontaneously as the *nimitta* moved—not the deliberately controlled manifestations of previous days but autonomous displays that seemed to arise from consciousness's creative depths when allowed to operate without specific direction or intention. These felt like glimpses into whatever visual libraries existed in awareness's deeper strata, random samples from vast archives of imagery that normally remained below the threshold of conscious access.

THE GEOLOGICAL BREATHING

My breathing had become so subtle it bordered on the imperceptible—each inhalation and exhalation slowing to rates that felt more geological than biological, with extended pauses between breaths that stretched across periods where ordinary respiratory rhythms would have demanded multiple air exchanges.

During these breath-pause intervals, my mind achieved states of tranquility so profound they felt like accessing consciousness's deepest possible settings—not the alertness and energy that characterized breakthrough sessions, but something approaching the cosmic calm that might exist at the foundation of awareness itself, where individual consciousness touched whatever universal peace underlay all mental activity.

THE DISABLED SUPERPOWERS

The evening group sitting brought disappointing confirmation that these profound states of tranquility came with specific limitations. Attempting to see the young monk's skeleton—a capability that had been reliably accessible just days ago—yielded only ordinary darkness behind closed eyelids. The X-ray vision that had made me feel like a meditation superhero seemed to have been temporarily disabled by whatever neurological changes the tranquility practice was producing.

But Sayadaw had warned that *nimitta* suppression was a predictable consequence of this particular exercise. Consciousness couldn't simultaneously access peak tranquility and generate spectacular visual phenomena. Different practices cultivated different capabilities, and today's assignment was specifically designed to abide in the deepest possible states of peaceful awareness rather than the energetic intensity that supported cosmic light shows and supernatural perception. This tranquility exercise was laying the essential foundation for *Vipassana* practice, preparing consciousness for the profound insights that would emerge once the mind achieved the necessary stillness and receptivity.

THE OPERATING MODES

It felt like learning that consciousness came equipped with different operating modes—high-performance settings that enabled extraordinary experiences, and energy-conservation modes that prioritized profound rest and internal healing over spectacular manifestations. Perhaps advanced practice required developing fluency in all of these modes rather than specializing in whichever capabilities felt most impressive or entertaining.

THE SACRED DISTURBANCE

As night approached, the recorded Buddhist chanting resumed its acoustic siege with the punctuality of a neighborhood alarm system that had been programmed by someone with no understanding of sound pollution's psychological effects. I attempted defensive measures, plugging my ears with Blu Tack that proved no more effective than the standard earplugs I'd been using to create barriers against this nightly invasion of mechanical devotion.

The irony was profound—Buddhist chanting, which should theoretically support meditative states, had become the primary obstacle to achieving the silence that deep practice required. Perhaps this was another teaching about accepting conditions beyond personal control, or maybe it was just evidence that even sacred practices could become sources of disturbance when applied without wisdom about timing, volume, and consideration for others sharing the same acoustic environment.

THE FOUNDATION OF PEACE

But lying in my mosquito net sanctuary while waves of recorded Pali syllables crashed against my windows like tsunamis of good intentions gone wrong, I reflected on the day's lessons about consciousness's infinite range of possible states and capabilities.

Today had revealed that profound tranquility was itself a sophisticated spiritual achievement—not just the absence of agitation but a positive state of awareness that required specific cultivation and came with its unique characteristics and limitations. While I missed the spectacular fireworks of recent sessions, there was something equally valuable about touching the deepest possible states of mental peace, discovering whatever calm existed at consciousness's foundation when all effort and striving finally dissolved into pure, effortless being.

Tomorrow would bring new opportunities to explore whatever territories of awareness remained unmapped in this accelerating curriculum of consciousness expansion. But tonight I went to sleep wrapped in tranquility so profound it could survive even the most determined external attempts to disturb the peace that intensive practice had been systematically cultivating in the deeper chambers of awakening awareness.

In this space where serenity had become both achievement and limitation, where the deepest calm came at the cost of spectacular phenomena, sleep finally claimed me—not as escape from the extraordinary, but as integration of a peace so fundamental it revealed itself as consciousness's natural resting state beneath all the cosmic fireworks and supernatural capabilities that had been merely expressions of awareness exploring its infinite creative potential.

Day 29 – The Great Deceleration

Four a.m. arrived with consciousness already settling into the deeper rhythms of tranquility practice that had been systematically recalibrating my nervous system's relationship with time, effort, and the compulsive drive toward spectacular spiritual achievements. The meditation cushion felt less like a platform for generating extraordinary experiences and more like a portal to oceanic depths where awareness could sink into profound stillness that had its own value beyond any phenomena it might produce.

THE ART OF WITNESSING

I watched my breath with the patience of someone learning to observe rather than manipulate, allowing respiratory rhythms to find their own natural pace while consciousness simply witnessed whatever patterns emerged without the interference of spiritual ambition or performance anxiety that had characterized earlier weeks of practice.

The *nimitta* manifested sporadically—appearing and disappearing like shy cosmic creatures that only emerged when conditions felt safe and non-threatening. When they did appear, images moved with the dreamy slowness of underwater ballet, each manifestation unfolding with geological patience rather than the rapid-fire displays that had previously characterized these luminous phenomena.

Small sun and moon *nimitta* occasionally graced my awareness with their gentle presence—not the blazing cosmic furnaces of recent sessions but modest, intimate displays that felt more like candlelight than searchlights, creating atmospheres of quiet contemplation rather than overwhelming spectacle.

By midmorning, concentration had found its sustainable rhythm, settling into stability that felt less like achievement and more like a natural consequence of allowing awareness to discover its preferred operating speed when freed from the constant pressure to produce impressive results.

THE AFTERNOON REBELLION

But the afternoon brought challenges that tested whatever equanimity the tranquility practice had been cultivating. Post-lunch restlessness invaded my system like unwelcome guests, transforming the subtle breathing that had become characteristic of deep states into harsh, rapid respiratory patterns that felt like someone had switched my lungs from meditation mode to emergency hyperventilation.

The harder I breathed, the more my nostrils protested this sudden increase in air velocity and volume. Soon my nose felt raw and inflamed, as if this return to ordinary respiratory mechanics was abrading the delicate tissues that had adapted to gossamer-light breathing.

As if sensing my vulnerability, mosquitoes launched coordinated attacks on exposed skin, their high-pitched whining and needle-sharp proboscis invasions creating multiple layers of distraction that transformed afternoon practice into an endurance test against biological annoyance. Each bite sent ripples of irritation through awareness that was supposed to be cultivating profound peace, while the itching that followed created additional focal points that competed with breath awareness for attention.

These accumulated distractions successfully sabotaged any attempt to generate *nimitta* before the five o'clock break—proof that even weeks of intensive training couldn't guarantee consistent results when conditions aligned against successful practice.

THE INCOMPATIBLE TECHNOLOGIES

But the break provided a necessary reset, and when I returned to formal sitting, *Metta* immediately produced a bright *nimitta* with the reliability of a spiritual technology that remained accessible even when other practices faltered. Yet this luminous display proved frustratingly incompatible with *Anapanasati*—I could generate the light through loving kindness, but couldn't integrate it with breath meditation because my nose had become paradoxically insensitive to the very sensations it had been hypersensitive to just hours earlier.

The afternoon's hard breathing had numbed the delicate nerve endings that detected subtle air movements, leaving me unable to feel respiratory sensations that had been registering with microscopic precision during recent sessions. It was like discovering that spiritual instruments required careful maintenance and could be temporarily damaged through misuse or excessive force.

THE COSMIC SLOWNESS

Most remarkably, my mind achieved even deeper levels of tranquility as the day progressed—not the alert clarity that characterized breakthrough sessions, but something approaching cosmic slowness that felt like consciousness learning to operate at entirely different speeds than ordinary awareness typically employed.

Everything was decelerating with the inevitability of natural law asserting itself: breath patterns slowing to geological rhythms, *nimitta* manifestations unfolding with patient grace, and my entire physical system settling into relaxation so profound it felt like discovering an alternative to the energetic intensity that modern life typically demanded.

I felt calmer than I could ever remember being, preferring minimal activity while paradoxically not feeling tired or depleted. This wasn't fatigue but a conscious choice to operate at sustainable speeds rather than the frantic pace that had characterized both ordinary life and the early weeks of retreat practice when every session felt like sprinting toward spiritual goals.

THE QUESTIONING OF SPEED

I didn't even feel motivated to write in my meditation diary—the compulsive documentation that had been tracking daily progress through territories of consciousness expansion suddenly seemed unnecessary, like someone had switched off whatever internal mechanism had been driving the need to capture and analyze every extraordinary experience.

The transformation felt like a fundamental shift in life philosophy enacted at cellular levels. It was as if I had been running without questioning why such urgency was necessary, then suddenly wondering: *Hey, why am I running? Why don't I slow down?* So consciousness had started walking instead of sprinting through spiritual practice.

But even walking began feeling unnecessarily energetic after a while, leading to the natural question: *Why do I need to walk? Why don't I just sit down instead?* That's precisely what the tranquility exercise had accomplished—teaching awareness that profound stillness was itself a legitimate spiritual destination rather than just preparation for more spectacular achievements.

This wasn't lethargy or apathy, but deep tranquility accompanied by complete contentment with being as is.

THE ULTIMATE PREPARATION

I understood now that Sayadaw had been systematically preparing my mind for *Vipassana*—insight meditation that required stable, unperturbed awareness. The extraordinary concentration I'd developed wasn't wasted effort but essential foundation, providing the lofty focus necessary for sustaining the precise observation that this ultimate practice demanded. These tranquility exercises were deliberately slowing down my consciousness so I could observe phenomena with the clarity necessary for insight to emerge.

At three o'clock, this preparation reached culmination when Sayadaw delivered the instructions I'd been working toward for twenty-nine days.

"Systematically examine your physical body," he instructed with the precision of someone who had guided countless students through this fundamental investigation. "Observe how your body manifests as sensations, and identify the three characteristics present in all phenomena: *anicca* (impermanence), *dukkha* (unsatisfactoriness), and *anatta* (not-self). These manifest in all bodily sensations—from the subtlest to the most gross forms."

The practice would begin with *rupa*—the Pali term meaning materiality, which paired with *nama* (mentality) formed the mind-body complex that would become my laboratory for investigating what I had always assumed was simply "me" and "my experience."

THE REAL WORK BEGINS

The transition felt significant—moving from preliminary exercises in concentration and tranquility toward the direct investigation of consciousness and phenomena that constituted the heart of Buddhist meditation practice. After twenty-nine days of developing increasingly sophisticated capabilities and experiencing impossible phenomena, I was finally ready to begin the real work of understanding what all these extraordinary experiences meant in the context of awakening to the true nature of existence itself.

As evening approached and I prepared for this new phase of practice that would use all the previously developed skills in service of fundamental insights about reality, I marveled at how systematically each day's assignments had been building toward this moment when spectacular abilities would be deployed not for their own sake but as tools for investigating the deepest questions about consciousness, identity, and the nature of whatever we call "real" in a universe that meditation was revealing to be far more mysterious and malleable than conventional understanding could accommodate.

In this space where urgency had dissolved into cosmic patience, where spectacular phenomena had given way to profound stillness, where all the extraordinary capabilities had been revealed as preparation for something infinitely more valuable, sleep finally claimed me—not as escape from the journey, but as the final rest before embarking on the ultimate investigation into the true nature of reality itself through the ancient practice of *Vipassana*, which would use every tool consciousness had developed to penetrate the deepest mysteries of existence and awakening. Tonight I went to sleep feeling like the most chilled person on Earth, wrapped in tranquility so profound it seemed to extend beyond my individual awareness into the very fabric of peace itself.

Day 30 – The Return of the Light

Day thirty arrived with the weight of profound anticipation. Today I would finally begin the practice I had chosen over supernatural powers—*Vipassana*, the thousand-dollar path that would deploy all my extraordinary capabilities in service of ultimate insight rather than spectacular display.

After twenty-nine days of systematic preparation, this was the moment everything had been building toward. All the cosmic light shows, the interdimensional travel, the X-ray vision—all of it had been training for this investigation into the true nature of reality itself.

The instructions Sayadaw had given yesterday were elegantly simple: focus on the heart region and observe whatever sensations arose anywhere in the body, investigating the actual moment-to-moment experience of being conscious in a biological form. This represented a complete shift from concentration practices that generated spectacular phenomena toward insight meditation that would examine the very fabric of experience itself.

THE MUTED SYMPHONY

Although my mind was clear and concentration felt good throughout the morning sessions, the *nimitta* were dramatically muted—weak, unstable manifestations that moved at slow-motion pace, bearing little resemblance to the spectacular displays I'd grown accustomed to. At the three o'clock interview, I reported this concerning development to Sayadaw.

His response surprised me completely. He laughed with genuine amusement rather than concern, explaining that the *nimitta* suppression was not only normal but deliberate. The tranquility exercises had been specifically designed to slow down my consciousness so I could observe phenomena in slow motion, as it were. Otherwise, he explained, things happened too fast and I wouldn't be able to witness them properly during *Vipassana* practice.

"It will come back," he assured me with the confidence of someone who'd observed this pattern countless times.

His certainty revealed something profound about traditional teaching methods. Teachers deliberately avoided explaining what practitioners should expect from specific exercises, understanding that advance knowledge could fundamentally contaminate the purity of direct experience. When students knew what phenomena they were "supposed" to encounter, their minds inevitably began manufacturing those experiences or generating anxiety when expected results failed to manifest.

This approach initially felt almost cruel in its refusal to provide the psychological comfort of knowing what lay ahead. My Western educational background had conditioned me to expect detailed explanations, learning objectives, and clear success criteria before attempting any new skill. The Buddhist method seemed to deliberately withhold the very information that would make the journey feel safer and more predictable.

But I was beginning to understand the profound wisdom embedded in this apparent withholding. Expectations created a kind of spiritual performance anxiety that transformed meditation from open investigation into achievement-oriented striving. Even worse, advance knowledge could trigger the mind's tendency to fabricate experiences that matched the expected template, leading practitioners to convince themselves they'd achieved genuine states when they'd actually created elaborate self-deceptions.

The traditional method preserved the authenticity of individual development by treating each session as a scientific experiment where consciousness was both laboratory and subject. Each practitioner's unique nervous system, karmic patterns, and spiritual accumulations would naturally produce their own sequence of experiences and insights. By refusing to impose standardized expectations, teachers allowed these organic patterns to unfold according to their inherent wisdom rather than forcing development into predetermined molds.

Here, ignorance was maintained as a spiritual asset. Not knowing what was supposed to happen meant approaching each session with genuine curiosity rather than goal-oriented striving, allowing whatever emerged to carry the shock of authentic discovery rather than the satisfaction of meeting expectations.

THE PROPHETIC RETURN

And return it did. Later that afternoon, robust *nimitta* began manifesting with approaching their former reliability. At four o'clock, both *Araham* and *Metta* produced blazing displays that confirmed whatever internal recalibration had been occurring was nearly complete.

By 5:45, familiar formations paraded through my awareness: blue circles transforming seamlessly into small suns, each manifestation flowing with the fluid grace of consciousness remembering how to operate its sophisticated features.

But the most dramatic confirmation came that night. The moment I lay down to rest, powerful *nimitta* began firing spontaneously from my nose like cosmic artillery operating on its own schedule. Blue and red flame displays erupted with such intensity that sleep became impossible—not from external disturbance but from internal illumination no longer under conscious control.

THE NEW RHYTHMS

My sleep schedule fragmented beyond ordinary patterns: bed at 8:30 p.m., awakening at 10:30, consciousness surfacing again at 1:00 a.m., then lying in luminous awareness until 2:00 when formal practice would resume. Yet paradoxically, I didn't feel tired despite minimal rest.

Whatever energetic recalibration had occurred was complete, leaving me with restored access to spectacular capabilities but fundamentally altered biological rhythms that no longer required conventional sleep to maintain optimal functioning.

As I lay surrounded by these involuntary fireworks, I reflected on how systematically each phase of training had built toward this moment—the integration of extraordinary phenomena with the ultimate practice of investigating reality itself. The thousand-dollar choice had led me here: consciousness equipped with cosmic capabilities, finally ready to turn them inward to investigate the fundamental nature of self and experience.

Tomorrow, the real work would begin.

Day 31 - The Liquid Body

The two a.m. session brought revelations about the fundamental nature of physical existence that challenged every assumption I'd held about the solidity and stability of the human form. Strong bodily swaying began immediately upon settling into meditation posture—not ordinary restlessness or fidgeting, but profound undulation that felt like my entire form had transformed into a bag of water being sloshed around on a moving boat navigating rough seas.

This wasn't imagination or visualization but a visceral physical sensation that seemed to be revealing something essential about the fluid nature of what I'd always assumed was solid matter. My body felt like it had lost its normal density and cohesion, becoming something more liquid than flesh, more oceanic than terrestrial in its fundamental composition.

THE ANCHORED LIGHT

Weak ring and moon *nimitta* gradually developed into stable ring and sun formations, their luminous displays providing steady anchors of light amid this physical liquefaction that was transforming meditation from stationary practice into navigation through internal weather systems that obeyed different laws than ordinary biology.

I continued working with *Rupa*—the *Vipassana* practice designed to investigate the true nature of physical sensation beneath the conceptual overlay that usually masks reality's actual characteristics. Each moment of observation revealed new aspects of how consciousness interfaced with whatever we normally called "body," though that term was beginning to feel increasingly inadequate for describing the fluid, dynamic, ever-changing phenomena that sustained biological existence.

By 8:20, despite the ongoing liquefaction, my concentration had achieved crystalline clarity while my mind maintained perfect alertness within profound calm—a paradoxical state where awareness remained sharp and focused even as the physical form it inhabited continued undulating like water in a cosmic container being gently rocked by invisible hands.

THE SCIENTIFIC DETACHMENT

The tranquility was exquisite in its depth and stability, creating conditions where consciousness could observe these extraordinary physical transformations with scientific detachment rather than alarm or resistance. It felt like discovering that profound peace and bizarre phenomena could coexist harmoniously when awareness developed sufficient equanimity to witness whatever emerged without needing to control or understand it immediately.

The 12:35–2:35 session intensified these revelations about the body's true nature. The sensation that my physical form was composed entirely of water became so convincing that ordinary concepts of flesh, bone, and tissue seemed like crude approximations of something far more fluid and dynamic than conventional anatomy could describe.

The sloshing motion moved in all directions—back and forth, side to side—creating internal tidal patterns that made me genuinely seasick despite sitting motionlessly on solid ground. It was like discovering that biological existence was oceanic, subject to currents and waves that normally remained below the threshold of conscious awareness but could be revealed through sufficiently refined attention.

Suddenly, I remembered Mr. Soemin's casual mention a day ago that I should sit in the middle of the bed when doing this meditation. It hadn't registered at the time, but now I understood! He'd known exactly what was coming—the intense swaying motions that would make sitting on the edge of anything precarious or potentially dangerous. His seemingly offhand comment had been practical wisdom disguised as casual suggestion.

THE SHIFT TO *NAMA*

At three o'clock, Sayadaw introduced *Nama*—a new exercise that maintained the same fundamental approach as previous *Vipassana* practice but shifted the internal noting cue from *Rupa* to *Nama*, directing investigation toward the mental aspects of the mind-body complex.

But the swaying motions continued throughout the day regardless of posture or activity—standing, sitting, lying down all produced the same undulatory sensations that seemed to be revealing something fundamental about the dynamic nature of physical existence. Sometimes only specific regions would sway—face, head, or torso moving independently—while other times the entire body participated in coordinated undulation like a single organism responding to invisible rhythms.

Most remarkably, even the *nimitta* themselves had begun swaying, their normally stable dots and formations rocking back and forth and left to right with the same fluid motion that was affecting my physical form. It was as if whatever force was revealing the liquid nature of the body was also demonstrating that luminous phenomena obeyed the same dynamic principles rather than existing as fixed, static displays.

THE ENDURANCE CHALLENGE

Despite these extraordinary physical transformations, I managed 9.5 hours of sitting meditation with excellent concentration and mindfulness—proof that profound practice could continue even when consciousness was discovering that the body's apparent solidity was a sophisticated illusion maintained by limited perception.

But sustained sitting brought its challenges that were becoming increasingly acute as daily practice duration extended beyond ordinary endurance limits. Sometimes my buttocks felt like they were literally on fire—not metaphorical discomfort but burning sensations that suggested prolonged pressure was testing the limits of whatever pain tolerance intensive meditation had developed.

I found myself constantly rotating between different postures throughout the day: cross-legged, half-lotus, kneeling, and sometimes even sitting in a chair with legs propped on the bed's edge when traditional positions became unbearable. Some of the most awkward and bizarre positions emerged from desperate attempts to give relief to body parts that had been screaming in pain. No position provided lasting comfort when maintained for hours, yet changing postures too frequently would disrupt the deep states that required sustained stillness to develop properly.

THE WISDOM OF ADAPTATION

The prohibition against lying down during formal practice created additional challenges—horizontal positions inevitably led to sleep, making them unsuitable for consciousness investigation that required alert awareness. So, enduring whatever pain arose became another aspect of practice, accepting physical discomfort as the price of accessing states that couldn't be reached through more comfortable but less conducive positions.

Through trial and error, I'd discovered that specific posture mattered far less than the ability to remain genuinely still once settled. Fancy positions like full lotus—which many people associated with advanced meditation—were often counterproductive torture devices that diverted attention from consciousness investigation toward pain management.

Many untrained practitioners made the mistake of assuming that traditional postures were essential for authentic practice, then spent entire sessions battling physical agony instead of observing the subtle phenomena that meditation was designed to reveal. The most elegant posture was useless if it prevented the sustained stillness that deep states required.

Some of my most profound sessions had occurred while sitting in decidedly inelegant positions—chair meditation with legs draped over the bed's side, cushions arranged in whatever configuration provided adequate support for extended sitting. I felt grateful for the privacy of individual room practice rather than group hall sessions where social pressure might have prevented the postural experimentation that allowed practice to continue despite physical limitations.

THE OCEAN OF EXISTENCE

As evening approached and I prepared for continued investigation of whatever *Nama* practice would reveal about the mental components of moment-to-moment experience, I reflected on how each day brought discoveries about the fluid, dynamic nature of what we normally considered solid, stable reality.

The swaying sensations had revealed that the body was far more oceanic than terrestrial in its fundamental nature—a collection of fluid processes rather than fixed architecture, subject to tides and currents that could be observed when consciousness developed sufficient sensitivity to detect the constant motion underlying apparent stillness.

Tomorrow would bring a deeper investigation of these discoveries about the liquid nature of existence. But tonight I went to sleep still gently swaying like seaweed in cosmic currents that flowed through dimensions where matter and energy were revealed as different names for the same endlessly dynamic dance of awareness manifesting as apparently solid forms that were as fluid as water in the vast ocean of consciousness itself.

In this space where solidity had dissolved into oceanic fluidity, where even luminous phenomena swayed with invisible currents, where 9.5 hours of sitting had become possible despite physical challenges, sleep finally claimed me—not as escape from the swaying, but as gentle rocking in the cosmic ocean where all separate forms revealed themselves as waves in the infinite sea of awareness itself.

Day 32 — Seismic Shifts

The pre-dawn darkness surrendered to consciousness at 3:43 a.m., not with the jagged violence of fragmented awakening that had become my nocturnal companion, but with the gentle insistence of natural emergence. Sleep had finally offered its benediction—hours of unbroken rest that felt like archaeological layers settling into place, each dream cycle depositing sediment that would support whatever was being constructed in the deeper strata of transformation.

Only twice had I surfaced from those merciful depths, brief appearances at consciousness's shoreline before diving back into restorative currents. The contrast was profound: where recent nights had resembled shipwrecks—consciousness scattered across temporal fragments—this morning felt like arriving at a harbor after weathering storms that had tested every timber of my being.

THE INVESTIGATION DEEPENS

Today's assignment marked another revolution in the curriculum of inner exploration. The investigation shifted from *Rupa*—that meticulous cataloging of bodily sensations that had been revealing the granular nature of physical experience—to *Nama*, the examination of consciousness itself. Like an archaeologist trading earth-caked tools for instruments capable of measuring light, I was being asked to observe the observer, to investigate the very mental phenomena that had been doing the investigating.

The practice required a delicate splitting of attention's beam: while maintaining awareness of the midpoint region between heart and navel, I was to note with internal precision whatever thoughts, emotions, or mental formations arose moment by moment. It was an attempt to witness the mechanics of consciousness in real time, to catch the mind in the act of creating the very experiences we mistake for solid reality.

But as consciousness turned its lens inward, the body began to demonstrate just how interconnected these seemingly separate domains actually were.

WHEN THE EARTH MOVES

What emerged was nothing short of geological upheaval occurring precisely where I sat in apparent stillness. My form began to move with unprecedented fluidity, as if the normal constraints that maintain physical coherence had been temporarily suspended. The usual boundaries that kept arms and torso within predictable ranges dissolved, allowing movements that felt both foreign and strangely familiar—as though I was remembering how to inhabit space before learning the limitations that civilization typically imposes.

Then came the tremors.

These were not the nervous shakes of anxiety or the gentle trembling that sometimes accompanies meditation. These were seismic events—earthquakes that seemed to originate from tectonic plates buried somewhere beneath the threshold of ordinary physical awareness. Each tremor would begin as a subtle vibration, a whisper in the bones, then crescendo into full-scale upheaval that left my entire system reverberating like a struck bell.

The tremors followed no predictable schedule. One moment, I would be sitting in relative stillness, observing the interplay between mental noting and physical sensation, and the next, I would be seized by forces that felt as impersonal and inevitable as natural disasters. My body became a seismograph recording disturbances in layers of reality I had never suspected existed.

During these episodes, the *nimitta* continued its mysterious appearances—those luminous displays that seemed to operate according to their own celestial schedule. Sometimes cascading images would arise like shooting stars across the interior landscape: faces without context, landscapes that carried emotional weight despite bearing no relationship to any place I could consciously remember, scenarios that felt simultaneously foreign and deeply familiar.

THE FAMILIAR BECOMES FOREIGN

As the hours accumulated, a pattern emerged that felt like a law of spiritual physics: initial wonder invariably gravitates toward routine familiarity, which, without careful attention, can collapse into the black hole of boredom. The *Nama* practice, despite offering unprecedented access to the machinery of consciousness, was beginning to feel as predictable as counting breaths or noting physical sensations.

This seemed to be another manifestation of the exquisite pedagogical timing that characterized traditional meditation instruction. Just as my engagement was beginning to wane, just as the revolutionary was threatening to become routine, Sayadaw introduced a practice that felt like being invited to attempt alchemy: the systematic recollection of past lives.

At three o'clock in the afternoon, while my enthusiasm for mental noting was ebbing like a retreating tide, I was suddenly asked to investigate whether consciousness could access memories that predated biological birth. The assignment felt both impossible and inevitable—the logical extension of an investigation that had already revealed consciousness to be far more malleable and extensive than ordinary experience suggested.

ARCHAEOLOGY OF MEMORY

From 4:30 p.m. onward, I entered territories that challenged every assumption about the nature of memory, identity, and the boundaries of individual awareness. Past life recall wasn't merely an exotic meditation technique; it was an empirical investigation into whether consciousness operated according to laws that transcended the apparent limitations of single-incarnation existence.

The practice required a delicate suspension of disbelief coupled with rigorous attention to whatever arose. I was to observe without attachment, neither grasping after dramatic revelations nor dismissing subtle impressions that might contain authentic information about previous existences. It was archaeology conducted not with shovels and brushes but with awareness itself.

Images began to surface with the unpredictable rhythm of deep-sea treasures rising from oceanic depths. Faces that carried the weight of recognition despite belonging to no one I could place in my current biography. Landscapes that evoked profound emotional responses—the kind of immediate, physical recognition that bypasses rational analysis and speaks directly to something deeper than memory.

I found myself witnessing scenarios that possessed the peculiar vividness of recovered memory: a stone courtyard where shadows fell with particular weight, hands that belonged to me but weren't quite my hands, conversations in languages that felt familiar despite being incomprehensible to my current linguistic repertoire.

Yet these images remained frustratingly ambiguous, like photographs taken through layers of ancient glass. Were these authentic glimpses into previous incarnations, or was I witnessing consciousness's remarkable capacity to construct compelling narratives from random neural activity? The practice demanded that I observe without premature interpretation, collecting data that might only become meaningful with additional investigation.

THE BODY'S REBELLION AND REVELATION

Throughout these explorations of expanded identity, my physical form continued its own revolt against conventional limitations. The seismic tremors persisted with undiminished intensity, as if consciousness investigation was triggering systematic dissolution of whatever mechanisms normally maintained bodily coherence.

The swaying motions that had become characteristic of recent sessions continued their hypnotic rhythms, while accumulated pain in legs and buttocks reached crescendos that demanded frequent negotiations between awareness and anatomy. Every few minutes required careful choreography—shifting weight without losing concentration, adjusting posture without abandoning whatever delicate states might be developing.

The irony was profound: pursuing investigation of consciousness that promised to reveal the illusory nature of physical boundaries while being constantly reminded of biology's very real constraints. The body served simultaneously as laboratory and limitation, the vehicle through which transcendent experiences became possible and the anchor that prevented those experiences from achieving sustained liftoff.

COLLECTIVE ALCHEMY

During the 7:15 p.m. group sitting, I attempted to apply past life techniques within the amplified field that the collective practice generated.

There's something alchemical about meditating alongside others—individual awareness somehow becomes more than the sum of its parts, creating conditions where extraordinary experiences feel more accessible and sustainable.

In that charged atmosphere, images arose with increased frequency and vividness. Visual fragments cascaded like autumn leaves, each carrying its own emotional signature, its own suggestion of narrative significance. But coherent revelation remained elusive. The mind seemed to be offering tantalizing previews of a movie whose full screening required additional development, patience, and perhaps guidance from teachers who understood how to distinguish authentic past-life material from consciousness's natural storytelling propensities.

THE ARCHITECTURE OF DISSOLUTION

As evening descended and I prepared for sleep that might or might not provide respite from the ongoing tremors, I found myself stunned by the precision with which each new practice seemed designed to dismantle specific assumptions about reality's structure. The earthquake sensations weren't random neurological misfiring—they felt like evidence that intensive *Vipassana* investigation was accessing foundational levels where the apparent solidity of existence revealed itself to be far more fluid and dynamic than conventional perception could detect.

Past life practice represented another vector in this systematic dissolution of boundaries. If individual identity could indeed access information from previous incarnations, then even temporal boundaries might prove more permeable than ordinary experience suggested. The practice was simultaneously humbling and exhilarating—offering glimpses of consciousness operating according to laws that transcended current scientific paradigms while remaining frustratingly incomplete.

Tomorrow would bring additional opportunities to explore whether memory could indeed breach the apparent boundaries of single-lifetime existence. But tonight, as geological forces continued their work in the depths of whatever I was still calling my body, sleep felt like another laboratory where transformation could continue its mysterious operations beyond the reach of conscious observation.

The tremors that accompanied me into darkness carried a strange comfort—evidence that something profound was being dismantled and rebuilt at levels far deeper than thought or intention could penetrate. In surrendering to forces that operated according to their own intelligence, I was learning to trust processes that revealed ordinary experience to be just the surface of an ocean whose depths remained largely unexplored.

What emerged from thirty-two days of systematic investigation was not answers but better questions—inquiries that reached toward the fundamental nature of consciousness, identity, and the mysterious relationship between awareness and the ever-changing phenomena it witnesses. The earthquake tremors were perhaps consciousness itself, vibrating at frequencies that revealed the temporary nature of every structure we mistake for permanent ground.

∼

Day 33 - Echoes from Ancient Lives

Sleep played its nightly game of hide and seek, consciousness surfacing repeatedly like a restless swimmer unable to find comfortable depths in the dark waters of rest. Yet when dawn arrived at 4:17 a.m., I felt neither depleted nor weary—as if the energetic machinery activated by weeks of intensive practice had evolved beyond conventional requirements for restoration, drawing sustenance from sources that bypassed ordinary biological necessity.

The morning began with the familiar *ritual of Anapanasati*, breath meditation serving as a reliable compass for navigating whatever uncharted territories the day might reveal. Two preliminary sessions functioned as stretching exercises for consciousness itself, preparing awareness for the archaeological expedition that past life recall promised to become.

THE VAULT OF MEMORY OPENS

At 8:50, I finally attempted the practice that challenged every assumption about the nature of memory, identity, and the temporal boundaries of individual existence. The instructions possessed the deceptive simplicity that often masks profound complexity: direct focused intention toward accessing memories from previous incarnations, trusting that consciousness contained archived information spanning multiple lifetimes, waiting patiently in neural libraries that proper attention could unlock.

The first attempt shattered expectations with immediate results that left me breathless with wonder and uncertainty. Three faces materialized and flew toward me with the velocity of shooting stars—too rapid for detailed cataloging but distinct enough to register specific features that carried inexplicable emotional weight. The first figure possessed a distinctive goatee beard that seemed to resonate with frequencies of recognition, as if this facial hair belonged to someone whose identity hummed in harmony with something deep within my own sense of self.

Emboldened by these initial discoveries, I requested what Mr. Soemin called "4D images"—asking consciousness to provide three-dimensional displays that would suspend in space with holographic clarity, revealing greater context about these mysterious figures and the historical circumstances they inhabited.

The response arrived like a flood breaking through ancient dams.

VISIONS OF FORGOTTEN KINGDOMS

A throne-like chair materialized first, its elaborate design suggesting royal ceremony and the weight of political authority. Multiple Buddha images followed, their serene presence indicating a Buddhist cultural context that felt as familiar as childhood memories. Then came a large bedroom dominated by an ornate four-poster bed that spoke of wealth and elevated social status—accommodations that belonged to an era when such luxury was the exclusive privilege of society's upper echelons.

. . .

Suddenly, perspective zoomed out like a cosmic camera pulling back to reveal the broader architectural context: a magnificent medieval European-style castle perched dramatically on a cliff top, surrounded by vegetation so lush and vivid it seemed to pulse with life. The entire scene possessed the kind of detailed authenticity that distinguished genuine historical documentation from fantasy constructed by imagination drawing on half-remembered movies and books.

Most intriguing was the appearance of an Asian man with a mid-length beard wearing a distinctive black square hat that immediately evoked ancient Chinese governmental regalia. His presence carried particular gravitational weight—not just visual clarity but emotional resonance that suggested personal connection transcending mere observation, as if I were recognizing someone whose face had been waiting decades to be remembered.

The lunch bell interrupted these revelations, leaving me suspended between amazement and skepticism. Had I indeed been that Chinese minister in some previous incarnation? Was consciousness somehow accessing actual historical archives, or generating compelling narratives from subconscious cultural information stored in the collective library of human experience?

THE PHYSICS OF TRANSFORMATION

Standing in the lunch queue brought its own extraordinary revelation about the ongoing physical metamorphosis that intensive practice was orchestrating at the cellular level. My body felt impossibly light and airy—not metaphorically but with the literal sensation of having been transformed into a helium balloon that the slightest atmospheric disturbance might carry away like cosmic tumbleweed.

The buoyancy was so convincing that I found myself gripping a bamboo railing to hold on to something, genuinely concerned that air currents might sweep me away if I didn't hold on to something. It was simultaneously absurd and undeniably real—consciousness investigation was producing alterations in bodily density that challenged basic assumptions about the relationship between awareness and physical mass, as if sustained meditation was gradually converting flesh into something approaching ethereal substance.

After lunch, the persistent swaying motions that had characterized recent sessions finally subsided, though accumulated pain in my posterior continued protesting weeks of extended sitting on surfaces designed more for monastic endurance than anatomical comfort. But any relief from physical discomfort proved short-lived when Sayadaw delivered new instructions at three o'clock that felt like being assigned spiritual torture disguised as advanced practice.

He requested that I attempt sitting in full lotus position for at least one hour.

THE CRUCIFIXION OF COMFORT

Full lotus—that most demanding of meditation postures, where each foot rested on the opposite thigh in symmetrical arrangement that looked elegant in Buddhist iconography but felt like medieval torture when attempted by bodies trained in Western chair-sitting rather than pretzel-like contortions. The very suggestion sent waves of preemptive panic cascading through my nervous system like seismic warnings of impending disaster.

From 3:55 to 4:55 p.m., I endured what felt like an hour-long crucifixion conducted through the medium of advanced yoga postures that my Western anatomy had never been designed to accommodate. The full lotus position transformed my legs into instruments of systematic torture, each ankle twisted into angles that sent lightning bolts of agony racing up through my nervous system with the efficiency of electrical storms.

Within minutes, intense burning and throbbing pain erupted simultaneously in ankles, calves, knees, and buttocks—every joint and muscle involved in this unnatural arrangement screaming protests that grew more urgent and desperate with each passing moment. My circulation began shutting down, feet going numb as the pretzel-like arrangement of limbs systematically cut off blood flow like tourniquets designed by sadistic anatomists.

At times, I opened my eyes to check the clock, convinced there was something wrong with it—surely the digital display was malfunctioning, surely time couldn't move this slowly. I would stare at the numbers, willing them to leap forward, then close my eyes in resignation. A few minutes later, the desperate thought would return: "Surely this has been hours." Another glance at the clock revealed the crushing truth—only three more minutes had crawled past like wounded animals seeking somewhere safe to die.

Yet determination overrode physical rebellion with the force of spiritual fanaticism. How could I face my teacher with reports of failure when he'd specifically requested this demonstration of postural commitment? The thought of admitting defeat felt more unbearable than whatever physical agony the remaining minutes might deliver. Spiritual pride had become a form of masochism, demanding completion regardless of consequences to the biological vehicle that was supposed to serve consciousness rather than be sacrificed to it.

When I managed exactly one hour—not a second more—I stopped with the precision of a timer reaching zero. But the ordeal was far from over. Untying those dead legs became its own elaborate choreography of pain and patience. My limbs had transformed into foreign objects—unresponsive appendages that belonged to someone else's body. Each attempt to move required negotiating with circulation that had completely abandoned its post, coaxing feeling back into extremities that had become as lifeless as mannequin parts.

VISIONS BORN FROM EXTREMITY

This fierce concentration born from necessity unexpectedly triggered cascades of extraordinary visions that transformed the torture session into inadvertent time travel through what appeared to be authentic historical landscapes populated by figures whose presence carried the weight of personal memory rather than mere imagination.

Magnificent palaces unfolded in architectural detail that exceeded anything my conscious knowledge could have constructed. Endless processions of armored soldiers materialized, dressed as medieval Chinese warriors, their authentic military gear—flags, spears, swords—rendered with museum-quality accuracy that suggested direct observation rather than creative visualization drawn from half-remembered documentaries.

Most marched on foot with the disciplined cadence of professional military forces, while others rode horses or stood atop horse-drawn carriages in positions that indicated rank and strategic importance. Along both sides of this martial procession, women and children carried household items—pots, pans, bedding—their presence suggesting mass migration rather than military campaign alone, entire communities relocating with the organized precision of civilizations in transition.

Then my consciousness zoomed in on one particular warrior standing prominently on a horse-drawn carriage positioned at the procession's center—a figure of significant authority radiating command responsibility. He was encased from head to toe in armor that reflected light with metallic authenticity, his protective gear concealing facial features but revealing a proud, mighty stance that communicated leadership and strategic competence earned through years of military experience.

I found myself wondering whether this armored commander represented another incarnation of whatever consciousness was currently struggling to maintain full lotus position while investigating memories that apparently spanned multiple lifetimes. The emotional resonance suggested personal connection rather than detached observation—as if I were witnessing my own historical presence rather than random scenes from Chinese military archives.

THE MONK'S REVELATION

Later sessions failed to produce faces with similar clarity until the 7:15 p.m. group sitting brought another figure whose presence carried unmistakable spiritual authority and ceremonial significance.

A regal-looking monk materialized holding an ornamental staff that indicated high ecclesiastical rank within whatever Buddhist hierarchy he represented. His headdress suggested a formal religious position rather than an ordinary monastic status, while his white, smooth face radiated the kind of serene authority that emerges from years of advanced spiritual development and the accumulated wisdom of sustained contemplative practice.

Could this dignified religious figure represent yet another echo from previous incarnations—perhaps a lifetime spent in Buddhist practice that had somehow prepared consciousness for the extraordinary capabilities being revealed through current intensive training? The monk's presence felt less like discovery and more like recognition, as if I were meeting an old friend whose face had been temporarily forgotten but whose essential qualities remained familiar.

QUESTIONS WITHOUT ANSWERS

As evening concluded and I prepared for whatever additional past life investigations tomorrow might bring, I found myself grappling with questions that challenged every assumption about personal identity, historical continuity, and the scope of individual memory beyond biological boundaries.

Were these genuine glimpses into previous incarnations, or was consciousness simply generating compelling narratives from archetypal imagery stored in whatever collective unconscious sustained human cultural memory? Did it matter whether these visions represented literal historical accuracy or symbolic representations of spiritual development that transcended ordinary temporal limitations?

The visions carried emotional weight and authentic detail that distinguished them from ordinary imagination, yet their implications were so extraordinary that accepting them as literal truth would require completely revising everything I thought I knew about consciousness, memory, and the nature of individual identity across multiple lifetimes.

Tonight I fell asleep wondering whether I was discovering that personal awareness extended far beyond the boundaries of current incarnation, or whether intensive meditation was simply revealing consciousness's infinite capacity for creating experiences that felt more real than ordinary reality while remaining fundamentally mysterious in their ultimate significance.

Perhaps the answer mattered less than the questions themselves—inquiries that opened doorways to territories of human experience that conventional psychology and neuroscience had barely begun to map. In the space between skepticism and wonder, between literal interpretation and symbolic meaning, something profound was being revealed about the nature of consciousness itself—its capacity to transcend the apparent limitations that ordinary experience suggests are absolute and unchangeable.

The hour of lotus torture had become an unexpected catalyst, demonstrating that extreme physical challenge could serve as a portal to realms of memory and experience that normal awareness couldn't access. Pain had become a strange teacher, forcing consciousness beyond its comfortable boundaries into territories where the impossible became temporarily visible, where the boundaries between past and present dissolved like mist in morning sunlight.

Day 34 – The Invasion of Light

Dawn arrived bearing witness to consciousness undergoing fundamental reorganization at depths beyond ordinary awareness. The mysterious, shining, multicolored rods that had made occasional appearances now materialized with the persistence of colonizers claiming new territory—not as fleeting visitors but as permanent residents weaving themselves into the *familiar* backdrop of inner vision like cosmic software updating itself without permission from conscious oversight.

These luminous invaders appeared to be conducting systematic integration, their brilliant colors threading through awareness with the determination of a new operating system installing itself. The process felt simultaneously natural and alien—as if consciousness was being upgraded to accommodate capabilities that belonged to more advanced versions of awareness than ordinary human experience typically accessed.

THE ARCHITECTURE OF ANCIENT WARFARE

The 4:15 a.m. session began with what Sayadaw termed "conditioning" practice—techniques designed to prepare consciousness for deeper archaeological expeditions into past life material and karmic patterns that required specific internal conditions to access safely.

Immediately, the martial processions that had been emerging during recent sessions returned with enhanced clarity and expanded scope, as if the conditioning practice had fine-tuned consciousness's reception of these historical broadcasts. Warriors in authentic metal armor materialized in perfect historical detail—helmets that gleamed with the dull sheen of hand-forged steel, long spears that spoke of specific military traditions and technological periods, faces hidden behind protective gear that distinguished professional soldiers from amateur fighters.

Some rode horses with the confident bearing of cavalry units trained for coordinated battlefield maneuvers, while the majority were foot soldiers marching in disciplined formations of three to four lines that stretched beyond the boundaries of inner vision. The endless procession moved with mechanical precision that suggested not just military training but cultural conditioning that made such organized movement as automatic as breathing.

Interspersed with these martial displays came scenes of magnificent palaces that rivaled anything imagination could construct from conscious cultural knowledge. Elaborate wooden carvings adorned walls and panels with intricate details that testified to master craftsmen working within artistic traditions that, though unfamiliar to my current incarnation, were somehow recognized as authentic expressions of specific historical periods and geographical regions.

Ornate thrones appeared with such realistic detail that I could almost feel the texture of their carved surfaces, their design suggesting royal or imperial contexts where power was expressed through architectural magnificence rather than mere functional necessity.

THE AUTONOMOUS REVOLUTION

As the day progressed, the relationship between focus and phenomenon began evolving in ways that suggested these experiences were becoming increasingly independent and self-sustaining. Initially, directing attention specifically to the midpoint region would reliably produce the familiar seismic sensations that had characterized recent sessions, along with whatever visual imagery emerged from these apparent investigations of karmic archives.

But by two o'clock, focusing on any bodily sensation would trigger the tremors regardless of their specific location—as if the geological activity that intensive practice was generating had spread throughout my entire system like mycelial networks, creating interconnected pathways that responded to attention regardless of where it was directed.

Most remarkably, by six o'clock, even passive awareness without any deliberate focus would spontaneously generate the shaking phenomena. The tremors had become background features of ordinary consciousness—seismic activity that continued regardless of whether formal meditation was being attempted or specific techniques were being applied. Consciousness was developing its own weather patterns, internal climate systems that operated according to their own meteorological principles.

Throughout every sitting session, images cascaded through awareness with the reliability of cosmic television broadcasts scheduled according to programming I couldn't control or predict. Past life material, architectural displays, and martial scenes flowed through consciousness like accessing some vast library of historical footage that existed in dimensions normally invisible to ordinary awareness.

REFRAMING SUCCESS AND STRUGGLE

The afternoon passed without the usual interview session since Sayadaw had returned late from whatever business had taken him away from the compound. While this meant no new instructions or guidance about

the intensifying phenomena, it also provided time for integrating the day's revelations about the autonomous development of visionary capabilities and the steady evolution of consciousness into something that operated according to its own mysterious principles.

THE CONTINUOUS CASCADE

As evening approached and I prepared for continued sessions where images would undoubtedly continue flowing through awareness whether invited or not, I reflected on the day's dual revelations: the internal revolution where visionary capabilities were becoming autonomous background processes, and the external validation that my experience fell within the normal spectrum of human response to both challenges and achievements.

The luminous rods continued their apparent integration with the normal *nimitta* background, their presence suggesting that consciousness was being systematically prepared for capabilities that

would require expanded internal infrastructure. Like renovating a house to accommodate new technology, awareness itself seemed to be undergoing architectural modifications to support whatever extraordinary functions might emerge from continued intensive investigation.

Tonight I fell asleep with consciousness operating on multiple simultaneous levels—the familiar awareness that observed and noted experiences, and the deeper intelligence that was quietly reorganizing itself according to principles beyond ordinary understanding. The tremors continued their background rhythm, the images flowed through their mysterious schedules, and the multicolored rods maintained their luminous presence like construction workers building something unprecedented in the depths of awareness.

Perhaps the most profound realization was that transformation was occurring not just despite the challenges of noise, physical discomfort, and psychological doubt, but somehow through them—as if consciousness required the full spectrum of human difficulty and achievement to catalyze whatever alchemical processes were turning ordinary awareness into something capable of accessing memories, abilities, and perceptions that transcended the apparent limitations of individual incarnation.

The invasion of light was not conquest but renovation, not replacement but integration—consciousness expanding to accommodate capabilities that had always been potential but required specific conditions and sustained effort to become actualizable features of lived experience. In the space between struggle and success, between ordinary awareness and extraordinary perception, something entirely new was being born from the ancient raw materials of human consciousness, investigating its own infinite depths.

∼

Day 35 – Glimpses of Tomorrow

Sleep had finally granted something approaching the mercy of normal patterns—restorative rest punctuated by only brief awakenings that allowed consciousness to surface gently around four a.m. without the exhausted disorientation that had characterized recent weeks. My nervous system felt more stable, perhaps adapting to whatever energetic reorganization intensive practice was orchestrating in the deeper chambers of awareness.

Morning brought the task of catching up with yesterday's missed instruction due to Sayadaw's late return. The new assignment challenged temporal boundaries even more audaciously than past life recall: "future lives prediction"—apparently, consciousness could project forward through time as easily as it could access historical incarnations, revealing whatever destiny patterns were already established in cosmic databases containing information about souls' evolutionary trajectories.

PEERING THROUGH TIME'S VEIL

The very concept felt simultaneously thrilling and terrifying. Past life investigation had at least dealt with events that had theoretically already occurred, but peering into future incarnations suggested that destiny itself might be observable through sufficiently developed awareness, raising profound questions about free will, predetermined karma, and whether individual choices could alter whatever trajectories these practices might reveal.

The 8:18 a.m. session brought immediate results that carried hopeful implications for whatever cosmic curriculum my consciousness was enrolled in across multiple lifetimes. Disembodied faces materialized within cloud formations, their ethereal appearance suggesting beings who existed in realms less dense than ordinary physical incarnation—consciousness inhabiting forms of light rather than flesh and bone.

Most significant was a figure wearing an ornate crown—not just royal regalia but the kind of elaborate ceremonial headpiece that suggested divine or semi-divine status rather than merely earthly nobility. The face beneath this cosmic crown radiated the serene authority that characterized enlightened beings who had transcended ordinary human limitations, their expression carrying the peace that comes from having solved the fundamental questions that drive most souls through cycle after cycle of incarnation.

I interpreted this vision as an indication that one of my future incarnations might involve existence as a "mind-only deity"—those beings in Buddhist cosmology who inhabited realms of pure consciousness without the dense physical bodies that characterized earthly existence. The prospect filled me with profound satisfaction and motivation—if consciousness could indeed glimpse its evolutionary future, this suggested that intensive practice was preparing awareness for eventually transcending biological limitations entirely.

THE REVOLUTION OF SENSITIVITY

The three o'clock interview brought a welcome transition to *Anicca* practice—investigation of impermanence through systematic observation of how bodily sensations constantly arose and dissolved in the endless flux that characterized moment-to-moment experience. This approach felt familiar, reminiscent of Goenka-style Vipassana that focused on sensations' transient nature as a gateway to understanding the fundamental impermanence underlying all phenomena.

But my capacity for detecting subtle sensations had been revolutionized by weeks of intensive concentration development. What had previously required tremendous effort to perceive now registered with crystalline clarity throughout my entire body—every microscopic fluctuation in temperature, pressure, tingling, warmth, coolness, and the countless unnamed sensations that constantly danced across the nervous system's vast network of sensitivity.

My *samadhi*—that foundation of concentrated stability necessary for detailed investigation—had evolved far beyond anything achieved during previous retreats. In those earlier attempts at meditation, I'd struggled like a novice swimmer fighting to stay afloat in choppy waters, attention constantly being pulled away by waves of distraction that made even five minutes of stable focus feel like a major accomplishment worthy of celebration.

Back then, simply maintaining awareness of breathing for an entire session had felt like trying to hold water in cupped hands. No matter how carefully I tried to contain attention, it would inevitably leak away through mental cracks I couldn't seal. My mind had been like an untrained puppy, constantly chasing after every sound, thought, or sensation that crossed its field of awareness, requiring constant correction and redirection that left me exhausted rather than peaceful.

But now, after weeks of systematic training that had been reconditioning consciousness itself, sustained attention operated with the reliability of sophisticated technology that had been calibrated for precision performance. I could encompass the entire body's sensory field—from crown to toes, skin to core—while simultaneously tracking the rapid appearance and disappearance of phenomena too subtle for ordinary awareness to detect.

THE MICROSCOPIC DANCE

This wasn't just improved concentration but a fundamental upgrade in consciousness's operational capacity. Where previous retreats had felt like trying to observe wildlife with broken binoculars that constantly went out of focus, current awareness functioned like high-powered microscopes capable of detecting cellular-level activity across vast territories of sensation simultaneously.

I could feel the microscopic dance of temperature variations as blood vessels dilated and contracted beneath the skin. The subtle electrical currents that accompanied nervous system activity registered as distinct phenomena rather than background noise. Even the barely perceptible pressure changes that occurred with each heartbeat created ripples of sensation that spread through tissues like tiny earthquakes whose epicenters could be precisely located and tracked.

Most remarkably, this enhanced sensitivity operated without effort or strain. Maintaining such comprehensive awareness felt as natural as breathing itself—no longer requiring the exhausting mental gymnastics that had characterized earlier attempts at systematic body observation. It was like discovering that consciousness came equipped with zoom functions and multiple simultaneous display screens that could monitor dozens of processes simultaneously without overwhelming the central processing unit.

The contrast with my previous meditation experiences was so dramatic that it felt like comparing a hand-drawn map with satellite navigation systems. Where once I'd struggled to maintain even rudimentary awareness of basic breathing patterns, feeling sensations as vague impressions that came and went like shadows, now I could simultaneously observe the arising and passing of thousands of subtle sensations while maintaining perfect stability and clarity. But the most revolutionary difference was that

I could now *see* these sensations rather than merely feeling them—the *nimitta* had transformed bodily awareness from a blind, tactile experience into vivid visual perception where each sensation appeared as distinct phenomena with their own colors, shapes, and luminous qualities.

THE FADING OF SPECTACLE

Several days of *Vipassana* practice had produced one unexpected side effect that felt like losing cherished abilities in exchange for deeper insights. The spectacular body visualizations that had been routine features of recent sessions—skeletal displays, organ examinations, internal architecture illuminated by cosmic light—were gradually fading as investigation shifted from concentration-based phenomena toward insight-oriented observation of natural processes.

The *nimitta* that had been revealing anatomical details with x-ray clarity was becoming less vivid and reliable, its luminous displays incompatible with the kind of receptive awareness that insight meditation required. It was like discovering that consciousness could operate in different modes—spectacular display generation or subtle investigation—but not both simultaneously.

This gradual fading felt like bidding farewell to supernatural abilities that had made practice feel like discovering cosmic superpowers. Yet perhaps this transition represented a necessary evolution from fascination with extraordinary phenomena toward understanding the more fundamental principles that governed all experience—something Sayadaw had already alluded to days earlier when discussing my practice options, suggesting he'd anticipated this natural progression from the spectacular toward the profound.

THE FAMILIAR MADE NEW

Today's practice was surprisingly relaxing, a welcome change from recent sessions that had pushed consciousness into increasingly challenging territories. The *Anicca* investigation felt like returning to familiar spiritual terrain where previous training provided an adequate foundation for whatever insights this approach might reveal.

The technique's similarity to methods I'd practiced before made the transition feel less like learning entirely new skills and more like applying enhanced capabilities to familiar frameworks—using the concentration and sensitivity developed through weeks of intensive training to investigate impermanence with depth and precision that hadn't been available during earlier encounters with this fundamental Buddhist practice.

THE CURRICULUM OF CONSCIOUSNESS

As evening approached and I prepared for continued investigation of sensation's transient nature, I reflected on how the retreat's curriculum seemed designed to systematically develop specific capabilities before deploying them in service of increasingly sophisticated forms of spiritual investigation.

Past life recall had revealed consciousness's ability to access information spanning multiple incarnations, while future life prediction suggested awareness could project forward through time to glimpse evolutionary destinies. Now, *Anicca* practice was using all previously developed sensitivity to investigate the fundamental impermanence that characterizes every aspect of experience—perhaps preparing consciousness for insights that would transcend even the spectacular phenomena that had been dominating recent sessions.

The progression felt deliberate, like a medical school curriculum that builds from basic anatomy through increasingly complex diagnostic and surgical procedures. Each practice seemed to develop specific capacities that would prove essential for whatever advanced investigations lay ahead. The past life work had stretched the boundaries of memory and identity, future life prediction had challenged assumptions about time and destiny, and now impermanence investigation was using microscopic sensitivity to reveal the fluid nature of reality itself.

Tonight I went to sleep carrying the day's vision of cosmic crown and divine destiny, wondering whether consciousness was indeed being prepared through systematic stages for eventual transcendence of every limitation that currently defined human existence. Perhaps these extraordinary practices were simply revealing capabilities that had always existed but which ordinary awareness lacked sufficient refinement to access and integrate into whatever we called normal life in dimensions where matter and spirit were still considered separate categories rather than different expressions of the same fundamental cosmic dance.

The future deity with the ornate crown felt less like a prediction and more like a promise—not of what would inevitably occur, but of what became possible when consciousness developed sufficient clarity to recognize its own infinite potential. In the space between past and future, between the solid and the flowing, something timeless was being revealed about the nature of awareness itself and its capacity to transcend every boundary that ordinary experience suggests is absolute and unchangeable.

Day 36 – The Soul's Architecture

Dawn brought immediate recognition that consciousness was transforming at levels far more fundamental than the spectacular but ultimately surface phenomena that had been dominating recent weeks. The moment awareness surfaced from sleep's depths, the shining rods materialized with the persistence of cosmic messengers delivering communications from territories beyond ordinary spiritual experience.

These luminous entities had evolved dramatically since their first tentative appearances—patterns and colors shifting daily as if following some predetermined evolutionary sequence, growing stronger and more vivid with each manifestation. They typically announced themselves first thing in the morning, often before full wakefulness had even been achieved, appearing during the liminal moments between sleep and ordinary awareness.

ENCOUNTERS WITH THE ESSENTIAL

Sometimes they manifested as rods—perfectly straight columns of concentrated light that pulsed with internal radiance. Other times, they appeared as ropes—more organic, flexible forms that undulated with living movement through the deeper chambers of inner vision. During deep meditation, these phenomena would show up briefly for just a few seconds. When they did, I noticed a complete inability to think—thinking became impossible, leaving only pure awareness. However, this was a different type of awareness altogether, something beyond ordinary consciousness yet more present than anything I'd ever experienced.

I raised this with Sayadaw, but we could not bridge the communication gap—both translation barriers and the inherent ineffability of the experience created insurmountable obstacles. How do you describe a state where thought ceases to exist, yet awareness becomes more vivid than ever? The very attempt felt like trying to paint wind or sculpt silence, made even more challenging by linguistic and cultural gaps.

When they appeared, I felt I was witnessing the very substance of which I was made at the deepest level—not flesh or thought or memory, but the luminous core that animated them all. Mystery, strangeness, and terror mingled into compound sensations that defied description. These weren't just visual phenomena but encounters with the irreducible structure that would persist beyond biological death.

In their presence, individual consciousness seemed to disappear without a trace, like a shadow suddenly vanishing when clouds moved across the sun. *Where has it gone?* The question carried existential weight, suggesting these experiences provided direct encounters with the mystery at the foundation of personal identity.

THE COSMIC MIGRATION

Typically, these shining rods would flash briefly—seconds-long revelations that consciousness could barely register before the normal *nimitta* background would reassert itself. But this morning brought unprecedented developments suggesting these phenomena were becoming more integrated with regular spiritual displays.

A "window" appeared within the normal *nimitta* background—an actual portal revealing these luminous entities existing in the same space as familiar spiritual phenomena but operating according to entirely different principles. As I observed with fascination mixed with apprehension, some of the shining rods began slipping through this cosmic window like a procession of luminous worms migrating from one dimension to another.

Their passage transformed the normal *nimitta's* white background into a glossy dark blue and green mass that pulsed with collective radiance.

The occupation continued for extended periods—sustained presence suggesting these phenomena were establishing permanent installations. Eventually, the familiar white background would reassert itself, but the shining rods returned in frequent flashes that felt like reconnaissance missions preparing for more complete integration.

THE RHYTHM OF EXISTENCE

Before departing for two days of business, Sayadaw assigned a new practice: *Udayababbaya Nana*—the knowledge of Rise and Fall. This represented another shift in focus—from examining extraordinary manifestations toward observing the basic rhythm of appearance and disappearance that characterized all phenomena, whether spectacular or mundane.

The Rise and Fall exercise produced profound tranquility that felt aligned with natural rhythms governing all existence at levels more fundamental than individual consciousness or biological processes. This came with expected trade-offs in terms of *nimitta* intensity and reliability.

As Sayadaw had warned, the luminous displays became much weaker and more sporadic than during concentration-based practices. Sometimes extended sessions would yield no *nimitta* at all, leaving only ordinary darkness behind closed eyelids.

But when *nimitta* did emerge, they appeared with startling intensity—flaring up like sudden supernovas powered by accumulated energy that had been building during periods of apparent absence.

GEOLOGICAL TIME

Most remarkably, everything in my perceptual field had begun operating at dramatically reduced speeds. Breathing slowed to geological rates where each inhalation and exhalation felt like seasonal changes rather than rapid biological processes. The familiar specks and background static of inner vision drifted with the patient movement of deep ocean currents. Even bodily sensations seemed to occur in slow motion, each arising and passing stretched across extended periods.

The Rise and Fall investigation was slowing down these processes so they could be observed clearly, allowing consciousness to witness each stage of manifestation and dissolution with unprecedented detail.

THE CAVE OF SOLITUDE

That evening, I chose to skip the group sitting, preferring the undisturbed environment of my meditation cave where these subtle investigations could proceed without collective energy and potential distractions.

The decision proved beneficial—nearly two hours of uninterrupted sitting allowed consciousness to settle into the profound slow-motion awareness that Rise and Fall practice was cultivating.

Everything continued progressing at speeds aligned with cosmic time rather than human urgency, revealing layers of experience that normally remained invisible beneath the surface turbulence of ordinary mental activity.

In that extended solitude, the shining rods made their periodic appearances like old friends checking in on a long journey. Each manifestation felt like a reminder that beneath all the temporal arising and passing, something eternal was observing—something that existed beyond the reach of time and transformation yet somehow expressed itself through these luminous displays.

THE FUNDAMENTAL PRINCIPLES

As I prepared for sleep while Sayadaw was away, I reflected on how each new practice seemed designed to reveal different aspects of consciousness's relationship to existence itself.

The shining rods were showing the soul's actual architecture—the eternal structures that persisted beyond individual incarnations—while the Rise and Fall investigation allowed me to witness the actual atomic processes constantly occurring—the perpetual flux in all phenomena where I could see each individual arising and falling away in real-time. Together, these practices suggested that intensive meditation was providing direct access to the basic operating principles of reality: both the timeless essence that survived death and the dynamic processes through which consciousness experienced the endless dance of arising and passing.

It was like discovering that existence operated on two simultaneous levels: the eternal dimension where souls maintained their essential structure across lifetimes, and the temporal dimension where everything continuously emerged from and dissolved back into the source. The shining rods belonged to the first category—glimpses of the imperishable architecture of individual consciousness—while the Rise and Fall practice revealed the second—the rhythmic breathing of the universe itself.

Tonight I went to sleep still moving in slow motion, consciousness operating at speeds aligned with geological time rather than biological urgency. In the space between the eternal and the temporal, between the soul's unchanging architecture and the cosmic rhythm of arising and passing, something profound was being revealed about the nature of existence itself.

The luminous entities continued their mysterious presence in the depths of awareness, patient messengers from realms containing the blueprints for individual souls, while the Rise and Fall rhythm pulsed through every moment like the universe's own heartbeat. In learning to perceive both simultaneously, consciousness was perhaps discovering its true nature—not just temporal awareness trapped in biological form, but eternal essence temporarily expressing itself through the magnificent dance of arising and passing that characterized existence in any dimension where souls chose to explore the infinite possibilities of conscious experience.

Day 37 – The Cosmic Dance of Particles

Dawn delivered the familiar greeting of bright multicolored ropes materializing the moment consciousness surfaced from sleep's depths—these mysterious luminous entities that seemed to exist at the intersection of soul and cosmos, waiting patiently for awareness to achieve sufficient clarity to perceive their presence. Today, they lingered longer than ever before, maintaining their enigmatic display for extended periods as if consciousness was developing increased capacity for sustaining contact with whatever realm they inhabited.

Eventually, like cosmic visitors who understood the protocols of ordinary awareness, they gracefully withdrew and allowed the normal *nimitta* background to resume its familiar patterns. But their extended presence felt significant—perhaps indicating that the barriers between different levels of consciousness were becoming increasingly permeable through intensive practice.

THE BREAKTHROUGH DISCOVERY

Today brought a profound discovery that would forever change my understanding of what it meant to be conscious in a universe composed of constantly changing phenomena. The Rise and Fall investigation, which had begun yesterday as an abstract technique, suddenly revealed its true purpose through direct visual confirmation of principles that Buddhist teaching had been describing for centuries.

Initially, I had no clear understanding of what to look for or how success might be recognized in this practice. The instructions seemed almost impossibly vague—observe the rising and falling of sensations—without specific criteria for determining whether genuine insight was occurring.

But discovery came through what seemed like a serendipitous accident, though in retrospect, Sayadaw may have orchestrated this deliberately—not telling me in advance how to observe these processes, allowing me to discover this fundamental truth through my own direct experience. When I focused intensely on powerful sensations—the more vivid and distinct the phenomenon, the better—something extraordinary occurred that transformed abstract investigation into direct visual documentation of reality's most fundamental processes.

THE QUANTUM REVELATION

Each focused sensation fired up a *nimitta* that displayed the most spectacular scientific demonstration I'd ever witnessed: I was actually seeing the Rise and Fall process itself occurring in real time—not just feeling sensations as I had in past retreats, but visually observing the fundamental mechanics of reality as they happened, rendered with clarity that made any university physics demonstration seem crude by comparison.

The display appeared initially like a massive solar flare erupting from some cosmic furnace—billions upon billions of tiny particles being emitted in continuous streams that shot outward like microscopic bullets fired from spiritual artillery. Most traveled straight upward in perfect vertical trajectories, while others swayed at slight angles, creating the overall impression of shooting stars exploding from a single point source in numbers that challenged mathematical comprehension.

The density of these particle streams was so overwhelming that from my "distant" vantage point, they appeared smoky at first—like observing steam rising from hot springs or fine mist drifting across mountain valleys. Sometimes the undulating movement resembled rice plants swaying in cosmic paddies where wind patterns obeyed different laws than terrestrial weather systems.

But when I used whatever zoom capabilities my enhanced *nimitta* vision had developed, the true nature of these phenomena became crystal clear: they were tiny electrical sparks, each one looking like miniature toothpicks that would jump upward with explosive energy before immediately dissipating into whatever void had given birth to them.

The recognition struck with the force of scientific revolution combined with mystical revelation: *these were electromagnetic excitations of subatomic particles*—consciousness was somehow accessing direct visual observation of matter's most fundamental level, where reality revealed itself as pure energy in constant motion rather than the solid, stable forms that ordinary perception typically assumed.

Witnessing this left me breathless with a mixture of scientific awe and spiritual revelation. I was observing the universe revealing its deepest secrets through the instrument of my own awareness.

THE MECHANICS OF OBSERVATION

What made this profound observation possible was the culmination of weeks of developing enhanced sensitivity. With the help of the *nimitta* acting both as an ultra-high microscope and telescope, consciousness could now see processes that normally occurred at the subatomic level. When I zoomed in on specific sensations, I could literally slow down these lightning-fast processes, stretching moments into observable sequences. When a particular sensation arose that caught my attention, I would turn the full focus of awareness toward it and watch these fundamental processes occurring in real-time—witnessing the birth, maturation, and dissolution of each phenomenon as it unfolded through its complete lifecycle, each sensation displaying its own unique visual signature as it moved through its phases of existence.

THE RISE AND FALL REVEALED

This was precisely what Mr. Goenka had described in his teachings about *Vipassana*: masses of subatomic particles arising and passing away instantaneously, the basic building blocks of existence revealed as temporary arrangements of energy that appeared and dissolved faster than the speed of light. They fired up like miniature fireworks before burning out almost instantly, each particle's entire lifespan compressed into a duration so brief it challenged conventional understanding of time itself.

Most profound was the realization about sensation's actual temporal nature. Even when these processes were slowed down by my *nimitta* for observation, the moment of rising was essentially identical to the moment of perishing. As soon as any sensation registered in consciousness, it had already begun its dissolution back into the quantum foam from which the next wave of phenomena would emerge.

Like soap bubbles that burst the instant they achieved sufficient coherence to be recognized as distinct entities, sensations existed for durations so brief that their arising and passing were virtually simultaneous events.

THE TEACHER'S RECOGNITION

When I reported this breakthrough to Mr. Soemin, his response carried the weight of someone recognizing genuine spiritual achievement rather than engaging but ultimately superficial experiences.

"Sadhu, sadhu, sadhu!" he exclaimed with enthusiasm that made my heart soar with validation and accomplishment.

The significance couldn't be overstated. The Buddha himself had declared that to witness the Rise and Fall of phenomena for a single moment was better than living a hundred years without such insight.

THE NATURE OF REALITY

To observe this process meant seeing through the illusion of permanence that usually obscured reality's true nature. We were composed of tiny particles in constant flux—not solid beings inhabiting a stable world but temporary arrangements of energy dancing in patterns so rapid they created the illusion of continuity and substance.

This revealed the body as a constantly changing constellation of sensations rather than the solid, stable form that conceptual thinking typically assumed. Every sensation had its lifespan—arising from apparent nothingness, intensifying to peak clarity, then dissolving back into the background flux from which the next wave of phenomena would emerge.

It was like watching a time-lapse film of a forest where each tree, each leaf, each blade of grass was constantly appearing and disappearing, revealing that what seemed solid and enduring was actually a river of change flowing so quickly that ordinary perception mistook motion for stillness. But now I could see the actual mechanism—the electromagnetic excitations, the tiny electrical sparks that constituted the foundation of all apparent solidity.

This was empirical investigation of consciousness and matter conducted through enhanced awareness rather than external instrumentation, revealing truths that belonged simultaneously to physics and metaphysics.

THE BODY IN FLUX

But these profound insights came accompanied by intensifying physical phenomena that challenged every assumption about the stability of biological architecture during intensive spiritual investigation.

The bodily swaying that had been occurring for several days reached unprecedented intensity today, transforming daily existence into constant navigation through internal weather systems that seemed determined to demonstrate the fluid nature of what I'd always assumed was solid matter

From morning until night, I felt like a bucket of water being continuously sloshed around by invisible hands that never tired of this cosmic agitation. The sensation was so convincing that genuine seasickness would periodically overcome me despite sitting motionlessly on dry land.

Most bizarre was the discovery that different regions of my body were swaying in opposite directions simultaneously—the lower half undulating one way while the upper torso moved in completely contrary patterns, creating internal conflicts that felt like being inhabited by multiple independent organisms that couldn't coordinate their movements.

Looking back, I remembered Mr. Soemin's seemingly casual advice several days ago to sit in the middle of my bed while doing this meditation "in case I felt swaying." His prescient guidance now revealed itself as practical wisdom about phenomena he'd witnessed countless times.

THE DELIGHT OF DISCOVERY

From afternoon onward, my concentration achieved excellence that felt directly connected to the morning's breakthrough in perceiving subatomic reality. The delight of having witnessed the Rise and Fall provided enormous motivation and confidence that intensive practice was indeed accessing the fundamental principles that governed existence at its deepest levels.

Each subsequent session carried the excitement of scientific discovery combined with spiritual accomplishment—consciousness was capable of direct investigation of reality's basic operating principles, revealing truths that belonged simultaneously to physics laboratories and meditation halls.

The satisfaction wasn't just personal but cosmic—like contributing to humanity's understanding of reality's true nature through individual investigation that accessed universal principles governing all existence. I had become both the scientist and the laboratory, the observer and the instrument, consciousness using itself to investigate the very foundations of conscious experience.

THE DANCE CONTINUES

As evening approached, I carried the day's discoveries like treasures earned through systematic development of capabilities most people never knew existed.Tonight I went to sleep still swaying like seaweed in cosmic currents, consciousness operating as both microscope and telescope for investigating reality at scales from subatomic particles to universal principles.

The tiny electrical sparks continued their dance in memory—billions of phenomena arising and passing away in each moment, revealing existence as a magnificent fireworks display where every sensation was both birth and death, beginning and ending, eternal creation and instantaneous dissolution.

In witnessing the cosmic dance of particles, I had discovered that consciousness itself was not separate from this fundamental process but was the very capacity through which the universe could observe its own deepest nature. The observer and the observed were revealed as different aspects of the same cosmic dance, temporary arrangements of energy investigating their own eternal source through the magnificent instrument of awakened awareness.

Day 38 – Bhanga Nana

Sleep had come like a benediction, wrapping around me with uncharacteristic tenderness. When consciousness crept back through the pre-dawn darkness, something shimmered at the periphery of my inner vision—a *nimitta* unfurling like fabric caught in an otherworldly breeze. Squares of color tessellated before my closed eyes: burgundy bleeding into ochre, emerald dissolving into violet, the pattern of some cosmic tablecloth spread across the dining hall of eternity. Yet today it possessed a strange dullness, its usual luminous sheen replaced by something matte and earthen, as if the very light had grown weary.

THE STILLNESS BEFORE

The morning sessions passed in unexpected stillness. Where usually my body would rock and sway like kelp in underwater currents, now it sat motionless as carved stone. The familiar tremors and electric cascades that typically coursed through my limbs had vanished, leaving behind only a gossamer lightness, as though my flesh had shed its gravitational burden. I fixed my attention on the ancient rhythm—Rise and Fall, Rise and Fall—

watching breath move through me like tides through empty channels.

But the final session before the lunch bell shattered this tranquility with visions that blazed across my inner landscape like fire across dry grass. First came the severed head, crowned with gold and jewels, its dead eyes staring with regal indifference—some monarch's final moment frozen in grotesque majesty. Then the world opened beneath me, and I was soaring, weightless, over continents that stretched like wrinkled skin.

Cities sparkled below like scattered diamonds; oceans unfurled their blue-black silk; bridges arced across chasms with impossible grace. These were not mere images but holographic realities so vivid I could taste the salt spray, feel wind against my face, and hear the distant hum of civilizations far below. For those moments, I inhabited two bodies—one sitting cross-legged on a meditation cushion, another flying through dimensions that defied cartography.

THE RHYTHM OF EXISTENCE

The afternoon brought me back to the fundamental mystery: Rise and Fall. What extraordinary choreography this was—the billions of subatomic particles arising and passing away in each moment, the electromagnetic excitations firing up like microscopic fireworks before dissolving back into the quantum foam. Each sensation was a small universe born and dying, born and dying. How many thousands of these cosmic cycles had I witnessed? Yet each one remained as fresh as the first snowfall.

By now, my *nimitta* had become more than a companion—it was an instrument, a lens, a gateway. I could manipulate it with the precision of a master craftsman adjusting his tools, zooming into the microscopic theaters where cells danced their molecular ballets, then pulling back to survey the vast architecture of consciousness itself.

I recalled one of our group seminars at Pa-Auk, where a senior monk had said that just as scientists require microscopes to study cellular structure, we develop the *nimitta* as our microscope to see the truth, He had explained so casually that I thought he meant it metaphorically rather than literally. Now I understood he had been speaking with absolute precision—this was indeed a microscope beyond anything Western science had conceived, capable of examining not just matter but the very foundations of consciousness itself.

THE TEACHER RETURNS

At three o'clock, I found myself facing Sayadaw again, studying the lines etched deep around his eyes like calligraphy written by decades of meditation. He had just returned from his pilgrimage, and the exhaustion hung on him like a worn shawl. Two nights without sleep—forty-eight hours of sustained wakefulness while his seventy-one-year-old body endured the punishment of long-distance travel. The bus journey alone had devoured sixteen hours, eight each way, carrying him across landscapes I could only imagine.

How did he do it? I, who complained after a single restless night, marveled at this quiet demonstration of human endurance wrapped in saffron robes.

"*Bhanga Nana*," he said, his voice carrying the weight of ancient knowledge. "Knowledge of dissolution."

The words settled into my consciousness like stones dropped into still water, their ripples spreading outward into implications I couldn't yet fathom.

THE GREAT DISSOLUTION

When I returned to my cushion and began this new practice, the world transformed—or perhaps dissolved is the more accurate word. The familiar sensations that had become my constant companions simply... weren't. The *nimitta* faded to barely perceptible whispers of light. The swaying that had marked my deeper states stilled completely. Even the parade of visions retreated, leaving behind something that felt less like meditation and more like a gentle slide into unconsciousness.

Yet it wasn't sleep. It was something else entirely—a dissolution so complete that the very architecture of selfhood began to crumble, brick by brick, until I could no longer locate the meditator who had sat down on the cushion. The familiar landmarks of consciousness—the sense of "I am here," the feeling of "this is my body," the certainty of "these are my thoughts"—simply vanished like smoke dispersing in windless air.

At first, there was a gentle erosion, as if the edges of my being were softly fraying. The boundary between my skin and the air around it became gossamer-thin, then disappeared altogether. My breath was no longer something I possessed but something that breathed itself through a space that had once been called "me." The cushion beneath seemed to extend upward, merging with what had previously been my sitting bones, my spine, my skull, until cushion and sitter became a single, continuous phenomenon.

THE VANISHING OBSERVER

Then came the deeper unraveling. The observer—that persistent witness who had catalogued every sensation, every vision, every fluctuation of the *nimitta*—began to dissolve like salt in warm water. Without this central reference point, experience became pure process: arising without an ariser, knowing without a knower, dissolving without anyone to mark the dissolution.

It was as if I had spent years studying my reflection in a mirror, only to have the mirror suddenly vanish, leaving neither reflection nor the one who had been looking.

Colors bled beyond their boundaries, sounds echoed without source or destination, and the very notion of "inside" and "outside" became meaningless—like trying to locate the edge of a sphere from within its perfect center.

Time stretched into taffy, then snapped back on itself, then ceased to flow in any recognizable direction. Minutes could have been hours; hours could have been heartbeats. In this state, duration became as obsolete as trying to measure the weight of silence.

CONSCIOUS UNCONSCIOUSNESS

The most unsettling aspect was not the absence of sensation, but the absence of the one who would usually register that absence. It was a kind of conscious unconsciousness—awareness aware of its own dissolution, knowledge knowing its unknowing. Like a candle flame observing its own extinguishing, I was simultaneously the witness and the witnessed vanishing, the observer and the observed becoming indistinguishable, until even the distinction between presence and absence lost all meaning.

In this space beyond selfhood, there was no suffering because there was no self to suffer. No fear because there was no entity to be threatened. No desire because there was no one to want. It wasn't bliss in any recognizable sense—bliss implies someone to experience it. This was something prior to experience itself, the pregnant void from which all experience emerged and to which it inevitably returned.

THE RETURN

When fragments of ordinary consciousness eventually began to coalesce again—like scattered mercury finding its way back into droplets—I found myself grasping for words that could never adequately contain what had occurred. How does one describe the color of transparency? How does one map a territory that exists only in the absence of the cartographer?

The return wasn't dramatic but gradual, like dawn slowly distinguishing itself from night. First came the faintest sense of spatial orientation—up and down reasserting their meaning. Then the whisper of breath moving through what was slowly remembering itself as a body. The cushion beneath began to separate from what sat upon it. The boundaries of skin quietly rebuilt themselves, defining once again an inside and an outside.

Yet something fundamental had shifted. Having witnessed the dissolution of every construct I'd considered essential to existence—the observer, the observed, even awareness itself—I could never again take the solidity of ordinary experience for granted. The self that returned was more like a convenient fiction than an absolute truth, a useful story consciousness told itself to navigate the world of forms and boundaries.

KNOWLEDGE OF DISSOLUTION

Bhanga Nana—the Knowledge of Dissolution—had revealed itself not as something to be understood intellectually but as a direct encounter with the impermanent nature of existence itself. Every structure, every sensation, every thought, every sense of identity was revealed as temporary arrangements of consciousness, patterns that arose and passed away like waves on an ocean that itself had no fixed form.

This wasn't the dissolution of matter into energy that I'd witnessed in previous practices, but something far more fundamental—the dissolution of the very framework through which any experience became possible. It was as if I'd been watching a movie my entire life, completely absorbed in the story, only to have the screen itself slowly fade to black, revealing that even the capacity to see had been just another temporary arrangement of awareness.

Tonight, as I prepared for sleep, I carried with me the profound recognition that everything I considered real—this body, these thoughts, even this consciousness that seemed so central to my existence—was as ephemeral as clouds forming and dissolving in an empty sky. Yet paradoxically, this recognition brought not terror but a strange peace, the relief of finally seeing through an illusion that had never been as solid as it appeared.

In discovering the knowledge of dissolution, I had encountered something that couldn't dissolve—not because it was permanent, but because it had never been constructed in the first place. The space in which all arising and passing occurred was itself beyond coming and going, the eternal witness to the cosmic dance of temporary forms appearing and disappearing in the vast theater of consciousness.

Day 39 – Entering the Void

Sleep had been a gift—eight unbroken hours of darkness that cradled me from half past eight until the monastery stirred at four. Such uninterrupted rest felt like a minor miracle in this place where consciousness perpetually teetered on the edge of dissolution. I woke feeling strangely hollow, as if the night had excavated something essential from within me, leaving behind only empty chambers where familiar sensations once resided.

THE LUMINOUS VISITORS

The morning brought familiar visitors: those enigmatic rods of light that pierced the darkness behind my eyelids like luminous needles threading through black velvet. They appeared without fanfare, hung suspended for moments that felt eternal, then vanished as mysteriously as they had arrived, leaving behind only questions and the fading afterimage of their impossible geometry.

These manifestations felt different now—more distant, as if observing them from across some vast metaphysical chasm that had opened during the night. They seemed to belong to a realm of experience that was becoming increasingly remote from whatever

I was transforming into through this systematic dissolution of ordinary consciousness.

THE CONSCIOUS DEATH

Settling into *Bhanga Nana* once more, I found myself adrift in a peculiar emptiness. This wasn't the gentle dissolution of yesterday, but something more complete—a kind of conscious death. My body felt like a corpse floating through the infinite vacuum of space, untethered from gravity, from purpose, from the very notion of being alive. There was no peace in this state, no blissful transcendence—only a vacant quiescence that stretched like a moonless night across the landscape of awareness.

The familiar *nimitta* had transformed into something primordial: pure blackness, the color of space between stars, an absence so complete it became presence. Against this cosmic backdrop, sensation had been pared down to its most essential elements. The usual symphony of bodily experience—the electric tingling, the waves of expansion and contraction, the rhythmic thrumming that normally coursed through my limbs—had been silenced. In their place, only heat and pressure remained, isolated islands of feeling in an ocean of numbness.

GLIMPSES THROUGH THE VOID

Rise and Fall appeared sporadically, like distant shore lights glimpsed through fog. The subatomic processes that had been so vivid and spectacular just days before now seemed to flicker at the periphery of consciousness, barely visible through the profound emptiness that had settled over my awareness like cosmic dust.

Occasionally, images would materialize from the void: golden Buddhas seated in eternal contemplation, their serene faces emerging from darkness; ancient pagodas rising like prayers made of stone; sprawling cities viewed from impossible heights, their lights twinkling like earthbound constellations. But these visions felt remote, as if viewed through the wrong end of a telescope, beautiful but fundamentally disconnected from whatever I had become.

THE TEACHER'S VALIDATION

When the afternoon bell summoned me to Sayadaw's quarters, I carried this strange emptiness with me like a shroud. He sat waiting, his eyes holding that familiar depth that suggested he could see straight through to whatever remained of my soul.

"I felt like a dead man floating in space," I confessed, the words tumbling out before I could consider their strangeness.

To my amazement, his weathered face creased into something approaching a smile, and he nodded with the satisfaction of a teacher whose student had finally grasped a difficult equation. "That's exactly what you should experience with this meditation."

Relief flooded through me—or through whatever vessel I had become. In this place where ordinary reality held no dominion, even the sensation of being dead could be progress. The validation was profound: what felt like spiritual failure was actually spiritual success, what seemed like dissolution was actually advancement along the precise trajectory that these ancient practices were designed to produce.

KNOWLEDGE OF FEAR

"Today we begin *Bhaya Nana*," he announced, his voice carrying new gravitas. "Knowledge of fear." He paused, studying my face with the attention of someone gauging readiness for dangerous territory. "This should have been yesterday's teaching, but..." He gestured vaguely, encompassing his absence, the bus journeys, the sleepless nights that had kept him from our appointed rounds.

Bhaya Nana. The words themselves seemed to cast shadows as they settled into my understanding. Knowledge of fear—not fear itself, but the deep recognition of what fear truly was, what it protected, what it revealed about the architecture of selfhood that was so systematically being dismantled through these progressive stages of insight.

The progression made sense: first, the dissolution of the observer through *Bhanga Nana*, then the confrontation with what that dissolution revealed about the fundamental groundlessness of existence. Fear was the natural response to discovering that everything one had considered solid and reliable was actually ephemeral arrangements of consciousness with no more substance than morning mist.

THE ABSENCE OF TERROR

Yet when I returned to my cushion and attempted this new practice, fear remained conspicuously absent. I waited for the terror that others experienced, the sensation of losing one's physical body entirely, of confronting the fundamental groundlessness of existence that supposedly lay beneath all conditioned experience. Instead, I found only more of the same vacant floating, the same cosmic emptiness that had characterized the morning sessions.

Perhaps the profound dissolution I'd experienced through *Bhanga Nana* had already carried me beyond the psychological structures that would normally generate fear. Or maybe my technique was still developing, my consciousness not yet refined enough to penetrate the veils that protected me from encountering the raw terror that supposedly lay at the heart of conditioned existence.

The absence of expected experience became its own teaching. In this territory beyond ordinary psychological categories, even the lack of fear could be significant data about the state of consciousness being explored.

SCATTERED ATTENTION

As evening approached, my attention scattered like leaves in autumn wind. The day's strange emptiness had left me feeling unmoored, unable to anchor awareness in any stable experience. Even the familiar rhythm of breath seemed to elude my grasp, dissolving before I could properly observe it.

This dissolution of concentration felt different from the systematic dissolution of *Bhanga Nana*. Where that had been precise and controlled, this was more like the aftermath—consciousness struggling to reassemble itself into functional patterns after being thoroughly deconstructed by practices that revealed the fictional nature of ordinary selfhood.

REFUGE IN DARKNESS

For once, I welcomed the early retreat to my sleeping mat, grateful to surrender this peculiar day to the darkness that had, paradoxically, become both my enemy and my refuge. Sleep promised temporary relief from the strange liminal space between existence and non-existence that these advanced practices were revealing.

In the darkness before sleep, I reflected on the day's journey through territories that had no names in ordinary language. The conscious death, the cosmic emptiness, the teacher's validation that dissolution could be progress—all of it pointed toward a systematic deconstruction of every assumption about the nature of consciousness, identity, and the relationship between awareness and the phenomena it observed.

Tomorrow would bring further exploration of fear's knowledge, deeper investigation into what lay beneath the comfortable illusions that normally shielded consciousness from recognizing its own groundless nature. Tonight, I surrendered to the void that was becoming both destination and departure point, the space in which all experience arose and into which it inevitably dissolved.

The luminous rods continued their mysterious presence at the edges of awareness, patient witnesses to this systematic dismantling of ordinary reality. In their light, I glimpsed something that existed beyond construction and destruction, beyond presence and absence—the eternal stillness in which the cosmic dance of arising and passing played out its infinite variations on the theme of temporary existence, exploring its own impermanent nature.

Day 40 – Bhaya Nana

The monastery's silence shattered at 1:48 a.m., not from any external sound, but from the sudden blazing of consciousness itself. I found myself thrust into wakefulness with surgical precision, my eyes opening to darkness while something far more remarkable illuminated the landscape behind them. There, without any effort or intention on my part, the Rise and Fall process materialized like dawn breaking over an inner horizon—the subatomic particles arising and passing away in their cosmic dance, accompanied by the familiar backdrop of my *nimitta* shimmering like aurora against the darkness of sleep.

THE RECOGNITION

The recognition struck me with startling clarity: this phenomenon had been there before, lurking at the periphery of awareness during those liminal moments between sleep and waking. How many times had I glimpsed this spontaneous arising without recognizing it for what it was? How many mornings had this cosmic breathing revealed itself while I, still caught in the web of ordinary consciousness, had dismissed it as mere hypnagogic hallucination?

My body had become a vessel adrift on invisible currents. Each attempt to lie still on the narrow sleeping mat felt like trying to remain motionless on a boat caught in rough seas. The swaying began as gentle rocking, then intensified until waves of motion rolled through my torso, my limbs, as if some unseen hand were testing the flexibility of my spine. The sensation grew so intense that nausea crept up my throat—my body's primitive protest against this supernatural seasickness.

But the swaying was only part of the symphony. Scattered across my skin, localized tremors erupted like tiny earthquakes—buzzing sensations so precise they felt as though someone were pressing electric massagers against specific points on my arms, my back, my legs. Each spot vibrated with its own frequency, creating a percussion ensemble of flesh and nerve that seemed to play compositions I had never heard but somehow recognized.

THE CROSSING

When I reported to Sayadaw about my continued absence of fear during *Bhaya Nana*, his response carried the weight of ancient maps being redrawn. "You may have already crossed into *Adinava Nana*," he said, his weathered hands gesturing as if tracing invisible boundaries in the air between us.

Adinava Nana—"knowledge of defection." The very phrase seemed to carry the weight of cosmic disappointment, as if consciousness itself were filing a formal complaint against the conditions of existence.

"Contemplate all conditioned phenomena," Sayadaw instructed, his voice taking on the cadence of someone who had delivered this teaching countless times to countless seekers. "Everything we experience in this world—every sensation, every thought, every moment of joy or sorrow—examine their true nature."

THE UNIVERSAL COMPLAINT

His words opened like a map of universal suffering, each syllable revealing territories of impermanence I had never dared to explore. Everything, he explained, existed in perpetual flux, not just the obvious changes we could witness, but the relentless microscopic dissolution occurring beneath every surface.

Mountains that appeared eternal were, in truth, surrendering themselves grain by grain to wind and rain, their granite faces crumbling imperceptibly with each season's passage. Stars that had blazed for billions of years were burning through their nuclear fuel toward inevitable collapse, each moment of their brilliant light bringing them closer to the cold darkness of death.

Even closer to home, our own bodies were engaged in a constant war against entropy—cells dividing and dying in cycles we barely noticed, organs gradually losing their efficiency, bones growing brittle, skin accumulating the geography of time. The face in the mirror was never quite the same face as yesterday's, though the changes were too subtle for our desperate need for continuity to acknowledge.

THE SUBTLER DISSOLUTIONS

But it was the subtler dissolutions that cut deepest. Every moment of happiness, Sayadaw explained, carried within itself the seeds of its own destruction—not as punishment, but as natural law. The ecstasy of a lover's touch would fade not because love failed, but because the nervous system that registered pleasure was itself subject to change, adaptation, the inevitable dulling that comes when any sensation meets the architecture of impermanence.

The satisfaction of achievement would sour with time, not because success was meaningless, but because new iterations of need and desire were constantly replacing the self that had once hungered for recognition. Even beauty existed only in the context of its dissolution. The sunset's magnificence came precisely from its transience. If the sun hung forever in that perfect position, casting those exact shadows, painting those identical clouds with gold and crimson, it would cease to move us. We loved it because we knew, somewhere beneath conscious thought, that this particular arrangement of light and shadow would never occur again.

THE ARCHITECTURE OF IMPERMANENCE

He gestured toward the meditation hall around us, its wooden beams dark with age and incense. "This building stands now," he said, "but termites work in its foundation. The wood contracts and expands with each season. The very atoms that compose these walls are slowly redistributing themselves according to laws we cannot control. One day, this place will be dust, and the dust will become soil, and the soil will nourish trees whose wood may become another meditation hall for seekers not yet born."

His eyes held mine with uncomfortable intensity. "And you," he continued, "the one who sits here listening to these words—where is the child you were twenty years ago? Where are the cells that compose your body, then? Where are the thoughts that seemed so important, the fears that kept you awake, the dreams that felt eternal? That person is gone as surely as last year's snowfall, yet something persists that calls itself by the same name, claims the same history, suffers the same illusion of continuity."

THE SOURCE OF SUFFERING

The teaching expanded outward like ripples in a pond. Every relationship, every possession, every plan for the future—all of it built on the fundamental misconception that anything could remain unchanged. We constructed elaborate castles of expectation on foundations of sand, then wondered why we suffered when the tides inevitably came to reclaim what had never truly been ours.

"This is why we suffer," Sayadaw concluded, his voice carrying the weight of countless similar conversations with countless seekers. "Not because change happens—change is neither good nor evil, it simply is—but because we expect permanence where none exists. We demand that rivers flow backward, that flowers bloom forever, that our loved ones never age, that our moments of joy stretch into eternity. And when reality refuses to comply with our demands, we call it tragedy, we call it unfair, we call it everything except what it truly is: the natural order asserting itself against our beautiful, impossible dreams."

"We suffer," he continued, "not because change happens, but because we expect permanence where none exists. We cling to snowflakes and wonder why our hands come away wet and empty."

THE RESISTANT UNDERSTANDING

The teaching lodged itself in my consciousness like a splinter of truth too sharp to ignore. Yet when I returned to my cushion to practice this new meditation, the intellectual understanding refused to transform into visceral realization. I sat there contemplating impermanence, trying to feel the inherent suffering in all conditioned existence, waiting for some profound shift in perception that would unlock the knowledge Sayadaw described.

Instead, I found only more swaying—my body continuing its mysterious dance with invisible forces, rocking back and forth like a human metronome keeping time with rhythms I couldn't quite decipher. The tremors continued their precise vibrations across my skin, each spot maintaining its own electromagnetic frequency as if my nervous system had become a cosmic radio receiving signals from dimensions beyond ordinary perception.

The lack of dramatic revelation left me wondering, once again, whether my technique was flawed, my concentration too shallow to penetrate the veils that separated intellectual knowledge from direct insight. Perhaps the profound dissolution I'd experienced through *Bhanga Nana* had carried me beyond the psychological structures that would normally generate the defection response. Or maybe consciousness was still integrating the previous stages before moving into this new territory of recognizing the inherent dissatisfaction in all conditioned existence.

THE CLINGING TO AWAKENING

Perhaps, I thought as the afternoon light slanted through the small window of my quarters, the very fact that I expected some grand awakening was itself another form of clinging—another way of trying to grasp the ungraspable, to make permanent what was, by its very nature, as transient as everything else in this endlessly changing world.

The irony wasn't lost on me: here I was, learning about the futility of expecting permanence, while simultaneously expecting my understanding of impermanence to arrive and remain stable. Even spiritual insight, it seemed, was subject to the same laws of arising and passing that governed everything else. The knowledge of defection might itself be temporary, a way station rather than a destination, another phenomenon arising in consciousness only to dissolve back into the vast space of awareness from which all experience emerged.

As evening approached, I continued the gentle swaying that had become as natural as breathing, my body keeping time with cosmic rhythms while my mind slowly digested the profound implications of Sayadaw's teaching. In recognizing the universal nature of impermanence, I was beginning to understand that even this recognition was impermanent—that the very consciousness exploring these territories was itself subject to the same laws of change it was investigating.

The Rise and Fall continued its spontaneous manifestation, those subatomic particles dancing their eternal dance of arising and passing, indifferent to whether anyone was watching, indifferent to the significance I assigned to witnessing them. In their simple, relentless rhythm, I glimpsed something that needed no validation, no permanence, no meaning beyond the sheer fact of its occurrence—existence exploring itself through temporary arrangements of awareness that arose, flourished, and dissolved back into the infinite creativity from which they had emerged.

Day 41 – Talking

Sleep arrived like an old friend, carrying me from nine o'clock until 1:45 a.m. with the gentle precision of a well-practiced ritual. When consciousness returned, it brought with it a *nimitta* unlike any I had witnessed—a luminous golden-yellow that glowed with the warm radiance of an omelet fresh from the pan, hovering in the darkness behind my eyelids like some celestial breakfast prepared by gods who understood the poetry of simple things.

THE COSMIC PENDULUM

By three in the morning, I had settled onto my cushion, only to discover that my body had transformed into a living pendulum. The swaying had intensified beyond anything I had previously experienced—great rolling motions that seemed to originate from some cosmic center of gravity I couldn't locate. Even my *nimitta* participated in this cosmic dance, swinging sideways across my inner vision like lanterns caught in a metaphysical wind. Yet paradoxically, as the movement increased, sensation itself seemed to retreat. The usual chorus of bodily experience faded to whispers, and my *nimitta* dimmed as if viewed through layers of gauze.

THE ENDURANCE TEST

The retreat was entering its final movement now, like a symphony approaching its concluding notes. Some participants had already departed—empty spaces at meals marking their absence like missing teeth in a familiar smile. I couldn't fault them for leaving. Forty-three days of enforced silence were an endurance test that pushed beyond the boundaries of normal human experience, demanding sacrifices that weren't merely physical but reached into the deepest chambers of the psyche.

Bodies ached from endless sitting on hard surfaces, spines compressed under the weight of motionless hours, joints stiffening into geometric protests against unnatural stillness. Sleep became elusive when minds refused to quiet, when the constant vigilance of meditation practice made true rest feel impossible. The physical torments paled beside the psychological crucible.

The silence that surrounded us wasn't the peaceful quiet of solitude—it was the suffocating muteness of being surrounded by dozens of people yet unable to connect, creating a peculiar form of communal loneliness that gnawed at the soul. The ache of missing loved ones grew sharper with each passing day—no phone calls to bridge the distance, no familiar voices to offer comfort, no gentle touch to remind us we were still human and still loved.

THE MENTAL CRUCIBLE

Simple routines that had once provided structure and comfort vanished completely. There was no morning coffee ritual, no evening news to mark the day's end, no casual conversations to process the day's events, no familiar music to soothe frayed nerves. Instead, there was only the relentless march of meditation periods, each one demanding the impossible—to remain continuously alert, continuously observing, never allowing the mind to simply rest in the gentle stupor that usually cushioned us from life's sharper edges.

The mental exhaustion was perhaps the cruelest burden of all. Every waking moment required concentrated attention on the breath, on sensations, on the Rise and Fall, on whatever meditation object had been assigned. There was no permission to let the mind wander freely, no lazy afternoons of pleasant distraction, no mindless entertainment to provide respite from the intensity of constant self-observation. The very act of relaxation—something most people took for granted—became a forbidden luxury.

Emotions cycled through territories most people never voluntarily explored—waves of inexplicable sadness that seemed to arise from cellular memory, sudden surges of anger at the smallest inconveniences, moments of terror when the familiar sense of self began to dissolve, periods of euphoria that felt both transcendent and somehow untrustworthy. Without the usual social outlets for processing these experiences, each emotional state had to be met directly, observed with the same methodical attention given to physical sensations, then allowed to pass without the comfort of external validation or support.

THE RETURN OF WORDS

Among those who remained, the quality of silence had begun to shift. Words started appearing in whispered conversations, tentative at first, like plants pushing through soil after a long winter. This gradual return to speech wasn't mere weakness or breaking of rules—it was deliberate preparation, a careful decompression from the depths of inner space. To emerge suddenly from this cocoon of silence into the cacophonous marketplace of ordinary life would be like ascending too quickly from ocean depths, risking a kind of psychological decompression sickness that could shatter whatever insights had been so carefully cultivated.

THE UNEXPECTED RECOGNITION

The revelation came through one of my fellow meditators, delivered in the casual tone of someone sharing pleasant gossip. "Sayadaw speaks of you often in the morning seminars," he said, his eyes holding that particular brightness of someone bearing good news. "He uses your progress as an example to inspire others."

The words landed with unexpected weight. Here I was, the foreign interloper who had spent the first weeks convinced I would be the retreat's spectacular failure. I had arrived like a fish gasping in air—unprepared for the relentless heat that pressed against the skin like a living thing, unaccustomed to humidity that transformed simple breathing into a conscious effort, completely unprepared for the acoustic chaos that had nearly driven me to pack my bags in defeat.

While the local practitioners sat with Buddha-like equanimity amid the construction noise, motorbike engines, and endless human chatter that seemed to penetrate every supposedly sacred space, I had writhed in my seat like a spoiled child, my Western expectations of monastic tranquility crashing against the reality of meditation practiced amid life's relentless din.

THE SILENT TABLE COMPANION

The morning brought an encounter that perfectly encapsulated the strangeness of our situation. A man who had shared my table for over forty days—someone whose presence had become as familiar as the wooden spoon I used for rice, whose quiet gestures I had observed through countless silent meals—approached me with words for the first time. The transition from silent table companion to speaking human being felt surreal, like watching a statue come to life.

His English flowed with the careful precision of someone who had learned it in classrooms rather than playgrounds. He told me about his retirement from office work, about a daughter who had emigrated to Australia, and about the systematic way he approached his spiritual practice. I had noticed his notebook during our shared silence—the way he would carefully extract it during group sessions, his pen moving across pages with the methodical attention of a scholar cataloguing discoveries.

While I had used the evening Dharma talks as additional meditation time (the Burmese flowing over me like a river in an unknown language), he had been taking notes, transforming every teaching into written wisdom he could review and integrate. His courtesy carried the weight of old-world formality, each interaction carefully measured and respectful. There was something deeply moving about this—two strangers who had shared space and silence for over forty days, finally exchanging the basic human gift of conversation as our peculiar journey approached its end.

THE DEMOCRACY OF STRUGGLE

Another conversation revealed how profoundly I had misunderstood the retreat's dynamics. A fellow practitioner shared his own struggles with the practice, and our exchange led to a liberating discovery about the noise pollution that had been testing my equanimity throughout the retreat. I learned it was affecting everyone, not just foreigners whose nervous systems might be less adapted to Myanmar's acoustic environment. When I confessed that I'd assumed locals were accustomed to such sound levels and that my disturbance marked me as spiritually weak or overly sensitive, he gave me a look of amazement mixed with disbelief.

"*Who* could get used to noise like that?" he asked, his voice rising with genuine incredulity, as if I had just suggested that humans could adapt to breathing underwater or sleeping on beds of nails. His expression conveyed the kind of astonishment reserved for encountering truly absurd assumptions about human adaptation to impossible conditions.

His question dissolved weeks of self-criticism about my inability to maintain perfect equanimity in the face of constant acoustic assault. Even experienced local practitioners found the neighborhood's audio environment challenging enough to require defensive measures that went far beyond ordinary coping strategies. This explained the bright yellow workman's earmuffs he'd been wearing halfway through the course—industrial-grade hearing protection that he'd specifically requested from his brother, indicating the noise levels were genuinely problematic rather than personal sensitivity.

The conversation had completely revised my understanding of both personal progress and group dynamics through the simple act of honest communication with a fellow practitioner. What I'd interpreted as personal inadequacy in dealing with noise was a normal human response to genuinely challenging conditions. Simultaneously, achievements I'd assumed were routine were quite exceptional within the group's overall experience.

The combination of these realizations created a more realistic and compassionate framework for understanding both the difficulties and successes that intensive practice was generating. I was neither as weak as I'd thought when struggling with external distractions nor as ordinary as I'd assumed when accessing extraordinary states.

THE FINAL ENCOUNTER

When five o'clock arrived, I found myself in Sayadaw's presence one final time, offering the traditional donation that acknowledged the teaching received, submitting the profile he had requested like a student completing an assignment. The finality of this encounter pressed against my chest with unexpected weight

—sadness mingling with a peculiar sense of loss I hadn't anticipated.

For over forty days, I had existed under his careful guidance, each afternoon bringing his measured wisdom, his precise adjustments to my practice, his quiet authority navigating me through territories of consciousness I could never have explored alone. Now, suddenly, I would be without this daily anchor, this steady presence who had become as essential as the breath I observed.

The prospect of his absence created a strange combination of emptiness and abandonment that surprised me with its intensity. I would miss these daily encounters more than I had realized—the way he would study my face as I described my experiences, the slight nod that indicated understanding, the careful questions that revealed depths I hadn't known existed in my practice.

THE SPIRITUAL FATHER

Somewhere over these forty days, he had become like a father figure to me—not in any sentimental way, but in the truest sense of spiritual parentage, guiding my consciousness through its first tentative steps into territories I could never have navigated alone. I felt profoundly indebted to him for his teachings, honored beyond measure to have been under his tutelage.

What struck me most was his inexhaustible patience in dealing with my relentless curiosity—I had bombarded him with questions every single day for the past forty days, arriving at each afternoon session with new observations, new confusions, new wonder about the strange phenomena unfolding in my practice. Yet he had never shown the slightest irritation, always greeting my eager interrogations with that same gentle smile, that same careful attention to whatever confusion or breakthrough I had brought to his door.

Despite the melancholy of parting, gratitude flooded through me —profound appreciation for his generosity in sharing knowledge that felt almost sacred in its rarity. This wasn't mere meditation instruction but esoteric wisdom accumulated through decades of practice, teachings that could only be transmitted from teacher to student in the intimate space of direct guidance. How many seekers throughout history had longed for such access to the deeper mysteries of consciousness? How many had spent lifetimes searching for what he had offered so freely to a foreign stranger who had arrived knowing nothing of these profound territories of the mind?

THE FINAL TEACHING

"The swaying comes from your changing *nana*," he said, his weathered hands gesturing as if tracing invisible currents in the air around my body. "When consciousness shifts between levels, the physical form responds. It cannot be controlled or prevented—it simply happens by itself, like water finding its level."

His words settled into my understanding like the final piece of a puzzle I hadn't known I was solving, explaining days of mysterious motion that had transformed my meditation into an elaborate dance with forces I couldn't see or comprehend. The swaying wasn't a distraction or malfunction—it was evidence of consciousness itself undergoing fundamental reorganization, the physical body responding to shifts in awareness that operated according to their own natural laws.

As I left his quarters for the final time, carrying this last teaching like a precious gift, I realized that the true transmission had been occurring not just in our formal exchanges but in every moment of patient guidance, every adjustment of technique, every gentle correction that had shepherded my awareness through territories it could never have explored alone. In learning to navigate the deeper levels of consciousness, I had also learned what it meant to receive teachings that could only be given in the intimate relationship between teacher and student, wisdom that could only be transmitted through the patient alchemy of direct guidance and sustained practice.

The retreat was ending, but something had been planted that would continue growing long after I returned to the ordinary world—seeds of understanding about the nature of consciousness itself, and profound gratitude for those rare beings who dedicate their lives to shepherding others through the magnificent, mysterious territories of awakened awareness.

Day 42 – Last Interview with Sayadaw

Sleep had granted me another night of deep rest, yet when consciousness stirred in the pre-dawn darkness, my inner landscape had shifted once again. The strange *nimitta* that greeted my awakening wore a different face today—its colors and patterns rearranged like furniture moved in a familiar room, creating new geometries I couldn't quite decipher. Notably absent was the skeleton that had been appearing with such regularity; it had vanished from my inner theater several days ago, leaving behind only its memory and the questions of what its disappearance might signify.

THE BODY'S REBELLION

I dragged myself to the cushion at 3:40 a.m., determined to maintain the discipline that had carried me through forty-one days of practice. But my body had other plans. Despite the restorative sleep, drowsiness clung to me like humidity, thick and inescapable. My eyelids felt weighted with lead, my spine kept collapsing despite repeated attempts to straighten it, and my attention scattered like leaves in a windstorm.

Desperate to shake off this lethargy, I abandoned my cushion for a walk in the cool morning air, hoping the movement and change of scenery would rouse whatever alertness remained within me. But even the ritual of walking meditation—the careful attention to lifting, moving, placing each foot—couldn't pierce the fog that had settled over my consciousness. By four o'clock, I admitted defeat and surrendered to the body's demands, allowing myself to sink back into the strange luxury of unscheduled sleep.

The morning continued its rebellion against serious practice. Despite having enjoyed what should have been adequate rest, sleepiness haunted me like a persistent ghost, appearing whenever I tried to settle into meditation. Between 3:40 and 9:30, I managed only two hours of actual sitting—a pathetic showing that would have mortified me in the retreat's earlier phases. Now, so close to the end, it felt less like failure and more like the natural entropy that settles over any intensive endeavor as it approaches completion.

THE DEFECTION OF INTEREST

Only after lunch did some semblance of concentration return, as if the midday meal had finally provided whatever fuel my system had been lacking. Yet even then, the meditation subject that had once fascinated me with its revelations now felt flat and unengaging. *Adinava Nana*—the knowledge of defection—seemed to have become defection itself, as if the practice were demonstrating its teaching about the inevitable dissolution of interest and engagement.

I found myself doing something that would have been unthinkable weeks earlier: watching the clock, counting minutes until the session would end, sharing the same restless energy that I could sense radiating from my fellow meditators. The irony wasn't lost on me—experiencing firsthand the very defection from all conditioned phenomena that the practice was designed to reveal.

THE UNRAVELING CONTAINER

The retreat's social fabric had begun to unravel in ways both liberating and destructive. Now that conversations had resumed, the intense focus that had bound us together in shared silence was dissipating like morning mist. Words that had been bottled up for weeks were spilling out in eager torrents, and with them came all the ordinary concerns and distractions that meditation practice had temporarily held at bay. The sacred container that had preserved our collective concentration was developing cracks, allowing the outside world to seep back in drop by drop.

Most disruptive of all was the growing presence of home in our thoughts—not just as an abstract concept but as a vivid reality waiting to reclaim us. The mind, which had learned to exist in the eternal present of breath and sensation, now found itself pulled forward into imagined futures: familiar faces to reunite with, comfortable beds to sleep in, favorite foods to taste again, the blessed relief of privacy and personal choice.

These thoughts of return carried their own magnetic pull, making it increasingly difficult to remain present with whatever wisdom the final days might still offer. We were like students in the last week of school, physically present but mentally already walking out the door.

THE GLOW OF LIBERATION

The evening brought a special closing talk by Sayadaw, his final teaching to our diminished but determined group. As I looked around the meditation hall, I could see a particular glow on every face—not the serene radiance of deep meditation, but the unmistakable brightness of people contemplating liberation from what had become, despite its profound gifts, a kind of self-imposed prison. The joy was infectious and entirely justified.

Whatever else we had or hadn't achieved in these forty-two days, we had proven something valuable about human resilience. Each person in that room had demonstrated a form of stoicism that would have impressed ancient philosophers—the ability to endure discomfort, uncertainty, and the relentless pressure of self-observation without fleeing to familiar consolations.

They had shown determination that bordered on the heroic, returning to their cushions day after day even when the practice felt impossible, even when every cell in their bodies screamed for distraction, comfort, or simple rest. The self-discipline required to maintain such intensive practice was something anyone could be proud of—a testament to capacities most people never discover they possess.

THE NATURAL LONGING

They had earned the right to look forward to reuniting with their families, to reclaiming the freedom to speak when they wished, to eat what they craved, to sleep when tiredness overtook them rather than when the schedule decreed. As Sayadaw spoke his final words to us, I could feel the collective anticipation in the room—not disrespectful of his teaching, but the natural human longing for home that even the most profound spiritual insights couldn't entirely transcend.

In this final gathering, we were witnessing the completion of a profound human experiment. These people had voluntarily subjected themselves to conditions that challenged every assumption about comfort, convenience, and the necessity of constant stimulation. We had discovered that consciousness could function in territories most people never explore, that awareness could be refined to perceive realities normally invisible to ordinary perception.

Yet we had also discovered the limits of such intensive practice—how even the most dedicated spiritual effort eventually encounters the gravitational pull of ordinary human needs and desires. The longing for home wasn't a failure of spiritual development but a reminder that even transcendent insights must ultimately be integrated into the messy, complicated, beautiful world of relationships, responsibilities, and everyday life.

THE FINAL RECOGNITION

As I sat there listening to Sayadaw's closing words, I felt profound gratitude mixing with relief, accomplishment blending with exhaustion, wonder at what had been revealed merging with simple human hunger for the familiar comforts we had temporarily renounced. The retreat had been a journey to the edges of human consciousness, but it was also a circular path that led inevitably back to the ordinary world—transformed by what we had seen, but still fundamentally human in our need for connection, comfort, and the basic freedoms we had willingly surrendered in service of this extraordinary exploration.

The last interview marked not just the end of the retreat, but also the conclusion of this particular chapter of spiritual discovery. Tomorrow, we will begin the delicate process of re-entering a world that would seem both foreign and familiar after forty-three days of intensive inner investigation. We carried with us insights that could never be fully explained to those who hadn't made this journey, along with a deeper appreciation for both the possibilities and limitations of human consciousness when pushed to its edges through sustained, systematic exploration of its own infinite depths.

Day 43 – Closing Ceremony

My final night in this sacred place granted me one last gift of restorative sleep, carrying me peacefully until consciousness stirred around four o'clock. I lay in the predawn darkness for nearly an hour, reluctant to begin the rituals that would officially mark the end of this extraordinary chapter. When I finally rose at 4:45, it was with the bittersweet awareness that this would be my last awakening in these simple quarters that had witnessed so many profound transformations.

THE FINAL SITTING

I offered myself one final sitting before breakfast—not because the schedule demanded it, but because some part of me wasn't ready to release the practice that had become as natural as breathing. On my cushion for perhaps the last time in this place, I found myself trying to memorize the quality of morning silence, the particular way light filtered through the windows, the familiar weight of my body settling into the posture that had carried me through forty-three days of inner exploration.

. . .

In that final session, the *nimitta* appeared one last time—not with the spectacular fireworks that had marked earlier stages, but with the gentle familiarity of an old friend offering a quiet farewell. The Rise and Fall revealed itself with subtle grace, those subatomic particles dancing their eternal dance of arising and passing, indifferent to whether anyone was watching, yet somehow blessing this moment of departure with their timeless presence.

THE CEREMONIES OF COMPLETION

The formal ceremonies began with the "sharing of merits"—that beautiful Buddhist tradition of offering the spiritual benefits of our practice to all beings. As we gathered in the main hall for the presentation of certificates acknowledging our donations, the atmosphere thrummed with an almost electric happiness. Faces that had grown familiar through weeks of shared silence now beamed with the unmistakable radiance of completion, of having survived something that had tested every aspect of their being.

The eagerness to return to ordinary life was palpable and, frankly, amusing. Some of my fellow retreatants had been counting not just days but hours until this moment—immediately after breakfast, they appeared with bags already packed, eyes bright with anticipation, bodies practically vibrating with the need to step back into the world they had voluntarily abandoned. Their haste was infectious, a reminder that even the most profound spiritual experiences eventually reach their natural conclusion.

THE FINAL FEAST

Lunch arrived as a final feast, more generous than our usual simple meals, as if the kitchen itself wanted to send us off with abundance. Afterward, Mr. Soemin appeared with his characteristically thoughtful gestures—printed photographs of Sayadaw and the group photo he had captured several days earlier. These small mementos suddenly felt precious beyond their simple paper and ink, tangible proof that this extraordinary time had occurred, that we had endured and thrived in this unlikely community of seekers.

The packing of my belongings felt surreal, like dismantling a temporary home that had somehow become more real than the life waiting for me outside. Each item I folded and placed in my bag carried memories: the meditation shawl that had witnessed countless hours of sitting, the simple clothes that had seen me through the most intensive period of self-examination I had ever undertaken.

THE GRATITUDE ROUNDS

When the time came for gratitude, I found myself moving through the monastery like someone paying final respects, offering thanks to Mr. Soemin and his family, to the servers whose quiet kindness had sustained us through the most challenging days. These people had held space for our transformation without asking for recognition, providing the practical foundation that had allowed our inner work to flourish.

Each expression of thanks felt inadequate to capture what had been received. How do you thank someone for facilitating the dissolution of your ordinary self? How do you express gratitude for being guided through territories of consciousness you didn't know existed? The words felt thin compared to the magnitude of what had been shared, yet they were all I had to offer in that moment.

THE DEPARTURE

The offer of a ride to Chinatown should have felt like liberation, but as our vehicle pulled away from the monastery grounds, an unexpected wave of loss washed over me. Through the rear window, I watched the buildings grow smaller, taking with them the sacred container that had held my most blissful moments and most profound insights. Already I was missing the presence of those remarkable people whose calming auras had created an atmosphere of peace I had never experienced in ordinary life.

Most acutely, I felt the absence of Sayadaw's constant, gentle presence—that man who seemed to carry within himself an inexhaustible well of compassion, whose permanent smile had become as reliable as sunrise. For forty-three days, he had been my guide through territories of consciousness I could never have navigated alone. His wisdom had been dispensed with the precision of a master physician, each teaching calibrated exactly to my capacity to receive it.

THE ULTIMATE TEACHING

But it was Mr. Soemin's absence that created the most disorienting void. This man had been my mentor, my translator between worlds, my steady anchor throughout the entire journey. He had taught me the ultimate lesson: to become "master of your mind"—yet now, faced with implementing that teaching without his guidance, I felt like a newly hatched chick pushed from the nest for the first time.

The irony wasn't lost on me: he had prepared me for independence by making me dependent on his wisdom, and now I had to learn to fly precisely when I most wanted to remain under his protective wing. There would be no one now to offer the daily encouragement that had sustained me through the most difficult passages, no gentle voice to redirect me when my practice wandered into confusion. The responsibility for my inner life had been handed back to me completely.

THE SACRED DEBT

Yet in that weight, I felt the full magnitude of what this extraordinary family had given me. Mr. Soemin's welcoming household had become more than shelter—it had been a sanctuary where transformation could unfold safely. His benevolent father, with his gentle eyes and weathered hands, had offered me wisdom that extended far beyond my personal journey.

"Share this knowledge with others," he had told me during one of our brief conversations, his voice carrying the authority of someone who understood the true purpose of spiritual insight. "Bring others here so they too can benefit from what you have received." His words had planted seeds I was only beginning to understand—the recognition that genuine spiritual experience creates an obligation to serve, to become a bridge between those still seeking and the wisdom that could guide them.

I felt profound gratitude for Mr. Soemin's sisters and the devoted kitchen staff, those unsung saints who had lovingly prepared our meals with a care that transformed simple food into daily acts of devotion. Each dish had been crafted not just to nourish our bodies but to support our intensive practice. Their cooking had been meditation in action—each ingredient chosen mindfully, each flavor balanced to support rather than distract from our inner work. Even now, the memory of those meals carries the taste of home, family, and unconditional care.

THE LINEAGE OF GENEROSITY

In the growing distance between myself and that sacred place, I felt the full weight of what had been freely given. Sayadaw had offered centuries of wisdom without asking for anything in return. Mr. Soemin and his family had opened their home to a stranger, trusting that the teachings would find fertile ground. The other retreatants had shared their silent journey, each of us supporting the others simply by showing up day after day.

This generosity created a debt that could never be repaid in conventional terms, only honored through the quality of my future life. The father's words echoed in my mind: *Share this knowledge with others*. Perhaps this was how the lineage survived—not through books or formal institutions, but through the lived example of those who had tasted freedom and could no longer remain silent about its possibility.

I carried within me now not just personal insights but a responsibility to those still searching, suffering, believing that peace was somewhere outside themselves rather than in the very awareness that was reading these thoughts.

THE BRIDGE BETWEEN WORLDS

As the city swallowed us completely, I closed my eyes and tried to hold onto the feeling of that sacred place for just a moment longer, knowing that while I could take its teachings with me, I could never truly return to the person who had first walked through those monastery gates forty-three days ago.

The person sitting in this car was fundamentally different from the one who had arrived six weeks ago, yet the world I was returning to remained unchanged. Therein lay both the challenge and the opportunity—to become a bridge between these two realities, to demonstrate that the peace discovered in meditation could survive contact with traffic jams and deadlines, with difficult people and disappointing circumstances.

The retreat had ended, but the practice of awakening was eternal, requiring no special place or perfect conditions, only the willingness to remember what I had learned about the nature of mind itself. In the space between the sacred and the ordinary, between the monastery and the marketplace, between the silence and the noise, lay the real test: could the consciousness that had witnessed subatomic particles dancing in cosmic emptiness also find peace in a traffic jam? Could the awareness that had dissolved into the knowledge of dissolution also navigate the solid world of schedules and responsibilities?

The answer would unfold in the days and years ahead, but in that moment, departing from paradise, I carried within me something more precious than any treasure—the unshakeable knowing that peace was not a place but a way of seeing, not a destination but the very capacity to be aware of the journey itself. The monastery was ending, but the monastery of mind was eternal, always available, always offering the same profound teaching to anyone willing to sit still long enough to listen to the silence that contains all sound, the stillness that underlies all movement, the awareness that witnesses all arising and passing with the same unchanging presence that had guided this entire remarkable journey.

Conclusion: The Monastery of Mind

Years have passed since that car pulled away from the monastery gates, carrying me back into a world that seemed both foreign and familiar after forty-three days of intensive inner exploration. The transition was not the spiritual emergency I had feared, but neither was it the seamless integration I had hoped for. Like a deep-sea diver slowly ascending to prevent decompression sickness, I found myself moving carefully between the profound silence I had known and the cacophonous demands of ordinary life.

The *nimitta,* that extraordinary microscope of consciousness, did not abandon me entirely. In moments of deep stillness—during early morning meditation or in the liminal space before sleep—it would occasionally appear, though never again with the spectacular intensity of those monastery days. Sometimes it offered gentle reminders of the subatomic dance underlying all apparent solidity, brief glimpses of the electromagnetic excitations that constitute the foundation of what we mistake for permanent reality.

The Rise and Fall, once witnessed with such crystalline clarity, became a more subtle teacher. In traffic jams, I could sometimes perceive the arising and passing of irritation itself—not just feeling annoyed, but watching annoyance emerge from emptiness, peak, and dissolve back into the space from which the next moment would arise. During difficult conversations, I occasionally glimpsed the birth and death of defensive thoughts before they could solidify into reactive words.

THE INTEGRATION

What proved most enduring was not the spectacular phenomena but the foundational insights they had revealed. The body scan that had once required tremendous effort became as natural as checking the weather—a quick internal survey that revealed tension before it crystallized into chronic pain, fatigue before it became exhaustion, emotional currents before they became overwhelming storms.

The concentration developed through weeks of systematic training provided an unexpected gift in daily life: the ability to be fully present with whatever was occurring, whether pleasant or unpleasant. Washing dishes became a meditation on warmth and texture; difficult work meetings transformed into opportunities to observe the mind's habitual patterns without being hijacked by them.

Most profound was the shift in relationship to impermanence itself. Where once the constant change of experience had been a source of unconscious anxiety—the fear that happiness wouldn't last, that security was always threatened—now it became a source of comfort. Knowing viscerally that all phenomena arise and pass away made it easier to neither grasp after pleasure nor resist pain. Both were temporary arrangements of consciousness, as ephemeral as morning mist.

FORTY THREE DAYS OF FIRE

THE TEACHING CONTINUES

Mr. Soemin's final lesson—to become "master of your mind"—revealed itself as not a destination but a daily practice. Each morning brought opportunities to choose awareness over automaticity, presence over distraction, wisdom over reactivity. The mastery was not in controlling thoughts and emotions but in no longer being controlled by them, not in stopping the mind's activity but in recognizing the space in which all mental activity arose and passed away.

His father's instruction to "share this knowledge with others" proved equally challenging and rewarding. How do you convey the taste of water to someone who has never been thirsty? How do you describe the relief of setting down a heavy burden to someone who doesn't realize they're carrying anything? The sharing came not through preaching but through presence—the way peace naturally radiates from those who have found it, like warmth from a fire that doesn't announce itself but simply offers comfort to anyone who draws near.

THE RIPPLE EFFECTS

Relationships transformed in unexpected ways. The dissolution experiences had revealed the fictional nature of the solid, separate self, and this knowing changed how conflicts arose and were resolved. It became harder to take personal offenses personally when you had witnessed the impermanent nature of the person being offended. Arguments that once would have lasted days were resolved in hours or minutes as the grip of ego loosened its hold on the need to be right.

The fear of death, which had lurked at the edges of consciousness for decades, underwent a quiet revolution. Having experienced the dissolution of every structure I had considered essential to existence—the observer, the observed, even awareness itself—

physical death lost its existential terror. What could die that hadn't already been revealed as temporary? What could be lost that hadn't already been shown to be on loan?

Work took on a different quality. The relentless pursuit of achievement that had once driven every decision gave way to a more sustainable rhythm of engagement. Projects were completed with the same care but without the underlying desperation that had made every deadline feel like a life-or-death proposition. Success and failure became equally temporary weather patterns in the sky of awareness.

THE DEEPER CURRICULUM

In the months following the retreat, I began to understand that those forty-three days had been not just a meditation intensive but a complete recalibration of human consciousness. Like a piano being tuned, every aspect of perception had been adjusted to resonate with frequencies normally inaudible to ordinary awareness.

The skeleton that had appeared so regularly in the early visions revealed itself as not morbid imagery but the ultimate teacher of impermanence—a reminder that beneath all flesh and personality lay the same fundamental architecture, the same temporary arrangement of minerals and space that would one day return to the earth from which it had been borrowed.

The swaying that had seemed so mysterious was consciousness learning to move with the natural rhythms of existence rather than against them. Like a tree that bends with the wind instead of breaking, awareness had learned to flow with the constant changes of experience rather than rigidly resisting them.

The light rods that had seemed like visitors from other dimensions were perhaps consciousness recognizing its own luminous nature—not metaphorically but literally, awareness discovering itself as the light by which all experience becomes visible.

THE ETERNAL RETREAT

What became clear over time was that the monastery had been a training ground for recognizing what was always already present. The peace discovered in those sacred halls was not unique to that place but was the natural state of mind when not obscured by the constant agitation of seeking something other than what is.

The retreat had not given me anything I didn't already possess; it had simply removed the obstacles that prevented recognition of what had always been there, like a sculptor who reveals the statue by removing excess marble, those weeks of intensive practice had chipped away everything that was not essential, leaving only the irreducible core of aware presence that had been witnessing every moment of the journey.

This awareness needed no monastery to sustain it, no special conditions to maintain it, no particular techniques to access it. It was as available in a traffic jam as in a meditation hall, as present during an argument as during transcendent bliss. The retreat had been a finger pointing at the moon, and the moon it pointed toward was the very consciousness reading these words right now.

THE CONTINUING JOURNEY

Months later, when people ask about the retreat, I find myself speaking not of the extraordinary experiences but of the ordinary moments that followed—the way morning coffee tastes when drunk with complete attention, how profoundly moving it is to witness rain falling on leaves when seen without the constant narrative of mental commentary, the peace that comes from no longer needing life to be different than it is.

The systematic progression near the *jhanas*, the breakthrough into subatomic perception, the dissolution of the observer—all of these had been profound and transformative. But they were also temporary experiences that arose and passed away like everything else. What remained was simpler and more valuable: the recognition that consciousness itself was the treasure that had been sought, the peace that had been pursued, the freedom that had been the goal of all seeking.

The monastery continues to exist, not as a place visited but as the very nature of awareness itself. Every moment offers the same curriculum: the invitation to wake up from the dream of separation, to recognize the luminous space in which all experience appears, to rest in the knowing that has been present through every change, witnessing every arising and passing with the same unconditional presence that makes all experience possible.

In the end, those forty-three days had been a love letter from consciousness to itself—a reminder written in the language of light and silence, dissolution and insight, that what we are seeking is what we are, that what we are running toward is what we are running from, that the peace we hope to find in some future moment is the very awareness that is hoping, seeking, and knowing right now.

The retreat had ended, but the retreat had also just begun. And it would continue, breath by breath, moment by moment, for as long as consciousness chose to explore its own infinite nature through the magnificent, mysterious adventure of being temporarily human in a world that was temporary too, but no less beautiful for its impermanence—perhaps more beautiful because of it.

A Quiet Invitation

If you have reached this page, then you have already walked these forty-three days with me.

You have sat in the heat, the noise, the doubt, the silence, and whatever stirred inside you as these pages unfolded.

This book was not written to persuade or impress. It was written to tell the truth of an experience that changed me — and perhaps, in some small way, to remind others that transformation is possible, even when it feels unbearable.

If this story resonated with you — whether deeply or quietly — I would be grateful if you shared your thoughts in a short Amazon review. It does not need to be long or polished. Honest words are more than enough.

Your reflection helps other readers find this book, and it helps me understand how this story landed beyond my own experience.

Thank you for reading.

Thank you for your time.

And thank you for being here.

Pali Terms Glossary

Adinava nana - Knowledge of danger; insight into the drawbacks and dangers of conditioned existence

Anatta - Non-self; the doctrine that there is no permanent, unchanging self or soul

Anapanasati - Mindfulness of breathing; a meditation practice focusing on the breath

Anicca - Impermanence; the teaching that all conditioned things are transient and constantly changing

Araham - Arahant; one who has attained enlightenment and is free from all defilements

Bhanga nana - Dissolution knowledge; insight into the passing away of phenomena

Brahmaland - Brahma realm; heavenly planes of existence associated with refined consciousness

Devaland - Deva realm; celestial planes where gods and divine beings reside

Dukkha - Suffering, unsatisfactoriness, or stress; the first Noble Truth

Maranasati - Mindfulness of death; contemplation on the inevitability of death

Metta - Loving-kindness; unconditional friendliness and benevolence toward all beings

Nama - Name; the mental aspects of existence including consciousness, perception, and mental formations

Nana - Type (classification) of experiential knowledge

Nimitta - Sign or mental image; a luminous mental sign that appears during concentrated meditation practice

Parami - Perfections; spiritual qualities developed on the path to enlightenment

Pa-Auk monastery - A prominent Theravada Buddhist monastery in Myanmar known for its systematic meditation training and scholarly approach to Buddhist practice

Piti - Joy or rapture; a mental factor arising in meditation and spiritual practice

Qi - (Chinese) Life force energy; the vital energy that flows through all living things according to Chinese philosophy and traditional medicine

Rupa - Form; the physical aspects of existence including the body and material phenomena

Sadhu sadhu sadhu - Well done, well done, well done; an expression of approval and blessing

Udayabbaya nana - Knowledge of arising and passing away; insight into the impermanent nature of all phenomena

www.ingramcontent.com/pod-product-compliance
Lightning Source LLC
Chambersburg PA
CBHW022024290426
44109CB00014B/742